Nature Spirits & Elemental Beings

~

Working with the Intelligence in Nature

Revised, updated and expanded edition

Nature Spirits &
Elemental Beings

~

Working with the Intelligence in Nature

Revised, updated and expanded edition

Marko Pogačnik

FINDHORN PRESS

© Marko Pogačnik 2009

The right of Marko Pogačnik to be identified as the author
of this work has been asserted by him in accordance with the
Copyright, Designs and Patents Act 1998.

Includes material from the first edition published by Findhorn Press in 1997.
Published in 2009 by Findhorn Press, Scotland

ISBN 978-1-84409-175-1

1997 first edition translated and edited by
Karin Werner and George MacNamara
Additions and changes for the 2009 second edition
translated, compiled and edited by Tony Mitton
Cover design by Thierry Bogliolo
Interior design by Damian Keenan

Printed in the USA

1 2 3 4 5 6 7 8 9 10 11 12 14 15 14 13 12 11 10

Published by
Findhorn Press
305a The Park, Findhorn
Forres IV36 3TE
Scotland, UK

Telephone
+44-(0)1309-690582
Fax
+44-(0)131-777-2177
info@findhornpress.com
www.findhornpress.com

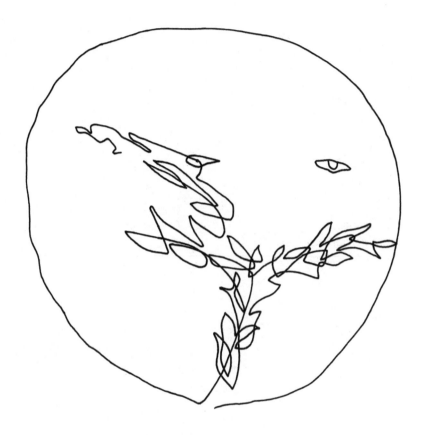

The elemental being of a plant.

Contents

Introduction to
Second Edition

THIRTEEN YEARS AGO I had completed the drawings and original German text of my book *Nature Spirits and Elemental Beings: Working with the Intelligence in Nature.* Now a new, up-to-date and essentially expanded edition is ready to go to press. The number 13 is like a magic number that opens the gates to the world of environmental spirits and elemental beings.

How, really, has this book come about? Its inception began with my long-felt desire to experience the consciousness planes of Earth and Nature – and that is what elemental beings and nature spirits really are. They represent different consciousness aspects of the Earth Soul – of Gaia. I was already professionally interested in a deeper interaction with Earth Consciousness, because since 1980 I have been concerned with the health of our planet, especially in relation to a kind of earth acupuncture called 'lithopuncture.' We have observed how bodily health among human beings depends quite largely on their state of consciousness, and this could also apply to Earth.

It has been 13 years since I first enjoyed real personal contact with elemental beings. That first contact, which occurred on the 26th of January 1993 – of which more in the next few pages – led me unexpectedly into a cycle of communication with their world. This lasted for precisely 13 months. I recorded my experiences from the start through till February 1994, and from these came the original book.

In those 13 months all the basic dimensions of the elemental world were shown and explained to me by the elemental beings themselves, i.e., by the consciousness of Earth. I felt myself like a guest who has been invited into an unknown world so he can report on its amazing beauty and authentic existence to his fellow men. In the succeeding years I have delved further into contact with the world of elemental beings and environmental spirits, making it an important part of the activity I direct to earth healing, geomancy and education. The 63 commentaries in the present book are based on the experiences I have gathered in the course of the past 13 years.

For the new edition, I re-read the original 1994 text for the first time in thirteen years. In doing so, I made a note of places where today I have developed a different perspective. In the intervening period, things have occurred between me and the elemental world that has led to a deeper understanding of their existence. In the end, it made sense to expand the original text with a newly written commentary.

So it is that a book has come into being with three levels or strata, which I hope will bring you joy and insight:

FIRST LEVEL: This is the initial report of my ramble through the elemental world in 1993-94. The text here is presented almost without alteration, and merely some formulations improved. I have rewritten the original introduction and replaced the previous last chapter, *Healing the Distortions in the Elemental World*, by a new one, *In the Turmoil of Change*. This last explains, in a comprehensible manner, the shift in my focus regarding the elemental world.

SECOND LEVEL: This comprises 63 Commentaries which are inserted at the appropriate places in the original text. In part they are concerned with my new discoveries, leading to a more complete understanding of already existing insights, and in part to self-critical reflections. Some 13 years later, I can better understand or categorise some of the things which I wrote earlier.

THIRD LEVEL: This is assembled from 56 drawings that for the most part I have sketched at the time and place of contact with the relevant elemental beings. There is a paradox connected with this: the elemental world has no physical forms, but can only find a place in human consciousness if it clothes itself in form. Thus, I have tried on the one hand to connect with the forms in which elemental beings were traditionally represented; and on the other to relax and liven up these overly dense forms that are antagonistic to etheric beings because they force the intelligence of Nature into roles that are projections of human imagination.

Give your inner child permission to enjoy my stories, and allow the grown-up within you to contribute to the universally evolving consciousness of our Earth's Intelligence.

Šempas. 16th March, 2007
Marko Pogačnik

Introduction to
First Edition

DWARFS, FAIRIES, NYMPHS—these figures are common in the fairy tales of many diverse cultures. But are these stories fact or fiction? My own experiences show that the elemental beings actually exist, and also that there is an intelligence in earth, nature and landscape which is real.

The experiences I report in this book show that it is time for the human species to take these beings and energies seriously, and to accept that they belong to the multi-dimensionality of life on this planet. For centuries our increasingly dominant human mind has driven them away into an unreal, separate fairy world. Yet I believe that meanwhile we have developed our consciousness to such an extent that we are now capable of approaching the elemental world on a new level, and we can experience it through the eyes of the modern mind, balanced by the emotional power of our hearts.

Within the thirteen months which passed between my first communication with the elementals on January 26, 1993, and the completion of this manuscript, the fundamental dimensions of the elemental world were shown and explained to me, mostly by the elemental beings themselves. I experienced myself as a visitor invited into an unknown territory so that I could report to my fellow humans about its vivid existence and surprising beauty. Of course, I did not disappear from the day-to-day world during these thirteen months; quite the contrary, I continued to live my normal life (which is centred around the work of earth healing) with even greater enthusiasm.

My first steps in the direction of earth healing were taken in the mid-'60s. The poet Iztok Geister and I founded an art movement in my native Slovenia (in the former Yugoslavia) called OHO,[1] which was concerned with the

---

[1] A monograph on OHO (1962-1971) was published by the Museum of Modern Art in Ljubljana in 1994 (the text is also available in English).

processes of transformation in art and culture. It was an attempt to change the fundamental principles upon which our modern human-centred culture is based. With the help of conceptual art, performances, and street- and land-art, we tried to open up ways to perceive the world around us which were free from human projection. At that time our tools were limited to artistic techniques.

The next step came about at the beginning of the '70s, when my wife Marika and I and a group of friends started a rural community at Sempas in Slovenia, north of Trieste. We left behind the urban environment and settled on a deserted farm in the Vipava valley to enter into conscious and loving communication with earth and nature. The 'Sempas Family' functioned as an organic farm and a spiritual centre at the same time.

Our interest in elemental beings was first kindled by a leaflet from the Findhorn Community in Scotland, which reported on a conversation with Pan. To follow this sign, we decided to visit the Findhorn Foundation in summer 1971. Once there, we realised that there were more fundamental things to learn from the Findhorn way of life than going deeper into knowing the elemental world. Our disappointment in this respect was diminished by the following experience.

On the way back home, Marika bought a packet of soya beans, which was a plant previously unknown to us. She sowed them at home to see whether they would grow in our country. For weeks the seeds did not germinate, and we were almost convinced that nothing would happen, since we had bought the soya beans for consumption and not for sowing. Then one night Marika dreamed that a horse-driven carriage came along—it had no wheels, yet it did not touch the ground, and there was a gnome holding the reins.

A very gentle maiden wrapped in green veils was dancing on the carriage to the rhythm of the 'Blue Danube Waltz' and singing, "I am soy... I am soy." My wife woke up and rushed out into the garden in her nightgown to look at our unhappy soya bean plot. She could hardly believe her eyes: in the moonlight she could just discern that all the soya beans had germinated. They were proudly poking their green heads out of the soil.

My true work with earth healing started in the mid-'80s when I developed my sculpture work into a kind of earth acupuncture which I call lithopuncture—the word comes from *lithos* (Greek for 'stone') and *punctura* (from Latin *pungere* 'to pierce'). To lithopuncture a place means to position stone slabs with sculpted signs—I call them cosmograms—on points of the earth's geomantic organism which are equivalent to the acupuncture points of the human body. The stone slab is positioned in such a way that it provokes a resonance on the energy level, while the cosmogram operates on the level of consciousness, i.e. the information level. During the years 1986-89, I first successfully implemented my lithopuncture method in all its complexity in the grounds of Türnich castle, near Cologne, where I was able to help the park regenerate in spite of the dramatically lowered underground water level caused by open-cast mining in the surrounding area, which had devastating effects on the life quality of the place.

To be able to do this kind of work, I had to develop a personal sensitivity to subtle dimensions of the landscape. In the beginning I was only interested in energetic phenomena like water lines, ley lines, aquastats and energy centres that function as chakras in the earth's body.[2] Later I discovered that a spiritual level of the landscape also exists, composed of invisible geometric structures which are usually called landscape temples. I have tried to present the laws of the spiritual level in a book published in German as *Die Land-schaft der Göttin* (The Landscape of the Goddess), Diederich, Munich, 1993. The present book on nature spirits and elemental beings introduces a further subtle aspect of the earth's body, the level of consciousness.

This multidimensional view of the landscape and nature could only have developed to its present wholeness thanks to the cooperation of my two daughters, Ajra Miška and Ana Pogačnik, each of whom communicates in her own way with beings from the angelic world. Through their channelled work they have been able to contribute a great wealth of knowledge which is seldom achievable in our modern world. With their help I have been able to re-examine and amend my experiences and understanding wherever there appeared to be weaknesses. I have quoted some of their channelled messages in this book, for which I am very grateful.

Whatever I have not been able to express through writing, I have tried to convey through my drawings. I have had to confront the strange aesthetics of the elemental world. On the one hand, elementals as spiritual beings are free from dense form; on the other hand, human consciousness can comprehend them only if they take on a specific shape through which they can be identified mentally. I have attempted to resolve this paradox by trying to discern and formulate the etheric forms of the elementals. Secondly, I have tried to build bridges between my own experiences and the forms traditionally ascribed to

---

[2] See a booklet called *Ley Lines and Ecology*, written with William Bloom, published by Gothic Image of Glastonbury in 1985.

the elementals: to loosen up the shapes where traditionally they have been conceived too densely, or to tie together energies in a corresponding figure where formlessness seems to be an obstacle to understanding.

To make the pictures as authentic as possible, I have drawn the 'formless forms' of some beings on the spot where they revealed themselves to me, receiving and taking into account feedback from my 'models' during the design process.

Three years after completing this manuscript, my advice to the reader would be not to take my concepts and comments too seriously. They are naturally limited by my consciousness at that time. What matter are my reports of my experiences, which are authentic and speak for themselves.

I hope you will enjoy this book and feel inspired to take your own steps into the wonder of the elemental world.

Marko Pogačnik
Srakane, 12th September 1996

ONE

My Entrance into
an Unknown World

IT WAS IN SEPTEMBER 1992 that I first came into contact with the nature intelligences which are mentioned in fairy tales and legends. At the time I was in Northern Ireland with my daughter and collaborator Ajra Miška. The previous year, the City Council of Derry (Londonderry) had commissioned me to carry out an extensive healing project for the landscape. The Derry/Donegal landscape has been painfully disrupted by the border between Northern Ireland and the Republic of Ireland. My aim was to re-create the original vital-energetic[1] unity of the landscape by means of stone sculptures on both sides of the border, and I had placed lithopuncture stones one-by-one at their appropriate sites in the landscape. Now we had returned to Derry for a dedication ceremony, and also to introduce this work to the public. We were to lead experiential group tours which were planned to the ancient sacred sites, marked by the lithopuncture stones.

Early one morning we travelled to the Beaghmore Stone Circles to prepare for the tours. The stones are situated in a wild moorland landscape, not far from Cookstown. There is a unique quality about these neolithic stone circles, for many centuries ago they were covered by thick layers of peat, and they are preserved in their original perfection. It was only recently that these examples of megalithic art were discovered by archaeologists. Today we can learn an immense amount from their pure, unaltered state.

This was the first time that I tried to sense the power structures in the stone circles just with my hands. A short while before, I had decided to stop using my dowsing instruments, and now it took courage for me to rely on my hands alone to sense the vibrations that indicated different radiations. It had always

---

[1]   The vital-energetic level within a landscape is at a higher vibrational level than the material level. It is also called the etheric or bioenergetic level. At these vibrations one can find power structures and other phenomena.

been my belief that I used the divining rod only to help make more obvious the subtle tremors experienced by a human body when it stands on a power point or moves through an energy field. It was twelve years before I was ready to release the rod as my 'crutch'. Since then I have simply allowed my hands to move freely within the vibrations of a place.

On that first day, I discovered that my hands followed the movements of certain patterns and laws, and therefore it was possible to distinguish clearly between different energetic phenomena. For instance, when I stood inside one of the seven simple stone circles, my hand swung backwards and forwards in a long regular rhythm which I recognised as a 'solar' rhythm. But when I climbed onto one of the round piles of stones (the so-called cairns which complement the stone circles), the rhythmic hand movements changed: the 'pendulum' swings of my hand became short, fast circles. These were lunar rhythms which I would call female, in contrast to the male (solar) power of the stone circles. The whole composition of the stone structures at Beaghmore was created to reflect the balance between the yin and yang powers of the universe.

But there are also individual stones near the cairns and the stone circles, seemingly strewn about without any order. On an earlier occasion, when I was still investigating with my dowsing instruments, I had not been able to find any point of reference to identify these as important parts of the structure of the old stone temple. Now I was quite excited to see if I could sense something with my bare hands from these mysterious single stones.

Relaxed but with inner concentration, I carefully put my right hand on the surface of one of the stones and let my left hand dangle. To my surprise my hand began to move very, very slowly. But it was not only this very slow hand motion that took me by surprise—it felt like it needed an infinitely long time to describe a backwards-moving arc—there was also a strange, deep feeling in the palm of my hand. It felt as if I was looking directly into the underworld through a narrow gap in the earth.

I was amazed by these perceptions, which I had never experienced before, and I turned to my daughter Ajra with an urgent request that she ask her Angel Master[2] what was going on. His answer was that I had encountered the presence of elemental beings.

---

[2]   The previous year I had asked Ajra to assist me while I was preparing the lithopuncture project. Recently she had discovered her ability to communicate telepathically with her Angel Master Christopher Tragius. I call him 'Angel Master', as he is one of those more highly evolved beings who accompany our human evolution from an invisible parallel reality from which they give advice and support the processes of unfoldment through their impulses.

This explanation would not have helped me much if my daughter had not written a book in the previous month, dictated to her on the inner levels by her Angel Master Christopher Tragius. There, among other things, the world of angels and elementals was described in detail. I had not yet had a chance to look at the book because it was still in the computer, but Ajra was able to give me two insights into this unexpected contact through her knowledge of the nature of elemental beings:

"First, elementals can exist on two levels simultaneously. Their bodies, unlike human bodies, have no material substance. Instead, they take the form of an energy vortex that vibrates on a vital-energetic level. Secondly, they have a consciousness which exists more on the emotional level,[3] not on the mental level as with human beings. Therefore, they cannot be reached through thinking processes, but only through a feeling connection."

The sensations in my hand exactly reflected this dual existence of elementals: from the extremely slow hand movements I could perceive the vibration of the vital energetic 'body', and through the feeling in the palm of my hand I was pulled into the deepest depth of a strange quality of emotional consciousness. My perception therefore was able to encompass both levels of the elemental's existence.

. . . .

1. COMMENTARY: The Elemental and the Cosmic Consciousness

Are we to talk about angels and elemental beings? Our rational mind may well rebel and hurl this book away. But wait a moment! We are not dealing here with simple concrete realities, but with different languages.

If one speaks in the language of the rational mind, one moves in the customary form of space and time. Simply put, the rational mind can know nothing of the extensions of reality that lie beyond this form. But here one is dealing with a language that knows totally different forms, for example, such things as elemental beings in the form of the genetic code of a plant.

If however one feels the urge to get to know these unrecognised extensions of life and allow oneself to be surprised by the levels of reality that are hidden from the rational mind, one's consciousness begins to articulate another language.

It then becomes plausible to admit that, parallel to the human, other levels of consciousness can also exist. For example, since we move on the planet earth,

---

[3]   Also called astral level.

we may expect that there exists a sort of consciousness that ensouls earthly life. Western tradition speaks of elemental beings and nature spirits.

Because the earth as a planet simultaneously plays a role in the wider universe, it follows that it must also participate in a cosmic consciousness. In the classical language of various cultures the cosmic aspect of consciousness is equated with the angelic.

Such a projection confuses the essential nature of both levels of consciousness. So, once again, wait! Can one imagine human consciousness without the existence of thinking human beings? It follows that the other two dimensions of consciousness could not exist if there were not beings to 'incorporate' the elemental and cosmic extensions of consciousness.

. . . .

Ajra also remembered how her Angel Master had talked about an awareness of the role of elementals in the landscape which still existed in the neolithic cultures. In every sacred place of this culture, contact points were built for the elemental kingdom, and this role is played by the 'randomly' scattered stones at the Beaghmore stone circles. A few days later I came across a second example of this at the Beltony stone circle, near Raphoe, Co. Donegal. There, one of the 66 stones arranged in a circle showed a number of round cup marks,[4] and with this stone I could perceive a similar deep and emotionally charged vibration, as with the single stones of Beaghmore. Obviously, of the 66 standing stones, this one had been chosen to be a specific link to the presence of the elementals.

During the following months, using this newly gained sensitivity in my hands, I discovered the presence of elementals in a number of different places, although I failed to progress beyond this basic experience. The following year, at the end of January, things went a step further when with my wife Marika I visited a healer in the Slovenian part of Carinthia. His name is Franz Mihelač, and he is a unique healer, for to carry out his healings he creates such a strong energy field in the room that one can barely breathe. The actual treatment was for my wife but I was allowed to be present and participate in the energy field. The almost unbearable pressure of these healing forces revealed two sensations in my body which had so far been slumbering in my unconscious.

---

[4] In Middle Europe this phenomenon corresponds to the so-called 'Schalensteine' (cup stones). According to my findings those are also dedicated to the elementals.

First I noticed with horror that something seemed to be missing in the region of my heart. I felt a tight band clasping this 'hole'. For years I had been searching for the cause of my recurring heart trouble, and I thought I had been quite successful in finding it. But now I was shown yet another unresolved problem.

The second manifestation occurred as a kind of vision: With crystal clarity I could see a tunnel opening at the lower end of my spine. It was beautifully faceted with a stone vault. There was a feeling that this tunnel led down diagonally into the depths of the earth. But when I tried to enter it with my consciousness I realised that the pathway was partly overgrown. On trying to go deeper I noticed that it was also blocked in places where the ceiling had collapsed.

. . . .

2. COMMENTARY: **A Threshold of Consciousness**

To help bridge the gap between modern language and what seems like fairytale, I will speak of a threshold of consciousness. My geomantic researches over the last few years have shown that there are places in the landscape that facilitate communication between the different levels of the physical body and the consciousness of earth. Such thresholds are a sort of tunnel in space and time that point to entrances and exits in the different levels of the under- and overworlds of earth.

When I speak of an entrance to the underworld, I can actually describe just such a geomantic phenomenon existing in the neighbourhood of our house – a threshold of consciousness that has enabled me to access information stored in the recesses of Earth.

This threshold was a tunnel that appeared obstructed because I was not clear in my own mind about why I should access Earth's subconscious. This is evidence that the phenomenon is not a left-over relic from a past epoch but a kind of consciousness tunnel. After my intention had become clear – see how the story continues – the entrance was freed.

To move through different dimensions of space and time in a consciousness tunnel, one must momentarily free oneself from our logical, result-oriented, space-time structure and trust oneself to the special nature of the particular threshold until one has reached the desired heights or depths of Nature Consciousness. In so doing, the individual consciousness remains alert to observe and guide the whole process, and of course to decipher experiences and translate them into logical form.

I could not come up with any useful ideas about this tunnel image, but as far as the heart trouble was concerned I began to suspect that the problem had its roots in one of my past lives. Until that time I had never wanted to regress into past incarnations, as I generally believe that all problems should be solved in the here and now.

But now I had a burning desire to unlock the secret connected to the 'hole' in my heart. I decided to trust Ajra with the supervision of my past life regression. Following her Angel Master's instructions she had developed a method of regression which includes the conscious cooperation of the person concerned, whereas most other methods use hypnosis. On January 26th, 1993, I lay on her sofa, and she guided me into the past through a dark tunnel. She let time fly backwards at great speed while I had to pay attention to the important events which approached. Then, as I focused my attention more sharply, time suddenly stood still, and I could calmly observe what was happening. First we passed through a lifetime which had no relevance to my heart problem. But at the start of the second experience I was filled with a premonition of its importance.

I could see myself as a very sensitive youth at the time of the Italian High Renaissance. My mother had died shortly after my birth, and my father was a powerful duke. As his only son I was destined to be his heir. But I had no interest in worldly power; I preferred to commune with nature in the wild grounds of the castle. Later, I became a monk to avoid my father's influence. Now time was speeding past. The monotony of monastic life gave no clues requiring close inspection, until suddenly I felt that something very decisive was about to happen.

. . . .

3. COMMENTARY: **Be Patient with my Fairytale Language!**

Please be patient! For centuries the rational human mind has suppressed the message emanating from this dimension of our world, and I use fairytale language because I want to protect this message from rational human control. The fairytale type of language, which I use throughout the book in relation to the subconscious halls of Earth, enables me to impart certain sensory and archetypical types of information that would otherwise be lost because of the one-sidedness of rational language.

For me, this relates symbolically to the two halves (hemispheres) of the brain that enable us simultaneously to think in a holistic and intuitive (right-sided) manner, and in a rational and specialised (left-sided) manner. My usual process is to describe my experiences of elemental and nature spirits in a fairytale (right-sided) manner and afterward translate them into left-sided rational language. In this way the holistic nature of the consciousness of the Earth and elemental beings is preserved, and due honour paid to the multiple layers of human consciousness.

. . . .

I stopped the flow of time. My father's envoy visited me in my monk's cell to tell me that my father was close to death and expected me to come home and take on his duties and title. It had all been arranged with the abbot. I went deep inside myself to ask whether I should follow this path of power. Finally I rejected the invitation. I wanted to stay true to my heart in all circumstances. I saw that my father's envoy went to see the abbot once again. They agreed to give me a poison from which I would faint and appear dead. Then I was buried alive. Obviously in this way the conspirators hoped that the sin of murder would not taint them, since I would clearly have died naturally.

When the air began to run out I woke up in my coffin. In the face of sure death I was surprisingly calm. Before I took my last breath I saw a group of dwarfs approaching—I could recognise them by their traditional costumes. They had come to take my heart away. It was the heart of a pure man.

. . . .

4. COMMENTARY: **The Holographic Fragment of Earth's Heart**

I have made a mistake here. When I wrote the original script, I had too little experience of the way the heart system of each human being is integrated into the body of Earth. Also, as regards the last sentence, I had accepted my rational mind's explanation that the purity of my earthly life was why the earth spirits wanted to keep my heart. Quite wrong!

In the meantime I have come to know that the human heart is valuable not only because our divine essence – the essence of our immortal soul – is anchored there, but also because it has a special relationship to the heart system of Earth. Because we have incarnated in the life systems of Earth, we are also part of the planetary heart system. And because we are 'children of the Earth', a holographic fragment (a self-aware fractal) of the Earth Heart is incorporated in us during the incarnation process. My daughter Ajra has called this concept 'the elemental heart'. From the time of our birth through the whole span of our incarnation we have the right and the capacity to vibrate in tune with the Heart of Earth.

What I saw in the events originally described is that moment in the after-death process when the elemental aspect of the human heart is merged back into the heart system of Earth. In a succeeding incarnation one can partake of it once more.

. . . .

In excitement I jumped up from the sofa and cried, "Ajra, we must follow the dwarfs to find out what they have done with my heart." Obviously the oppressive emptiness which I felt in the heart region was connected to this fairy-tale experience of the past.

Ajra asked me whether I knew a place connected to the dwarfs' kingdom. And sure enough, through the newly discovered ability in my hands, I had discovered such a place shortly after my journey to Ireland. It is located in the forest not far from our house in Sempas. There, a small rock wall rises out of the leaf-covered ground.

Now Ajra told me to imagine an archway lined with stones in the rock face. This was the threshold to a tunnel deep down into the earth. Then I was to imagine creeping into the tunnel, following a dark path into the depths of the earth. The black tunnel seemed endless but doggedly I went on further and further. Suddenly the path came to an end and I was in a lighted room, a spacious hall. I looked around me. Apart from a dim light I could not see anything at first until I suddenly looked down onto the floor. There I noticed a busy crowd of dwarfs running back and forth between my feet. I felt like Gulliver among the Lilliputians. When my first reactions of amazement had subsided I remembered why I had come down to this underworld. Then with a strong inner voice I told them who I was, and that I had come to visit my heart. To my surprise, the little folk must have known about the whole situation. A small group immediately left the crowd and started running in a certain direction. I followed with giant strides.

The path wound back and forth as if we were in a labyrinth. We had to travel a great distance. Finally, we stopped in front of a chamber in the rock. To my astonishment I saw my heart lying on a pedestal. It was the only object in the room. It seemed like it had been transformed into a precious stone. The form of the heart was so familiar to me that I grabbed it quite naturally and put it into my chest. It fitted perfectly the hole I had experienced in the region of my heart while visiting the healer in Carinthia. Immediately I felt renewed.

It was only when in my joy I tried to leave the room that I noticed there was a kind of disappointed silence around me. Immediately I understood what I had done. I was about to take away the dwarfs' holy relic, the heart of a pure man. With a heavy feeling I put it back on its altar. Then I had an idea. I told the dwarfs, "Yes, you are right. The heart is now your relic. But since it is my heart, I would like to ask you to grant me a favour—that I can visit it whenever my present heart is in need of regeneration." And, with the sense of justice for which dwarfs are well-known, my wish was granted.

. . . .

5. COMMENTARY: **Holes in the Heart**

A mother loves all her children. It is impossible for me to have been born on earth without a fractal of Earth's Heart beating within me. The holes that I discovered in my heart region can be better understood as an expression of my alienation from the Heart of the Earth, which I still had not recognised.

In that period of my life I was much occupied with a sense of renewing the human relationship with earth and nature. I had already formulated and publicly communicated the basic idea of a multidimensional consciousness ordering the operations of the life-forces in the landscape. Lithopuncture and other methods of ecological healing were already developed and manifest in different projects. The book *Landscape of the Goddess* had renewed the concept of landscape temples. Yet my emotional relationship with the Being of Earth had still not awoken, and I had not understood it in the sense of the holistic world picture. I still could not give the Earth Heart the expression it had so long wanted. Its fractal embodied in me still lay slumbering in the shadows of my unconscious.

. . . .

During the next few days, in the depths of my morning meditation, I returned regularly down this well-trodden path to fit the pure heart into my chest for a short while, and then to replace it on the altar. Then I stopped using the entrance into the underworld at the rock wall in our local forest. Instead, I began to use the tunnel which I had perceived at the base of my spine during the healing session in Carinthia. At that time I had seen the tunnel as being obstructed. As with most people, my ability to make any connection with the elemental world had been lost from my conscious mind.

For seven days my visits to the underworld in my morning meditation had presented no problems. But when I returned there on the eighth day the usual feeling of welcome from the pleasant grey atmosphere was missing. Instead, I found myself in a glaring light. I tried in vain to understand what was going on. I delved into the light to find out, and there I found myself deep inside the watery element. To my surprise I could breathe very well as I began to sink deeper and deeper into the water. I was gliding downwards next to a vertical rock wall, and I felt myself being drawn into the primordial depths of the water, until finally I came to the entrance of a cave. Inside it I saw a fish, a grey leaf-like giant fish. It did not seem to move from its position, although it was making slight movements back and forth to keep its perfect balance.

I looked into the eyes of the fish, and I recognised it as Faronika, the fish woman. A famous Slovenian folk ballad tells of her:

> Jesus is swimming in the sea, in a deep, deep sea.
> A fish woman is following him, it is Faronika.
> "O wait, fish woman, wait fish woman Faronika!
> We want to ask you what is happening in the world."
> "If I flap my tail then the world will perish.
> If I turn onto my back then the world will be flooded."
> "O don't do it fish woman, fish woman Faronika.
> Think of the little children, don't do it,
> and think of all women in childbirth." [5]

Silently I asked her what was her real function in the landscape. I received the clear answer from her that she is one of the water elementals, and that she works in waters and also in 'blind springs' within the depths of the earth. Her task is to keep the fundamental balance within the landscape. If she flaps her tail then there would be catastrophes above on the earth, just as the folklore tells. Each place and landscape has its own integrity, and each has a balance point which resonates with an elemental of her type. Then I asked her how I would be able to recognise such a balance point. Soon my hand began to align itself in the water, rotating anti-clockwise in front of me.

I gave thanks to Faronika and asked her to have mercy upon humanity for the ecological imbalances we have created. While slipping back into my everyday consciousness, I felt particularly grateful for this encounter because I had met a water being in a completely different dimension from that of the com-

---

[5] A fish, as guardian of the world, or 'world fish', is mentioned in the creation myths of many indigenous peoples. In the Germanic tradition, it is called the 'celebrant' or 'con-celebrant'. A folk song from the Eifel region tells us that the fish has similar powers to the one mentioned in this verse: "The fish is con-celebrant, / It should be called forth in every holy mass / If it is not called in every holy mass, / there will be earthquakes in this land."

mon fairy tales where undines or sylphs are mentioned. It made total sense to me that water should be the appropriate element for the elemental beings of balance, since water has the ability to form a flat and level surface in any given situation. We should protect our underground waters for the sake of the earth's balance.

. . . .

6. COMMENTARY: **The Fish Woman and the Earth Soul**

At that time I was absolutely convinced of the meaning of the fish woman Faronika's role. However, in the light of later experiences it became clear that she stands as the symbol of a multi-layered prototype. The archetypal fish is primarily a symbolic representation of the Earth Soul. The form of the archetypal fish symbolises not only its own equilibrium but the preservation of Earth's identity. As indicated, the Earth Soul is present everywhere in her watery depths as a holographic fractal of herself. We may speak about the soul of a place (in Latin, 'genius loci'). The watery element belongs to her because she operates through the emotional consciousness.

It is significant that I experienced the archetypal fish first among the archetypes of Inner Earth. Because she symbolises the Earth Soul, she also stands as the original mother of all nature spirits and elemental beings. They represent different manifestations of her thinking pathways. In this sense one could see nature spirits and elemental beings as executive intelligences that take the Earth Soul's plans and precautions, which are dedicated to the life on her surface, and translate them into deeds.

For the archetypal fish, one of the most important places in the whole world is the place where Venice stands today. Situated there is a planetary chakra that serves to maintain the equilibrium of the terrestrial force fields. It is significant that the body of the city of Venice, seen from above, has a fish-like shape, and also that it is constructed in the midst of the sea.

. . . .

Next morning, when I dived down into the underworld during my meditation, I was full of anticipation. Which of the fairy-tale beings would I encounter this time? Again I found myself in the element of water. I was carried down into the depths very quickly. Tiny water vortexes danced and swirled around me, pulling me directly into the primordial ocean. On reaching the bottom of the ocean I was met by a being of incomprehensible beauty. In her I recognised the empress of the watery element, called the beautiful Vida in Slovenian folklore. Her magical beauty enchanted me so much that I had already forgotten my task of getting to know the neglected world of the elemental beings. Just before she disappeared again I returned to my senses and besieged her with questions. She told me that the mysterious regenerative power of pure water was her gift to life. The fairy tales which mention the 'water of life' as a power that can bring the dead back to life refer to the elemental beings who preserve the power of water.

Then I was shown a vision of the surrounding nature in all its overwhelming beauty; normally a human being experiences such beauty only on very rare occasions. I was told that this heavenly quality of beauty is given to us by virtue of the regenerative power of water which the sylphs distribute throughout the whole of the created earth. This beauty is not only visible, but is perceived primarily through our feelings. When I felt ready to give thanks and leave Vida, the water woman issued a severe warning. The beauty given to the world by her and other elementals is not only an aesthetic quality but is in fact a fundamental quality of life. Through the progressive damage done to the environment, firstly by pollution and then later by the degradation of all water systems, this quality of life would be driven out, and the kiss of death would follow.

The third fairy-tale figure I encountered in my morning meditation was King Mathias, the most famous hero of Slovenian folk tales. People say that he slumbers with his great army inside Mount Peca, at the edge of Slovenian Carinthia. It had always been one of my special wishes to meet him, because I was curious to know what real powers he embodied compared to our heroic stereotypes for such figures.[6]

First a luminous sceptre appeared in the darkness, the symbol of kingly power. As I grasped the sceptre it led me into Mount Peca's underworld. Eventually I came to a huge hall where an old king was sitting. I was allowed to look into the face of this old king. Suddenly I knew that he was the prime intelligence of the elementals of earth, and his army were the sleeping powers of the earth, an immense number of gnomes wrapped in the arms of sleep.[7]

This deep sleep of these powers, which we imagine as soldiers, reminded me of the fairy tale 'Sleeping Beauty', which points out that awareness of the elemental world has sunk into the unconscious mind of humanity. Because of this complete forgetfulness, I was told, we experience the earth as a lump of non-intelligent matter. Since human consciousness is the decisive driving

---

[6] Similar stories are told in Britain about King Arthur who is said to be sleeping in certain places.

[7] Gnome comes from genomos (Greek): living inside the earth.

Fish woman Faronika —
a mythological figure depicting the spirit of balance.

force during the time of our evolutionary presence on earth, consequently the world of gnomes has been forced to retreat almost completely. The particularly sensitive people who created the folk tales long ago felt that the condition of the earth elementals was like someone lost in sleep.

After this I asked to be allowed another question. When this was granted, I asked about the event mentioned in many versions of the legends, where the soldiers of the king of the gnomes would awaken if a youth entered the great hall of the underworld and drew the sword from the king's sheath. Immediately the sword was pulled a third of the way out of its sheath. The blade was illuminated like one of the power lines on earth, which we call dragon lines,[8] which glow as they run through the landscape. Simultaneously, I received a message that the youth is a symbol for a new generation of human beings who will rediscover the earth's energy pattern: they will purify it and respect it. When this happens, the fully drawn sword is to be a sign for the elementals that the time has come to return from exile. They will transform the earth into a new Garden of Eden, co-creating it together with humanity. Therefore the legends end happily with the promise of an epoch of peace and bliss.

After these three encounters, I concluded that I had been meant to see the true functions of these fairy-tale figures, and to get an idea of the secret message in the fairy tales and an understanding of what they could mean for our lives today. Afterwards, there was a change of subject matter in my contacts with the elemental world. It seemed as if I was to be systematically initiated into all the different aspects of their existence.

. . . .

7. COMMENTARY: **The Primal Intelligence of Earth**

My first three encounters with the Earth Consciousness had not yielded any meetings with true elemental beings but instead with three facets of the primal intelligence of Earth. These are primal patterns that shape the processes on the earth's surface. However, one must understand that these primal patterns are simultaneously divine beings. That is why I could communicate with them and recognise them as mythical figures from the Slovenian folk tradition.

For the elemental beings on the earth's surface, these archetypical figures represent a sort of revered master intelligence that imparts vibrational instructions to direct their activities. These they follow constantly and in absolute trust. A kind of

---

[8] In the Chinese tradition acupuncture meridians are called dragon lines.
In the earth they carry cosmic power through the energy tissue of the landscape.

Beautiful Vida — ruler over the element of water.

heart relationship exists between the essence of the nature spirits and elemental beings on one side and the pantheon of archetypical figures on the other. I have only touched on this aspect here.

Later, I gave the name 'Arch-Elemental Plane' to the level, deep in Inner Earth, where these archetypical figures are to be found. The primal patterns that guided the construction of terrestrial creation on the surface are preserved there, and they are renewed in every moment. Pictorially speaking, elemental beings dive again and again into the Arch-Elemental plane to renew the power and knowledge that they need to carry out their specific functions on the earth's surface.

. . . .

The next phase was, in general terms, about the interaction of elementals with the life processes of the earth. The new phase also began with the water element. Water had carried me away and had left me on a river bank. I thought very hard about the kind of countryside in which I found myself. I was sure that I was in the middle of a typical cultivated European landscape. I saw brooks, lined with trees and bushes, meandering through fields. As was the custom in traditional agriculture, the fields were surrounded with colourful hedges teeming with plant and animal life. I immediately understood that I had not arrived in this landscape through my normal sense perceptions but rather through a doorway of the elementals, the dwarfs. So with great concentration I tried to observe where I could sense their presence. I realised that the whole landscape consisted of polarised energy fields like a chess board. It was not that one field was yin, the next field yang, but rather that each field was polarised within itself.[9] An intensified interaction occurred between the polarised corners which brought a dynamic energy to the whole field.

In practical terms, this polarisation stems from the hedges which frame the fields in a healthy agricultural landscape. As I have just mentioned, the hedges are polarised diagonally opposite each other, so that the dynamic interchange of the poles takes place in the centre of the field. The whole procedure is supervised by the elementals. In one corner of the hedge border the 'male' dwarfs have their focus, and somewhere in the polar opposite corner are the 'female' dwarfs. I could see their activity as an interplay between a reddish yin and a bluish yang type of wave energy, alternating from one focal point to the other, mixing in the field and mingling in a playful

---

[9] By this I mean that each field had a quality similar to a medieval cloister. The corners were polarised in such a way that one could experience a harmonising effect wherever one stood in the area.

Mathias — the sleeping king of gnomes as a symbol of earth powers.

knotwork. Simultaneously with this image I understood that, through the interaction which I had observed, the land would maintain its fertility quite naturally. Agricultural activity will continuously exhaust earth energy, but this draining of energy is balanced by the hedgerows.[10] Within the wonderful wilderness of hedges, the fertile powers of nature will regenerate endlessly. Polarised earth elementals have the task of initiating this process of regeneration and of irrigating the fields with renewed power through the yin-yang interplay.

While experiencing these glimpses into the mysterious activities of nature I realised that there was an impending danger for the long-term fertility of the earth. If all the hedgerows are destroyed in order to facilitate mechanised agriculture, then all the focal points for elementals will be eliminated. Their beneficial presence in the landscape will wither away. I had a sinking feeling that our planet was doomed to die.

In my next meditation after this precious insight into the work of the dwarfs, I began to get a sense of the possible relationships between the elemental world and the animal and plant kingdoms. With the animal kingdom, I remained in the dark for a long time. Quite obviously my consciousness lacked suitable concepts of the essence of animals for me to be ready for a revelation. Then I received a hint from the Walt Disney cartoon film of the fairy tale 'Beauty and the Beast', which I had watched the night before. The prince had been changed into an ugly animal because of his bad behaviour. During his change back, the prince returned to his beautiful form, and the strange animal mask fell away The handsome prince had been bewitched to wear a relatively ugly animal skin, and this was a striking indication of the fairy-like elemental which is somehow hidden in the animal form.

As an example, I wanted to be able to see the elemental soul of a bear. Subsequently, I perceived a transparent image of a bear which had a beautiful maiden's form shining through it. This maiden was a highly developed fairy being, and the bear served as a contact point for her with the material world. The difference between the two was baffling. The essence of the elemental is intertwined with that of the animal on the emotional level, and each helps the other. They learn from each other and therefore accelerate their spiritual growth.[11]

Then I asked whether the relationship with plants can be seen in a similar

---

[10] Hedgerows provide a living environment for an infinite number of animals and microbes. Stone walls or earth walls around fields have a similar function.

[11] Not all animal species live symbiotically with elementals; it is most common in the higher developed species.

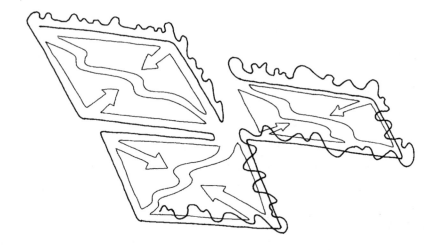

Part of a traditional cultivated landscape:
hedges around the fields maintain the effect of enlivening polarities.

way. The answer was: yes and no. Each plant will offer its physical body to an individual elemental as an opportunity for contact with the material level and for service. In that sense the relationship is similar to that with animals, although there is a difference which I want to talk about later (see Chapter Six). The 'no' refers to the different heritages of plants and animals. As with human beings, the evolution of animals is a kind of cosmic 'guest appearance' on Planet Earth, only the animals have gone deeper into expressing the variations of matter. Plants, on the other hand, are beings of the earth, and therefore are totally dependent on the cooperation of elementals, who in turn bestow on them increased levels of consciousness.

. . . .

8. COMMENTARY: **Spirits of the Environment – the Political Aspect**

Weird though it may sound, we have here to deal with a political question. For some time now, ecology has become a leading political theme worldwide. We go about protecting plants, animals and biotopes, and preserving the original character of individual landscapes. Can we then simply ignore and forget the soul and consciousness of these same natural worlds? Just when 'soft-ware' (consciousness) has become more important than 'hardware' (material) in the globalised world, the dimension of Nature's consciousness is being denied.

To address the political side of the elemental theme, I recently coined the expression 'environmental spirits'. It is time now to integrate the consciousness worlds of Nature with the various foci of environmental protection. Although they have no physical body, environmental spirits are no less real than plants, beasts, men and mountains. Consider. Are our thoughts real? Do they have a physical body? Are our gestures not seen as physical expressions of our thoughts? Similarly, environmental spirits can be seen as possessing a physical body, represented by their respective plants, mountains, beasts...

The theme of elemental beings is not only real in the political sense but it is explosive. Once we acknowledge that there is an environmental intelligence, we can no longer deal with plants, animals and valuable ores as objects to be bought and sold. It will be demanded of us that we communicate with them and respect their rights as integral beings.

. . . .

On another occasion, I asked my invisible guides to the worlds of elemental beings whether there was also a direct link between human beings and elementals. Their answer was difficult for me to grasp at that time. Therefore I asked them to show me in my own being how elementals act upon the human body. For a while there was darkness around me. Then I noticed the forces of the underworld working on my body. There was no direct contact; our interaction happened through resonance. Certain parts of the body seemed to be in resonance with complementary elemental forces. It seems plausible to me that these resonant relationships can become very disturbed when a human is alienated from nature. Then all sorts of illnesses might occur without an obvious cause on the physical plane.

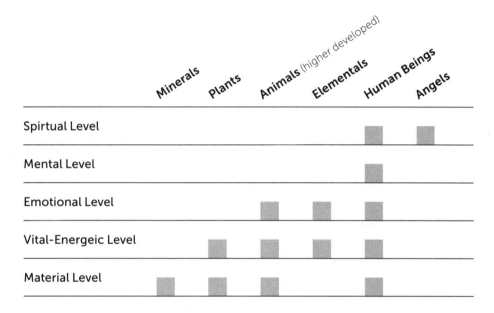

A comparison of how the energy of various elementals
is distributed on different levels of being.

In a second image I was able to see the kind of tasks the elemental world performs as a human being comes into incarnation. Again, I sensed the activities of elemental forces on matter by way of resonances in my own body. Then I saw how one elemental approached some matter which was already imbued with resonances, and moulded it according to patterns within its consciousness, so that the organs of the body were built. (This process is described in more detail in Chapter Seven—*The Personal Elemental of Animals and Humans.)*

There is another insight into the secret life of elementals which I would like to mention. It too was given to me in the winter of 1993. One morning in meditation, after taking my usual path into the underworld, I was immediately on arrival pulled in a curve to the right. I found myself on a path that spiralled vertically downwards, being drawn down deeper and deeper. In passing, I noticed two sideways-leading entrances on different levels but I was going at too great a speed to be able to leave the track and explore them.

. . . .

9. COMMENTARY: **Logical Consequences of a Fairytale Language**

I am aware that my research reports often seem like fairytales, and that the rational mind can hardly accept them as relevant. I make the contrary argument that if a scientifically oriented person is to investigate an almost completely unknown realm of consciousness, the only valid method is to settle oneself there and experience it in the language peculiar to it.

This is a type of spiritual investigation where the investigator identifies with the consciousness to be researched in order to collect direct qualitative experiences. The process demands that the rational mind translates spiritual experiences into a logical language that carries objective meaning to enhance our knowledge of the realm of environmental spirits and the general nature of the terrestrial world.

I have decided not to hide the process through which I have come to recognise our parallel evolutions. I speak on the theme openly in order to mediate to our rationally ruled culture the feeling that there are worlds which, although they appear to function by dancing and playing, yet bear an enormous responsibility for the fabric of life on earth. We humans should learn from them how we can overcome our stubbornly rational attitude towards our own problems and give greater expression to our emotional nature. Thereby we might also overcome the alienation from the life of earth from which our culture suffers.

. . . .

Eventually, at a third entrance at the end of the spiral I came to a halt. I entered to look around. In front of me there was a vast, beautiful landscape, but I could see no living beings. I asked myself what was the matter with this beautiful but lifeless country. In place of an answer I noticed how my body was slowly beginning to dissolve. Everything that had kept my body together was gently melting and dissolving into the beauty of the landscape. There was no pain involved in this process, rather a sense of solemnity as I became united with the forces of nature. It is interesting to note that my focus of consciousness remained whole.

Then I received a telepathic explanation: I was on the lowest level of a triadic cycle in the life of an elemental, a phase equal to 'death' in human beings. It should be understood that death is not just the dreaded moment when the soul leaves the body, but primarily means a continuation of life on the soul level. For the elementals, this phase is distinguished by the dissolution of the body which I had just experienced in my mind's eye. The elementals slip into total unity with the forces of nature, without losing their individual focus of consciousness. In this way they maintain a cycle of regeneration.

The two other entrances I had seen on my swift journey into the depths each lead to other phases in the life of elementals. The cycle begins with a phase of innocent pleasure and infinite joy within their own kingdom. We use the term underworld relative to the system of our own consciousness. If we consider the trinity of divine power, the underworld represents the 'Virgin' aspect of universal wholeness.[12]

After a time in the underworld, there follows a second creative phase, where elementals take on a certain task and carry it out in the real natural world. During this phase they leave the 'underworld' and connect their focal point with a particular plant, a hedgerow in the landscape or a river bank. In this book, it is mostly this phase which will be discussed, because it is the divine plan for nature, human beings and the elementals to be constantly in touch with each other.

It can take hundreds of years of continuous service for elementals to get to the third phase, which I had been experiencing in my body during this meditation. It is the phase of transformation which will finally take the elemental in its life cycle back to the threshold of the first phase. Compared to the daily rhythm of a human being, the first phase would be a mixture of food intake and pleasant play, the second a time of work, and the third one of sleep. However, the sequence of these three phases does not represent a rhythmic repetition of eating, working and sleeping as in the case of human beings. It is more like a cycle of three seasons in nature: spring, mid-summer and winter.

With these insights into the life cycle of elementals, my 'theoretical' cycle of revelations was complete. After this I was led towards the elemental world in more practical ways, and I was now to get to know the elementals in my

---

[12] On the spiritual-soul plane of a landscape the divine powers unfold as a threefold cycle. In their individual character the three phases relate to the threefold Goddess who was worshipped in pre-patriarchal times. I have observed her active power in the landscape as the virgin aspect, creativity aspect and transformation aspect.

own surroundings. The first encounter presents an example of the very awkward relationship we have with the intelligences of nature.

The first beings which I could directly perceive in nature were the elementals who accompany the growth of trees. I call them fauns, from the Latin term 'faunus'.[13] Traditionally they are depicted as young men with the lower body of a goat and horns on their head. This archaic image does not say much about the function of fauns but the half-man/half-animal form at least makes it clear that 'tree spirits' are on an entirely different path of evolution from the tree itself. As I mentioned previously, there is a symbiosis between plant and elemental.

I see the faun in a healthy tree as a spiralling energy which encircles the branches and also the roots deep down into the earth. This weaving of a power web by the fauns seems to precede the growth of branches and roots, and so can direct the growth into certain useful directions. The faun is able to manage this leading role because he possesses not only this energy body but also a relatively autonomous intelligence, so that he can constantly watch over the environment of his tree both above and below the earth. He is in complete harmony with the incoming information, and in his consciousness he can oversee the growth of the tree moment by moment. I perceive this dimension of consciousness in the faun as a face woven into the top of the tree, complementing the energetic structure of his body.

In classical antiquity fauns were perceived as running from tree to tree. This image reflects the estranged consciousness which can no longer recognise the laws of cooperation between tree and elemental. Through its plant body the tree provides an opportunity for the elemental to gain experiences in matter. In return, the faun offers his consciousness to help the tree grow harmoniously into its environment. Through this reciprocal action the faun is tied to the tree for its entire lifetime. It is a process almost equivalent to the way a soul joins the body of a person during incarnation.

The coupling is achieved by a kind of umbilical cord which ties the faun to his chosen tree. More precisely, this is the focal point of consciousness which the faun tacks onto the energetic fabric of the tree to build a bridge of mutual communication. Since elementals have no free will, but act as a part of all-embracing nature, the faun cannot untie his 'umbilical cord' as long as 'his' tree is alive and this means as long as there is life within its roots.

---

[13]   The Greek word 'dryad' is also used for a tree spirit.

10. EXERCISE: **Shaking Hands with a Tree**

This seems the right place to propose an exercise by which readers can experience for themselves the being of different tree spirits. Some mighty trees that stand in a park in the Italian part of Gorizia helped me discover this possibility.

At the time, I had been invited to give a talk about the power of Nature. The talk was to be given in the middle of the park, and I wanted to end it with some exercises with the surrounding trees. My usual perception exercises consume a lot of time, so I had the idea of asking the trees themselves what sort of contact they wanted. The reply was unambiguous: they look at people and constantly see how we shake hands with each other. But nobody would shake hands with them.

"How's that going to happen?" I wondered, and immediately felt myself turned around by a giant cedar so that my back was towards it. (I was standing under the edge of its crown). Next, my left hand was raised high (I am left-handed) so that it was held out over my shoulder towards the tree behind my back. At the same time, I felt a strong prohibition against turning around and observing any gestures on the tree's part. After a few moments, I felt a warm, tender touch on my fingertips. I understood at once why the tree spirit had desired this higher degree of intimacy. To be able to reach into the physical realm, it must circumvent certain defining rules that do not allow it to operate on the physical plane.

I have often repeated this exercise with different groups, and each time I experience something unexpected. The resulting communication ranges from conscious emotional impressions to very precise insights into the place's geomantic levels. One can even use this method to shake hands with mountains!

. . . .

During my first days of practising the perception of elemental beings, I was provided with two instructive examples. In mid-February 1993 I had a meeting with the mayor of the northern districts of the city of Ljubljana to discuss a lithopuncture project for the town. We were having dinner at the Forge Inn, a famous old restaurant on the outskirts of town. When the proprietress passed our table he introduced me to her. To our surprise she told us that she had read and very much appreciated my book about the spiritual dimensions of the townscape of Ljubljana. Later on she joined us to talk about a problem which worried her greatly. Her concern was about a centuries'-old linden tree in the yard of her restaurant. Her family wanted to cut it down, considering it dangerous to the foundations of the house and to the roofs of surrounding buildings. She herself did not dare to agree to this, fearing that it would bring misfortune. I promised to call again the following week to talk to the linden tree.

When I returned she led me to the inner yard where I encountered a shocking and terrible sight. Every single branch of the tall linden tree had been sawn off. Only the thick trunk towered six metres high. I asked the woman to leave me alone for a few minutes, and I went across to the tree trunk. To find a contact point for communication I placed my hand very lightly on the bark of the tree. Then I opened my emotional consciousness by radiating love, and so created a bridge over which communication with the being of the tree could flow.

As soon as the bridge was established, an image rushed into my consciousness of a crucified giant suffering terrible agony. With a spasmodic movement he rose up again and again as if he wanted to push off from the earth, but then he kept collapsing to the ground. Each upward thrust caused a repeat of this unbearable torment.

To be able to illustrate better the faun's suffering I want to draw an historical parallel. The Romans invented the 'perfect' method of crucifixion whereby the victim remained alive to endure his suffering for at least three days. They put a cross-bar underneath the feet of the crucified man on which the victim would instinctively seek support, pushing upwards at the moment of collapse and choking.

The situation of the poor faun was exactly like that of a crucified man. The enormous roots were still intact and sending a stream of life force up into the trunk. But up there the top was missing and could not take in this force. Consequently, the surge of power collapsed and plummeted back downwards again. Through a single image the faun had communicated to me the whole tragedy of his situation.

I went to see the worried proprietress and told her that this kind of torture should never be suffered by a tree. Since it was irreversible I would try and 'transplant' the faun. I asked her to show me the young linden trees she had planted around the house to replace the old tree in the future.

I tested each little tree with my hand to see whether or not it had a faun. And lo and behold by the car park I found a linden tree which had no faun. It looked quite miserable. Taking a beautiful gem stone from my pocket (I always carry some with me) I went to the tormented linden tree and held the small stone close to the trunk, explaining to the faun that I wanted to transplant him to another linden tree where he would be able to serve well. Then I asked him to transfer his focal point onto the stone and I carefully transported him to the young linden tree. There, once again, I put the little stone close to the thin stem and asked the unlikely traveller to alight, and to put his focus of consciousness onto the young linden tree.

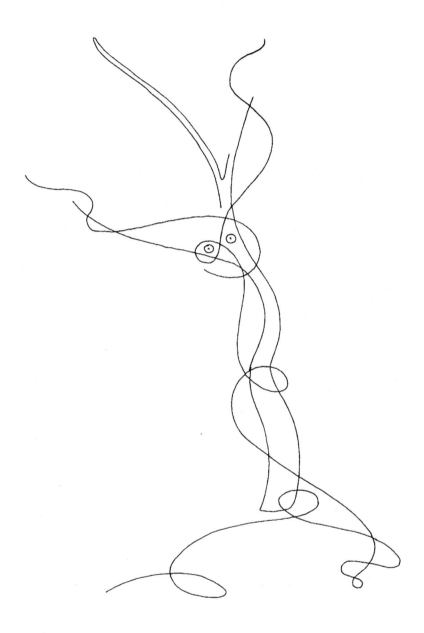

The faun of a young tree.

Afterwards, I recommended to the proprietress that she should fell the old linden tree completely as soon as possible. When I went to visit the 'Smithy' again in early summer, the woman told me that the young linden tree had never bloomed so beautifully as this year.

. . . .

11. QUESTION: **Can a Tree Feel Pleasure?**

After the original book on elemental beings was published, this story released an avalanche of questions from readers. I was asked whether, in general, it was right to fell trees, whether one should transfer the spirit of every tree felled to another tree, etc.

Above all, one should trust the consciousness of nature to take care of the trees and other beings of nature independently. If a tree is felled, its spirit experiences a kind of liberating impulse that enables it to return to the wholeness of Earth Consciousness. As related above, this is a natural process in the life cycle of a nature spirit.

Naturally, the process will be made easier if people inform the tree spirit at least 24 hours before the cutting begins. How do you do this? To give an example, you may bow before the tree and thank the tree spirit for its service. Then you follow with the news, which the tree spirit can perceive through the accompanying waves of gratitude. It can then withdraw before the painful sawing process begins. If a whole woodland is targeted, one can give the news (which is sad only for us humans) to the collective spirit of the wood.

There are exceptional cases as here described when, instead of being freed from a service it no longer desires, the tree spirit feels tortured by the good intentions it can no longer fulfil. Trees that perform a special task in the landscape are also exceptional cases. For example, they may represent the seat of a higher environmental spirit. In such a case, one should, whenever possible, plant a substitute tree beforehand. Since a young tree is really too weak to serve as the focus point for such an elevated being, one should bury a stone or powerful crystal nearby. In this case, the spirit concerned should transfer to the new focus point. However, one must inform it of the possibility.

In all circumstances, one should go forward creatively, be open to any ideas and fearlessly forge new paths. If the solution is not exactly right, nature will adapt. A clear and pure intention is always decisive.

. . . .

Meeting with the suffering faun in the topless linden tree.

A few days later I was giving a workshop in the old Slovenian town of Koper. Originally, this town was built by the Venetians on an island, and the houses were placed so close together that there was no space for a green area. But by the end of the 19th century a fortified tower at the tip of what used to form the island had been torn down and in its place they had put a tiny park. The trees they planted then had now grown into beautiful giants. Among them I had noticed in particular a plane tree from which a strong branch stretched out horizontally for eight metres brackets (8ft), at which point it turned upright again with full power. The point above which the branch was now growing was one of the local balance points that I had learned about from the fish woman Faronika.

The faun in charge of the growth of a tree is not only aware of the biological-geological conditions of the tree's environment, he also knows about the energetic phenomena. He can direct the growth of the tree in such a way that it is able to relate to power points within its reach, as in this example of the plane tree at Koper. Such branches are particularly worth protecting, because the vitality of the tree normally depends on them.

When I arrived in the small park with the participants in my workshop to practise communication with fauns, I discovered with horror that the park had been urbanised. Not only had the landscape gardeners paved the paths but they had also cut off the unusual long branch of the plane tree, because in their eyes it was a disturbing feature.

After I had used this example to explain the ignorance of people regarding trees, and their consequent wrong decisions, each participant went off to choose a tree to communicate with. I decided to leave it to the others to experience the mutilated plane tree. Instead I went to a different plane tree.

Although I approached it with deep love, there was no response from his side. For a long time everything was quiet, then something like a wild dog jumped on me from the top of the tree, barking frightfully loudly. I looked up to the top with surprise. And what could I see? The reckless landscape gardeners of the park had sawn off all the lower branches of this old plane tree. They simply wanted a tree with a high top. What arrogance!

All of a sudden I could understand the faun's message: because of this disastrous surgery to the middle section of the trunk, the faun had lost his connection with the roots, and now was desperately isolated up there in the remaining part of the crown. To be able to help him I went deep into meditation and created with my consciousness a bridge of light to connect the faun above with the roots below. I kept this inner picture for quite a while to allow this much-abused elemental to reconnect with the roots. At the end of this meditative 'action' I received a gentle feeling of gratitude before I resumed further work with the workshop participants.

Very soon it became clear to me that the fauns would be my first guides in any domain of ecology where elementals are present. I simply began to ask the trees about anything I could not understand. I had often done this before, but I had not then been ready to perceive the slight distinction between a tree's 'plant being' and the faun 'incarnated' within it. Nor had I known that the faun represented the tree's intelligence, and that this was the level at which communication was possible.

Next, my thoughts began to turn towards a tragic situation where I felt a faun could help me. This situation had arisen not far from our house eight years previously, during a period when farmland was being redistributed. The environment in our valley had been badly damaged at this time, in the first half of the 1980s. A small piece of woodland behind our house was turned into a field. It was cut down and the roots of the trees were even pulled out using heavy machinery. In theory, this should not have posed a problem for the fauns, because with the removal of the roots they were free to take on new jobs in the surrounding forests.

However, there were many signs of a problem. A farmer had unsuccessfully tried to grow corn in the new field, and then had never tried again, and the field had remained as fallow land. Also, when passing one day, I inwardly perceived that the whole area of these former woods was blackened, as if there had been a fire there. A flock of very distressed beings hovered nearby, but I could not identify them.

To find an explanation I went to an old hornbeam situated close to this unhappy field. In answer to my question about what was going on in the neighbouring field the faun impressed on my consciousness a very clear picture. I saw the organic form of a white kernel, squeezed inside several layers of distasteful grey and partly black matter, and the whole formed a sort of hard-baked lump. The faun showed me the lump in cross-section to help me understand its content.

Unfortunately I did not have enough experience of elementals at that time, and therefore I could not interpret the picture. I asked my youngest daughter Ana to pass on my request for an explanation to the Angel of Earth Healing, with whom she had been in communication since 1992. A short while later Ana wrote down the Angel's answer. His name is Devos, and he is completely dedicated to the problem of healing disruptions to the earth's energy web. His message was:

"This is a typical human act. They remove whatever is in their way. Nature and all those beings who will lose their home through the destruction of their habitat are of little importance to them. Humans only value what is pleasing to themselves. Trees which are in the way must disappear, they are of no use. (They think) there are enough woods around, and it would not matter if the small forest in question were to be cut down. Our lamentations and complaints could go on endlessly but it is too painful and too distressing. People do not realise that they are destroying a great number of beings, and in the last analysis also a part of themselves, because humans are also part of nature.

"It is better for us to look at this situation now. As Marko knows, certain elementals and other beings are able to break free from such a place to find new homes and tasks after a while. Angelic beings who hover over such a complex area are of such a type. They take care of the proper unfolding of life forces, balancing the elements which are present, and they direct energy and other beings. But they can also drift about for a while to look for solutions in difficult circumstances. Eventually they will reorient themselves. Nevertheless, there are certain beings tied to a place, so much so that they don't know what to do after an interference with nature such as this. For instance, the water beings responsible for a spring, a stream or a river, are part of these water systems and form its life. They cannot leave their responsibilities after such a disaster and move to another place. They are tied to a particular water environment. This is the reason why they are affected so deeply by such an act of destructtion. They continue to try and help a spring or a stream. But these culverts, created by machines and human coarseness, are foreign to their nature. That is why they hover above the water in an unhappy state: they cannot exist in the watery substance any more, and they are doomed to watch its degradation. In this unfortunate state they turn very dark, even black. This means the end of their habitat, and left to itself it will degrade.

"This is the case with the tiny forest behind your house. The water beings have withdrawn from the site since all their efforts to make contact with the place have been in vain.

The space will harden and then crumple and become a dead place without energy and without life. You can help the situation by trying to find the point where the beings had their centre, their focal point, and from which they spread the energies of the spring water into the environment. Find a way to help them gather and live again at their source point. Then they do not need to be scattered all around. At least this point could have life again, where all the beings and all their energies have their source. The place will be able to breathe again when it is not plagued by lost beings constantly wandering about."

The root of my inability to understand the picture which the hornbeam faun had put into my mind was the fact that I had expected possible problems only with the tree ele-mentals, and I had entirely forgotten that at the edge of the forest there had been a marshy area with a small spring. From there, a tiny stream had meandered through the meadows. With the reorganisation of land this natural damp area had been drained and the spring blocked. To deal with the spring water which still trickled out, a culvert more than a metre deep had been dug in place of the stream. All the natural forms of the water element had been destroyed, and the water elementals, the nixies, were deprived of any possibility of fulfilling their life's work.

In the same way that a faun ties his energetic body to a certain tree by an 'umbilical cord', the nixies who take care of a spring are connected to it. They tie their focal point to the source, and this indicates that they are responsible for the spring. If the spring is destroyed by human interference, then they lose their 'body' but are still tied to their task. Unlike a tree which dies but whose seedlings can grow nearby, a spring is a permanent part of the landscape. Even when it is destroyed, a spring stays present in the inner landscape along with its guardians, the nixies. They must forever hover over the place in their dis-embodied misery, confused and darkened through destructive human actions. My image of a lump that was caked together with light on the inside and more and more black towards the outside was an accurate depiction of the tragic situation.

Together, Ana and I took care of the lost flock of nixies. First we thoroughly purified the whole area of the old marshland using a combination of medita-tion and visualisation of healing colours. Then we placed at its edge a beautiful big stone and aligned it to the right vibration. We asked the water elementals to gather around this stone as their focal point. The Angel of Earth Healing had suggested that this at least should help to overcome the chaotic condition of the nixies, until such a time when the spring could flow there again.

. . . .

12. EXERCISE: **Perceiving Water Elementals**

Since that time I have developed various exercises to help perception of the envi-ronmental spirits of the water element. Over the past ten years my aim has shifted from relaying information on my personal experiences to encouraging personal responsibility in others. Everyone who desires their own experiences of the world of elemental beings should be helped to achieve them. The proposed exercises will afford this help.

The first exercise is based on its resonance with the traditional image of a mermaid, the lower part of whose body is portrayed as covered with fish scales. You should stand at the rim of a watery biotope and for a little while imagine that your thighs are covered with fish scales. Don't just visualise this but feel how the fish scales are characteristically hard and cool. Finally, you can flap your 'own' fish tail back and forth a few times.

These procedures build the resonance bridge to those water elemental beings that are present. You should now forget what you have imagined and at the same moment open your perception.

The second exercise starts like the first, at the rim of a watery biotope. You should imagine yourself raising a few drops of water high enough to touch your solar plexus region. Then raise the water still higher to the edge of the heart chakra.

After a few moments, let go of the water you have imagined and at the exact same time, open your perception. Every second's delay weakens the capacity to perceive the invisible extensions of the water world, because it allows the rational mind to re-establish control.

In the sense meant here, perception means letting the water world work on our bodies, feel it emotionally, even let it lead us into an inner dance...

. . . .

TWO

The Realm of Elemental Beings

IN EUROPEAN FOLK TALES we often encounter strange creatures, and I would automatically classify them as elemental beings if I had not had such sad experiences as those mentioned in Chapter One. These experiences have shown me how we have demonised and perverted the essence of nature spirits. I now understand that many of the figures in the old legends are above all an expression of distorted human thinking rather than true stories about elementals and their qualities.

For example, there are numerous stories about dragons, but I have never been able to observe a dragon-like elemental. On the other hand, I am familiar with many energy aspects of Planet Earth that are of a fiery nature, and which mark the landscape with a strange pattern of power. It would be very easy to build a dragon-like image into them. Our familiar ley lines (which distribute cosmic power within the landscape) are even called dragon lines in the Chinese geomantic Feng-Shui[1] tradition. If we could see the invisible fiery vortexes of such a power line as it runs in a straight, radiant axis up and down the landscape, then it would most certainly be symbolised by a dragon figure. We would then understand that the dragons in fairy tales and legends are a reminder of the power structures within the landscape. When human beings could no longer perceive them, they sank into the unconscious realm.

There is yet another group of forms which has found its way into the lore of fairy tales and legends, although superficially it seems to belong to the elemental kingdom. The goddesses were mostly banished from human consciousness when patriarchal structures came into power, and a veil was drawn over their presence; they sank to the lower ranks of mythology and could only exist in an altered form through legends and fairy tales. An example of

---

[1] Literally translated: wind and water.

51

this is the tale of 'Berchta with the Iron Nose' who watches over the winter solstice as the bearer of transformational power, in this small way upholding the tradition of the Black Goddess. In Slovenian folklore she is known as Pehta, and in parts of the German-speaking countries as Frau Holle, who is the maker of snow.

There is a third group of mythical figures which should not be confused with elementals. They exist because for centuries Christian teachings have veiled their true identity in human consciousness. However, the folk soul of each region has intuitively recognised the weak points in standard Christian beliefs, and has compensated by creating certain symbolic figures. I believe that in this way demonic figures have developed, like the 'returner' (German: *Wiedergänger*) who returns again and again in the form of a ghost or animal, although no longer part of the living world. He seems to represent a response to the Christian taboo on ideas of reincarnation. In addition, the suppressed dimensions of the individual soul might take on a demonic form in dream life, a *night-mare*.

On the other hand it is possible to find the true nature of dwarfs, fairies and nixies revealed in some legends. For instance, we can discover something in a Slovenian legend about the work of fairies. Here they are seen as wise women: "It happened in winter. There was still snow on the ground when there was a loud call from the fairies: 'Sow broad beans, sow broad beans.' But the farmers thought it would be crazy to sow beans in the snow. All of them were of this opinion except for one, who was bright enough to follow the wise women's advice. He grabbed his hoe, made a furrow in the snow and sowed his beans.[2] In early summer, the clever farmer had to use a ladder to pick his broad beans. They had grown miraculously tall!"

Nowadays we can work with the biodynamic seed-planting calendar and so we know that certain days, and even hours, are more suitable than others for planting because a certain constellation of stars and planets in the sky will enhance the growth of plants. In my experience, fairy beings are the kinds of elemental spirits which mediate life processes between heaven and earth. It is definitely in their domain to signal the right sowing times. The purpose of the legends is to make farmers less susceptible to the reasoning of their minds, and rather to trust the old ways of nature. The clever ones will obey the traditional guidance of the nature beings and will listen inwardly to their call.

---

[2] Broad beans were one of the staple foods in Europe before the potato was introduced from America. Normally they do not grow taller than 120 cm (4 ft).

To strengthen the credibility of the above messages from the myths, I would like to tell the story of a host of fairies which I watched in summer 1993. I was on the Isle of Srakane, a small, stony island which is part of a group in the Adriatic Sea (the group includes the other tiny islands of Susak and Srakane Male).

I perceived that the focus or 'umbilical cord' of the fairies was a tall, thin pillar of power on top of the central hill, which I named Venus Hill because of its inner connection to the Planet Venus. The pillar of power was anchored inside the earth and was glistening with all the colours of the rainbow as if it were woven from delicate coloured threads. In my consciousness I immersed myself in the pillar of colour to be carried upwards by the ascending power. At one point, about a hundred metres high (328ft), the pillar of power resolved into a group of dynamic beings. I identified them as fairies of place for this location. They expanded from their centre in a gliding motion until they covered the entire area above the group of islands. As soon as they reached the borders of their territory they would return in a big sweep to their source at the focal point. In this resting phase they resembled the closed bud of a flower. After a pause, these white fairy figures would expand outwards again and glide through space on the same route. It resembled the movement of a constantly opening and closing flower bud.

I tried to count the number of individual beings within the host of fairies, and got a surprise: there were 13 of them. To be honest, I must confess that I had been quite certain that, in accordance with the normal rules of invisible reality, the number would be the solar 12, and I felt a certain resistance when it turned out to be 13. When I asked within for a reason for my resistance I was led downwards in the pillar of light. Deeper and deeper I followed the fairies' focus, through the crust of the earth and into the underworld. There I saw the thirteenth fairy circling like a shadow through the underworld spaces. At first I believed that I was seeing a demon, and I was afraid. But I soon realised that the work area of fairies of place could not be restricted to the air *above* ground. To be complete, their sphere definitely had also to encompass part of the dark world below.

I immediately remembered the dark, thirteenth fairy in 'Sleeping Beauty'. She was not invited to the birth celebration of the newborn princess, but nevertheless appeared to tell the princess that she would die at the age of 15. This thirteenth fairy reminds us of the moon rhythm[3] and the old world order.

---

[3] The ancient lunar calendar with 13 months was replaced by the sun calendar with 12 months.

Within her own being she was not negative at all; rather she represented a darker part of our world sphere together with the underworld aspect of the fairies which had been banished from our consciousness at a time when memories were still fresh of these fairies of place in their light bodies.

I asked myself what it does to the life of a landscape when fairies of place dance in concentric circles, since this kind of fairy dance is often mentioned in fairy tales. In response I recognised four levels on which the fairies of place were active. On the uppermost level the fairies would show themselves in harmony with the rhythm of the stars and planets. These rhythms were reflected in the fairies' consciousness and would put them into a state of ecstasy. They would transfer this state of being to their surroundings and at the same time would imprint the cosmic time pulse onto all living beings.

The next level below this one I can only compare with the feelings of ecstatic love-making. This derives from the fairies' constant gliding through their area, and the scent of unconditional love which they wrap around even the tiniest living particle with which they come into contact. The whole area is repeatedly bathed in the love of these divine beings.

On the next level, the fairies take care of all the different life processes which occur within 'their' space. It also entails the alignment of the earthly life rhythm with the universal rhythm, as well as the orchestration of various patterns of events within the nature kingdom to guarantee the most harmonious life atmosphere.

Then I was able to see the fourth level which connects their work to the underground spaces. Here there is a feeling of grounding and deep rootedness within the being of Planet Earth.

. . . .

13. COMMENTARY: **Fairies and the Space of the Underworld**

It is time to fill a gap in this discourse. Compared to the other three levels, the fourth level of fairy activity in the landscape has received short shrift, because it has only been during the past two years that I have really come to grips with the Inward Spaces of Earth. Beforehand, I was still partly fixed on the idea of Earth being a dense ball. As related in the previous chapter, I was then merely able to drill some holes of consciousness into the Inward Earth.

In the meantime I have come to see the Inward Earth as a cosmic space that does not get narrower as one penetrates deeper but becomes ever broader. This means that life in the Inward Earth is no less wide-ranging and intensive than life on the earth's surface, or even further out in the universe. Earth's inner and the

Dancing fairies of place above Venus Hill (Isle of Srakane);
the thirteenth fairy is circling through the underworld.

outer lives differ in that as you proceed inward into ever broader regions, the life-realms settled there display a more predominantly ensouled and spiritual charac-ter. The realms of life that strive for incarnation and materialisation stretch toward the outside. The bases of the life processes are stored towards the inside, but their realisation in matter towards the outside. (See my book *Touching the Breath of Gaia*, Findhorn Press, 2008)

The fourth level of fairy activity operates in facilitating the exchange that takes place between the inner and outer worlds of Earth. On this level its circling path resembles an upright lemniscate (8). The lower circle of the lemniscate represents its path through the archetypical world of Inward Earth where it gathers from the cosmic storehouses of the inner worlds the information that is important to the cycles of life on earth's surface. The upper circle symbolises the dance of the fairy consciousness as it distributes the acquired qualities into the airy space above the surface and into successive extensions of the outer cosmos.

. . . .

Finally, I must stress that we should not imagine the four levels of fairy consciousness as being four hierarchical layers; rather they are expressed in each moment as four interweaving vibratory qualities, and they are danced by the fairies.

Since we humans hold more and more power over our shared living land-scape, the fairies of place are no longer able to limit their function to the na-ture kingdom alone. During the past centuries, without being conscious of it, human culture has striven to shape and occupy spaces, and has had an impact on the fairies of place. The relationship between the two formative forces will become increasingly tragic because we human beings are completely ignorant of the function of these fairies. We force our egotistical will onto the land-scape without consulting the lawful intelligence of the fairies about the effects of our interventions. This is true even of some of the well-intended ecological projects of which we are so proud.

. . . .

14. EXERCISE: **Perceiving the Fairy World**

To understand the fairy world, it is best to gather together one's own experiences of their presence. There are various exercises for this. Since fairies are beings of the air element, Ajra suggests that we breathe with them. During your inbreath, be conscious that you are inhaling the fairy essence, which is distributed every-where in the air. Greet them with an open heart while you take them into yourself, and greet them too while you exhale, to honour their presence. After you have breathed like this a few times, forget about breathing and give yourself over to experiencing the heights and depths of the fairy world.

A second exercise is related to the fairy world's traditional symbol: the wings of birds. To resonate with the fairy world, you should imagine that your shoulders have sprouted a bird's wings. Stretch your wings out wide a few times, as birds do in a birdbath. By stretching your wings in your imagination, you begin to vibrate in tune with the fairy consciousness. In the same moment, open yourself to the experiences that come to you. Feel free to join in the fairy dance.

A third exercise was recommended to me by a sacred tree in a neighbouring wood. Imagine that you put both your hands under the soles of your feet and raise yourself high in the air. There, consciously breathe in and out a few times. Then feel free to perceive the expanses of the fairy world around you. Do not hesitate. Be open to what is unknown and never before experienced. Extend your imagination. Trust your heart's essence, which is your soul, that it would never lead you into illusions unless such an experience was important for you at that moment. Let yourself enjoy the quality of the fairy world.

. . . .

Folk tales often tell of attempts to reunite the two divergent worlds. An interesting example of this is an experience I had when visiting the church of St Anna in the far northeast corner of Slovenia. The church is situated in a clearing in a forested hilly landscape, at least three miles away from the village which it serves. This unusual site points to a secret.

We were to learn more about this while preparing for a workshop on earth healing in Jeruzalem-Svetinje in August 1993. This included a visit to the church. During one of her communications, my daughter Ana had asked the Angel of Earth Healing to give her some information about the role that St Anna plays in this particular landscape.[4] The Angel considered the site of the church to be very important for the vital-energetic dimension of the Slovenian macro-landscape. The vital energy feeds different areas in the country. It is stored here and distributed from this focal point. The hill with St Anna's church and the two neighbouring hills form a threefold-layered triangular composition. Each of the three hills of different height is the anchor point for one of three triangles which are piled on top of each other. The three hills

---

[4]   Here we are dealing with the vital-energetic level which is closer
to the material level than the highest spiritual-soul level.

and their respective triangles differ in the spiritual-soul qualities they embody. These qualities are love, synthesis and connectedness. The three triangles act as channels for the life force which is received from cosmic realms through a central pillar of light within the triangles.

Once the energy has flowed through one of the triangular channels, it is directed via ley lines to many different points of distribution in the Slovenian landscape. The function of this triangular energy structure may be compared to that of the heart in our human body.

In neolithic times, about five thousand years ago, people still understood the significance of this place. Therefore they constructed circular temples of standing stones on the three hills, which they constantly re-energised by means of ceremonial rituals. As the early stone age culture of the Goddess became more and more suppressed in Europe by the intrusion of Indo-Germanic patriarchal tribes, the awareness of the interrelationship between different parts of a landscape faded, and the sanctuary circles on these three hills were no longer cared for. Now, only the church of St Anna (built much later) remains of this complex structure of the holy shrine. However, Christian rituals have been celebrated there over the centuries and have kept the quality of the place relatively pure until now.

When I began to understand how precious this church was, I cautiously asked the warden of St Anna's whether he knew of any tradition that could explain why the church and the cemetery were built so far away from the village which, after all, was a 25-minute walk through the forest. He said he did not but he did remember some stories about an incident. There was a time, probably in the 18th century, when there was a plan to rebuild the church on a new spot in the centre of the village. All the necessary materials were soon obtained, brought to the place and left there, but then, during the night, fairy beings—the 'White Women'—carried all of it back to the old location of St Anna's. After receiving this clear message, the people decided to leave the church in its original place.

If we combine the information received from the Angel by my daughter with this miraculous story told by the warden, we can draw conclusions about the great precautions that the fairies of place take in caring for the landscape entrusted to them. These fairies of place not only enhance and harmonise the life processes in nature, but also know about power inlet points and the significance of powerful places within their stewardship. They try to protect places such as St Anna's from neglect, and try to motivate the currently dominant culture to preserve their sacredness.

As long as nature alone dominates the landscape, the power points are made use of only to the extent necessary to support the elementals of place. But if human civilisations develop in this area, there will be a much greater demand for life energy and certain cosmic powers. The human culture then needs to take responsibility for further development of the places of power because of its own need for additional supplies of energy. The fairies silently pray that this responsibility may be practised in cooperation with the rhythms of the fairies of place.

In the Western tradition, the first book to bring together all the different species of elementals into one coordinated system, and which described their unique characteristics, was *About Nymphs, Sylphs, Pygmies*[5] *and Salamanders and Other Spirits*. It was first printed in 1589, 48 years after the death of its author, the famous physician, scientist and theosophist Theophrastus Bombast of Hohenheim, also known as Paracelsus. Paracelsus stated that the elemental spirits were equal to human souls in the value of their evolutionary development. He talked about two ancestral lines of descent whereby one, the human being,… "is of the lineage of Adam and the other one, the nature spirits, is not". For the first, redemption through Christ is guaranteed but for the other it is not. Nevertheless, Paracelsus always reiterates that the elementals should not be seen as demons or devilish spirits; they too originate from the incomprehensible diversity of divine creation.

To emphasise that nature spirits are of equal value to humanity, and to differentiate the elementals from 'devilish' creatures, the author describes the elementals in a very anthropomorphic manner, which is not in accordance with my own observations, although I believe that in fact they have the potential of taking on such a form. It is also possible that they *did* appear to him in humanoid form to support him in his vision of two parallel original essences. Paracelsus even maintained"… they have blood, flesh and bone, they bear children, are fertile, and they talk, eat, drink and travel." All these things are not possible for the spirits known as demons. However, all the characteristics ascribed to nature spirits are not manifested in matter, as with human beings, but exist on a level of finer materials.

I can see in the works of Paracelsus a courageous attempt, in the face of the Inquisition, to rescue the rich lore of the Middle Ages about elementals. He used an almost scientific method to preserve it from the future mind set of denial in the age of rationalism. I am grateful for the systematic approach which

---

5   From: *pygmaios* (Greek)—the height of a span or a kind of goblin

he established in his work. He divides nature spirits into four kinds, each belonging to one of the classic elements. He calls the beings of water *nymphs or nixies*; the beings of air *sylphs*; the earth spirits *pygmies*; and fire beings *salamanders*. During my own observations I was able to verify that individual elementals actually belong to one of the four elements in nature. Paracelsus also wrote about giants, mermaids and the 'Venusburg', which are themes I want to return to later.

Element	Name of Being (after Paracelsus)	General Purpose
Powers of water	Nymphs	Quality of life
Powers of air	Sylphs	Quality of space
Powers of earth	Pygmies	Quality of physical manifestation
Powers of fire	Salamanders	Quality of transformation

A system of elemental beings developed according to Paracelsus.

. . . .

15. COMMENTARY: Environmental Spirits of the Five Elements

I have described the world of nature spirits in terms of the four elements, but with the ongoing process of earth change, which I will describe in more detail in the final, newly written chapter of this book, that model has become too narrow. During the last ten years elemental beings have appeared that cannot be categorised in one of the four elements. They move freely between the four elements and show themselves as belonging to different elements in different situations. These are the environmental spirits of the fifth element.

The five element system plays an important role in the Eastern World, for example in Feng-Shui. Furthermore, we forget that the old, four element model really recognises a fifth element, which is ether.

The ether element takes precedence over the other four. Water, Air, Earth and Fire represent the manifested world, but the ether element expresses the life-promoting powers that operate in the invisible realm to shape the environment gener-ally. We can distinguish between a watery, airy, earthy and fiery ether, from which we may see that the fifth element carries the other four as powers within itself.

The essential characteristic of the environmental spirits of the fifth element is that they can move freely through the realms of the other four without having to belong to any one of them.

We will speak more of this later, but basically we can see them as spirits of communication that are prepared to mediate between the hostile worlds of na-ture and humankind, which is engaged in selfish globalisation. They often serve as mirrors of the qualities that should really be incorporated in us, but from which we are now far distant; for example the quality of brotherly love. They mirror them-selves back to us, reminding us of who we are in the inmost core of our being.

. . . .

Of the four elements, I have so far described gnomes and dwarfs as the earth elementals; I have also introduced the water spirits and the fairies who repre-sent the air element. As the fire spirits are often neglected, I had better describe them now to avoid upsetting them.

My first encounter with these awesome beings came quite unexpectedly after a workshop on earth healing in Kiel in April 1993. Ilse, my host, has a small plot of land on the outskirts of town, and she asked me to investigate a peculiar event. The previous winter she had pruned the crown of an old apple tree. The clippers suddenly seemed to jump from her hands for no apparent reason, and the back of her hand was cut so severely that she had to go to hospital for stitches. She was bleeding so profusely that the doctor expressed surprise that her hand was not badly damaged, for no nerves or ligaments had been severed.

I climbed to the top of the apple tree—and what did I see on one of the uppermost branches? A dozen small beings, each of them somewhat crow-like. They looked like the horrible figures in the paintings of Hieronymus Bosch. Some of them had long, badly proportioned noses, reminiscent of the beaks of vultures, others were squatting on thin insect-like legs ... I recognised them intuitively as fire elementals. The surrounding atmosphere felt unhappy and almost hopeless. I asked Use what she thought had happened and why these salamanders were sitting high up in the apple tree in such a desperate state. Was there anything wrong with the spot where the apple tree was growing? After a long pause she recalled that there had once been a compost pile un-derneath the tree. The previous autumn she had decided to move it to the opposite side of the garden. One day, with the help of two young men, the old compost heap had quickly been moved.

Suddenly, I was able readily to understand the problem of the fire spirits. As they are spirits of transformation, their field of action is centred on dying, decay and regeneration. In every garden their most cherished work place is the compost pile: it is their temple and their palace. There they work with the forces of death, but also with the forces of regeneration. How could human beings just come along and take away their sacred place, and how could the poor fire spirits know that there was a new compost heap for them at the other end of the garden, which to them is a universe away?

In search of their sacred compost the salamanders had climbed the nearest apple tree, and finally they sat and waited on the highest branch. The only possible way they could see to draw attention to their predicament and despair was to inflict some noticeable pain on Use when she was unthinkingly working with her clippers high up in the tree.

We modern people are accustomed to operating constantly on the mental level with our consciousness. For instance, if we think about transplanting a shrub the following day, we make a plan to do so, or we organise ourselves to shift the compost pile on a particular day. But we are totally unaware of the fact that elementals are responsible for plant growth, or for transformation within the compost, and that they are unable to follow our thinking. Their consciousness works on the emotional level. They 'think' the way we feel, and the opposite is also true: our mental level is like a foreign language to them.

If we need to decide on something which interferes with an area of responsibility of the elementals, we should try to give them an early warning. It is sufficient to go to the area in question about 24 hours beforehand, tell the elementals of our intentions and ask their permission. It would also be wise to consider that nature spirits do not understand our thoughts in words, but rather read our messages from the feeling vibrations which accompany the spoken words.

· · · · · · · · · · · · · · ·

16. COMMENTARY: **Caring for Many Levels of Relationships**

No one should feel obliged to give literal heed to my advice, i.e. to give timely information to the elemental world. That runs contrary to the change in our joint approach to Earth and the dimensions of her soul and consciousness.

This change can be accomplished if we base it on a specific discipline. In the text above I have proposed such a discipline: we undertake to inform the relevant

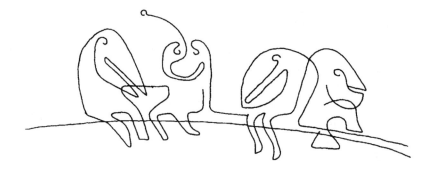

Lost fire spirits on top of the apple tree.

environmental spirits of wood or garden of our plans in timely fashion. However, we should realise that our decision to communicate cannot remain one-sided. Given that we are communicating with a live being, sooner or later there will be specific feedback. It is this feedback, in whatever form and not the discipline itself, which can introduce the change in our lives. This disciplinary path can yield success if one is prepared to stay with it for a minimum of several months.

If a discipline has enabled one to reach a degree of attunement with the elemental world, the techniques that served as introduction may become useless. One's attitude is then naturally attuned to the elemental world. This means that what one does in the garden, for example, is done in harmony with the Deva of the garden. This means that the Deva of the garden and her elemental beings already know of your plan at the moment that the thought occurs: they have shared the thought with you.

There are people who simply live and put into practice this sort of direct attunement with the elemental world. Good for them! And yet I should like to emphasise the importance of conscious communication with elemental beings at this specific time. Just now, when relations between humankind and nature are becoming so dramatically involved and a monstrous alienation yawns before us, it is imperative that some people at least try to renew the conversation with nature.

. . . .

This means that people need to communicate lovingly with elementals, and then they can be understood. The feelings of love and affection which accompany the message will form a sensitive aura around it, and allow it to come across to the elementals in ways which are comprehensible to them. A good example of how to do this is to watch grown-ups talking to very small children. They gesticulate, they make grimaces, they jest and laugh, because intuitively they know that intellectual talk would be of no avail. In some sense, elementals are like small children compared to human beings.

There is a happy ending to the sad story of the salamanders in Use's garden. I asked her for a crystal and she brought me a beautiful amethyst. Once again I climbed to the top of the apple tree, first of all to apologise for the mistake. Then I placed the crystal close to the branch where the fire spirits were sitting, and I asked them to transfer their energy focus onto the amethyst. Afterwards I carried the stone very carefully to the first of the four new compost heaps, asking the 'crew' on the stone to take up residence.

When I tested with my hand a little later to see whether the crystal was empty, I found to my surprise that some of the salamanders had remained sitting there. At the same time, I understood intuitively that they wanted to be distributed evenly on all four compost heaps. So I carried the amethyst from one pile to the next. Each time I would wait a little, until some of the demanding passengers had disembarked. Eventually, the crystal was empty again.

. . . .

17. EXERCISE: **Perceiving Fire Spirits**

The ability to perceive fire spirits yields a very special experience. To do so, a short exercise is necessary. Any compost heap is an ideal place for it.

My daughter Ajra has suggested an exercise for perceiving the elemental beings of fire. It follows the principle of resonance. The warmth of our blood and body resonates with the world of the fire spirits. The warmth signals that the person is alive.

You should concentrate for a little while on the warmth of your blood and the pulse beating in your body. When you feel yourself ready, you should quickly turn your attention to any part of your surroundings where you sense the presence of fire beings. Then allow for the collection of impressions and insights.

I also use another exercise that is of a different sort, but can still bring success – provided that one maintains a deep respect for these mysterious beings. They are beings of transformation and know the path from death and decay to rebirth and new beginnings.

Keeping this in mind, the perception exercise runs as follows: you imagine – but for no more than a moment – that your physical body is turned inside out. All of the organs and liquids that are internal are moved to the outside. In the very same moment you should forget this image and turn your attention to your perceptions.

In exercises of this sort it is important to accustom the rational mind to take up a 'stand by' position and not involve itself in the perceptive process while the supersensory perception is ongoing. Afterwards it is welcome to help sort through the meanings of what has been perceived.

. . . .

Almost four hundred years have passed since Paracelsus laid down his philosophical framework for the nature of the elemental spirits, and only recently have the first steps been taken to resume a conscious communication with these unusual beings. In the early 1960s a small group of people settled near the village of Findhorn in the north of Scotland. They felt the inner urge to develop a project which they called 'an experiment in cooperation between the three kingdoms'. By this they meant the evolutions which contribute to the creative processes on Planet Earth: the angelic world, the human world and the elemental world.[6]

From these beginnings a wonderful garden was created on barren sand dunes along the rough North Sea coast. When I and my family visited Findhorn for the first time in 1971, we were able to enjoy the garden in all its splendour. We were astonished not only by the unusually large vegetables grown in the desert-like dunes, but also by an almost sweet atmosphere in and around the garden, which filled it with vitality. Apparently the elementals were present all around, only I was not yet ready to perceive and differentiate them from the general feeling of the place.

Three exceptionally sensitive people were needed to establish such a garden, with the addition of Peter Caddy who initially played the role of gardener. They were able to communicate with intelligences from the three worlds. Peter's wife Eileen received daily guidance from a source she called 'the voice of God'. R. Ogilvie Crombie (called Roc) was a retired scientist from Edinburgh who, almost by accident, had begun to talk to a faun in the city's Botanical Gardens. Through him the contact with the earth elementals began. Later he also developed communication with a higher nature intelligence which he identified as Pan. Dorothy Maclean, the third person in the group, developed a special gift of communicating with devas. From my own experience, I would call the devas highly developed plant fairies.

The term 'deva' has been taken from Hindu philosophy and means a radiant being. It has been used to describe any great intelligent being in the nature kingdoms. A little later Dorothy contacted another high being which she called the landscape angel, who is responsible for a whole area of landscape. Both terms indicate an expansion of the representation of angels in the Christian tradition, where angels are implied to exist on a spiritual level superior to nature. When Dorothy describes a landscape angel, in my view it is the equivalent of the fairies of place which I observed on top of 'Venus Hill' on the Isle of Srakane.

. . . .

18. COMMENTARY: Landscape angels and Space Fairies

My experiences over the last few years have shown me that space fairies cannot substitute for the role of landscape angels or vice-versa. We are looking at two similar but essentially different types of task that have to do with the landscape.

---

[6] *The Findhorn Garden*, Findhorn Press, 1988 (2nd edition),
is a book about the Findhorn Community.

As elemental beings, fairies have the task of bringing the impulses of the Earth Soul and the wisdom of the terrestrial formative powers to the earth's surface and distributing them out through space. They work in cooperation with the inner worlds of Earth.

Landscape angels work in the opposite direction. They are the bearers of inspirational thoughts 'down' from the broad universe towards the earth's surface. They represent the role of the cosmic consciousness in respect to developments on the earth's surface and further on downwards into Inward Earth.

The Earth is an autonomous cosmic system. It is because of this that Gaia has evolved her own consciousness, which elemental beings and environmental spirits carry to the earth's surface. At the same time, Earth is tied into the wider universe of our galaxy and therefore participates in the cosmic consciousness. Landscape angels represent an aspect of the cosmic consciousness that watches over the inclusion of the cosmic dimensions in a given landscape. So it happens that in a single landscape one can find the focal column of a host of fairies as well as the anchorage point of a landscape angel. The fairies watch over the unfolding of the space—and time—conditioned life processes in a given landscape. Landscape angels concentrate more on the maintenance and further development of the original identity of their particular realm.

. . . .

I was still not sure how to integrate Dorothy's devas into my own perceptions and evaluations. Then, on 13th October 1993, I noticed the figure of a white maiden in our vegetable garden in Sempas. She was standing right in the middle of a bed of fennel, and she revealed herself to me as the fennel deva. After I had marvelled at her beautiful presence for a while, I took the opportunity to ask her about her function in regard to the plant world.

First of all she explained that it was not her task to oversee the development of each individual plant. The nature spirits of the earth element would take care of this. (They are called elves in the English tradition.) When she began to talk about her real work I experienced a mental barrier in myself which was caused by thought forms that I had developed at Findhorn in the early 1970s. To overcome this I asked the deva to convey her function in pictures. She proceeded to put the picture of a plant into my consciousness. A plant can only thrive when it is sprinkled with rain from the clouds and is illuminated by beams of sunlight. The effect of raindrops on plants is equivalent to the impulses of the fairies of place on the landscape which they oversee. In contrast, the rays of the sun are symbolic of the connection an angel maintains with each plant species and its cosmic blueprint. The angel radiates the blueprint through its unique pattern of vibrations.

One of the deva's tasks is to receive the rhythmic inflow of impulses from the angel and translate it into a concrete patterning. This allows the elves to build each individual plant in accordance with its blueprint. However, the deva has a second task: she also needs to be aware of impulses from the fairies of place in their respective landscapes in order to weave the two patterns into a unique quality. Therefore, her overall function is to link the messages from a) a universal source and b) a place-related source, and to weave them into a unified energy pattern. The architects from the ranks of the earth elementals can then build the physical plants from this.

While my brain was busily weaving these inner pictures into a sensible explanation I had a feeling that I should ask another question about the devas, connected to the moon's influence on plant growth. The fennel deva responded with a complex feeling which showed me that there was indeed a third source for her impulses to serve. The effects of the moon cycles on plant growth are less obvious than those of sunshine and rain. This third source is definitely very important for their work on a more subtle level. I was able to feel the deep and loving affection of the deva towards the third source when she revealed her essence to me in the form of a fairy queen. Intuitively I understood that she was one of the master intelligences. She is far advanced on the developmental path of air elementals, and she teaches her 'younger' colleagues how to deal with unforeseen circumstances while they execute their tasks.

At first, I saw the fairy queen inwardly in the form of a white feminine figure of sublime beauty. After a while this picture of her identity dissolved and a deep silence descended. Then a second perception surfaced in my consciousness and I realised that this time she wanted to show me the vital-energetic dimension of her being. She resembled a wondrous blossom of light, slowly opening and radiating gentle tones of red-orange.

This picture too dissolved after a while and I waited expectantly in the darkness, wondering whether she would show me another aspect of her being; and so she did. I was given a third vision of the deva queen. At first I saw a regular network with strongly accentuated nodes. I was unable to understand this idea and begged her for an explanation. Then I discovered the deva in the centre of the network. She showed me how she would lean over to touch lightly a single crossing point with a kind of magic wand, thereby evoking a gentle tone (as in the fairy tales). Each node of this 'xylophone' made a differ-

Lettuce deva in our garden at Sempas.

ent sound. It dawned on me that the deva queen was in resonance with each individual deva in her domain, and it thus became possible for her to influence each deva quite purposefully with her individual guidance. This was all the information I received on the subject of the duties of a fairy queen.

When we look at the different relationships a plant deva needs to maintain in fulfilling her creative role then there seems to be an interconnection between two worlds, even though these worlds appear to be separate in our habitual view—if we are among the few who admit the existence of two worlds at all. The world of elemental beings is organised within the earth sphere, the world of angels in the spiritual sphere. But this story tells us about angelic beings who look after the processes in the material world through the medium of the elementals, and it also tells about elementals who have reached a high spiritual level of intelligence, even mastery. In light of this our usual polarities begin to dissolve.

In his book *Devas, Fairies and Angels* William Bloom[7] has completely rejected a polarised point of view, which is also expressed in the title of his short essay. The author sees the fairy elementals in the same world of light as the angels; he calls it the devic world. Their worlds can be recognised as one not only through the formlessness of their presence (in our understanding they lack a material body) but also through their parallel roles within creation. Their forms vary greatly—from the tiny light being of a gnome to the mighty mandala forms of the angels of the cosmic spheres.

According to William Bloom's insights, these beings share the task of building bridges between invisible creative impulses, patterns and thoughts and their realisation in matter. He illustrates this process with an analogy which I can confirm from my own observations. Somebody who whistles, says William, will produce a sound wave which will make the ear-drum vibrate. We perceive this wave not only as a vibration but also as a formed note, and we perceive a sequence of notes as music. Certain beings of the light realm (which he calls the world of devas) take part in transforming the chaos of vibrations into music.

Another of my experiences also relates to William's view. On 23rd July 1993, I was present when the world-famous violinist Miha Pogačnik gave a solo concert in Ljubljana cathedral to open the IDRIART Festival. Some solo violin sonatas by Bach were on the programme.

---

[7]   William Bloom *Devas, Fairies and Angels: a modern approach,* Gothic Image, 1986

19. COMMENTARY: **The Rational Mind and the Elemental World**

I am now attempting the impossible. I am going to present in logical language a process that does not conform to usual linear logic. If I were to choose a rational form of language, this would be really impossible. The processes of the formation of music as described run concurrently on different planes of our multidimensional reality. To be able to present them, I have to complement rational explanations with fairytale images. It is my hope that both together may enable people to understand these kinds of processes, and also sense their poignant depths.

This is why the rational mind shies away from the idea of elemental beings and environmental spirits. It is confronted by an ambiguity for which there is no common denominator. A person is required to combine the rational and intuitive modes of thought. It is my opinion that our global society is leery of the synergy that would result. It is quite scary to contemplate the quantum leap of consciousness that would then be possible.

Unfortunately, it is not hard to deny the existence of an evolutionary strand that has no physical form, even though it may provide a valuable service to living beings. Put the other way about, it would greatly serve the further evolution of human beings if our rationally moulded consciousness were given access to the sensitive, feeling quality of the environmental consciousness – that is, of elemental beings. We ourselves, as incarnate humans, are part of the Earth- and Elemental-Consciousness and we think, so to speak, with its brain. As cosmic souls we could not rightly find our way in the terrestrial world if a part of the elemental world had not put itself at our disposal to think and feel within material space. Recognition of the elemental world must be understood as an essential part of recognising oneself.

. . . .

It was the first time that I had attended a concert after my eyes had been opened to the elemental world, so I was very excited about what I might be able to see. Hardly had the first notes rung out when I saw a goblin sitting by the right leg of the violinist who himself was deeply immersed in the universal sound patterns of Bach's music.

The elemental reached only up to his knee. While the musician's effort was concentrated on drawing the right harmonies from his instrument, the elemental was completely focused on a different reality, but with equal devotion. In synchronisation with the rhythm of the music the goblin was giving a virtuoso performance with his fingers. It reminded me of the sign language with which the deaf and dumb communicate. While I was still pondering on the purpose of these hand gestures I noticed a fine thread of light leading upwards from the rapidly moving hands of the invisible 'co-performer'. Out of curiosity I followed this thread with my consciousness. It led to a focal point high above the cathedral. There I found a host of fairies dancing in geometric patterns. Their dance was finely attuned to the gnome's hand movements and to the rhythm of the music. Apparently I had received an insight into the invisible source where music is formed and where elemental beings play the role of mediator.

At first I interpreted their behaviour as if they were a kind of translator. But a few months later I had an opportunity to talk with an old sage of the elemental kingdom about my story. As usual, I received his response in a kind of mysterious mixture of projected images and inspired thoughts which I tried simultaneously to decipher in a state of attentive meditation. In the most striking picture I was shown the act of spinning: from a chaotic hank of woollen material emerges an orderly thread. One could compare the incomprehensible hand movements of the goblin with those of somebody spinning. In place of the hank of wool one would have to imagine an invisible vortex of vibrations springing forth from the instrument's resonant body.

I realised that I should not take the example of spinning too literally because the thread of light did not emerge as a result of the elemental's spinning hand movements but came from the instreaming power of cosmic blueprints which corresponded to the resounding music. These blueprints and cosmic harmonies (the 'music of the spheres') were presented to me in pictures by the muses[8] who danced their patterns above the cathedral.

The task of the goblin at the feet of the musician was to combine the vibrations from the musical instrument with the spiritual blueprints of a particular piece of music, and to wind them into a thread of light, which is a 'multi-dimensional' music. Music made in this way not only has the purpose of producing artistic sounds for us to consume, but has a creative, purifying and harmonising effect on the body, mind and soul of the listener and his or her environment, and even on the wider environment of the world. However, I am convinced that such holistic works of art, which are spun from the relationship between the different worlds, are only possible when the artists themselves can serve these invisible worlds more or less consciously, and when

---

[8] I will say more about the muses, who are highly evolved fire beings and who work in the field of the arts (see from page 155 onwards).

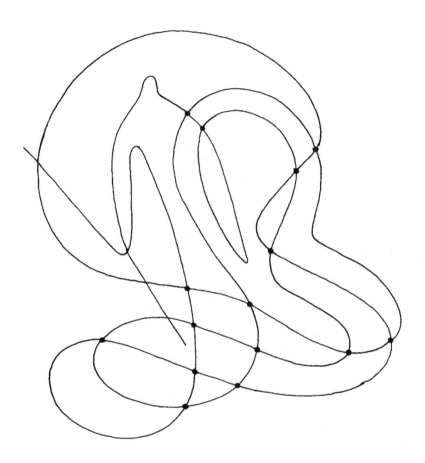

Female deva master with her magic wand,
touching the crossing points of her 'xylophone'.

musicians make music through direct physical contact with their instrument.[9]

There is a famous legend about the dwarfs of Cologne. It gives us an idea of the meaningful relationship between creative people and the elementals involved in their work. According to the legend, in the Middle Ages the craftsmen of Cologne were able to enjoy life in a relaxed manner throughout the day while the elementals – the dwarfs – did all the work at night. I regard this division into day work and night work as a symbolic representation of the dual function each craft formerly fulfilled. That is, human beings would work with physical matter in the daylight world, while elementals would integrate and synchronise this human endeavour into the blueprint of the whole world during the invisible night-world. We can imagine that the craftsmen of Cologne at that time had a daily festival of creativity and a joy in living, that each could express his inner fulfilment, and that their work and their tools were blessed each day by the cooperation of the elemental beings.

. . . .

20. COMMENTARY: Technology Invades the Elemental World

The language used in the story of the dwarves of Cologne is so like a fairytale that one would scarcely think that it has relevance to our modern technology, and indeed to the whole of consumer society.

How can one explain this to the rational mind? Everything that moves, be it an electric razor, an aeroplane or an ankle, is driven by an inner power. These living powers (powers of life) certainly take a materialised form when the movement is on the physical plane. However, what causes the movement lies beyond the physical. The movement that moves that which is moveable originates in the womb of the elemental world.

Because as a civilization we no longer have access to the source that supplies all sources, we have become a sacrifice to two dangerous developmental strands. On the one hand, we must produce ever faster, and consume just as fast, to hide the fact that our technical and agricultural production is destructively exploiting the bases of our existence. On the other, we are trying through aggressive scientific research, use of atomic energy, artificial intelligence, genetic manipulation, clone research and nanotechnology, to invade the life and consciousness realms reserved for the operations of elemental beings. This does not mean that the five areas mentioned are basically excluded from our research. Rather, the boot is on

---

[9] It seems relevant that I was able to make these observations with a musician who insists on performing his music personally and on principle does not allow recording through electronic devices. Similar observations of other musicians turned out to be less clear, or even distorted.

A spinning goblin by the side of the violinist.

the other foot. Because our researchers dismiss as non-existent the foremost elemental intelligences in these areas of knowledge, the results of the technology so developed can be unimaginably destructive, as for example at Chernobyl.

A healthy alternative would be to open up to the possibility of an intelligence in Nature, one that is familiar with atomic energy, genetic records and the cosmic memory, and to associate with it harmoniously in concordance with the intentions of the Earth Soul. Our scientists could learn the relevant technology from her, and develop it further in dialogue with the elemental world.

. . . .

The legend of the dwarfs of Cologne also explains how this wondrous union collapsed because of an interfering human mind. A tailor's wife was so driven by her curiosity that she wanted to see her husband's assistants with her own eyes. This is how the destructive power of the rational mind can force things. The woman sprinkled dried peas onto the stairs and made the dwarfs slip and tumble down the steps. In the light of her lamp (her mind) the woman was able to see them for a fraction of a second. But at that instant they vanished because they cannot exist on the mental level. And they will never return. The craftspeople must complete all their work by the sweat of their brow.

It is not my intention to blame a woman for this rift between the worlds, for the rift is caused by the increasing power of masculine attitudes. This tale pins down some of the tragedy in our human condition, as we are now strangers to the world of elemental beings. Certainly nowadays we may be able to produce whatever physical item the human mind is capable of imagining, but our work does not have the depth to enable us to unite in each instant with our own soul and with the joy of the living universe. Our intellect wants to plan everything we create, and the price we pay for this is our extreme emotional coldness. When this coldness is coupled with a complete denial of any elemental intelligence in nature, the elementals no longer accompany us in our activities, and therefore are not able to help make our work live. In a way, the outcome of our productivity and efficiency is primarily 'dead' substance, and this can easily rebound on both humans and nature.

. . . .

21. EXERCISE: **Using the Antennae of the Solar Plexus**
To perceive elemental beings and environmental spirits in the original quality of their lives, one should approach them on the level of feeling. This is necessary because direct perception enables one to develop not only an understanding of

their type of service but also a feeling for the unique quality of their identity. For that, the emotional level of perception is essential.

The best exercise that I can propose for this sort of perception takes the solar plexus for its starting point, or to be more precise, that aspect of the solar plexus which is entrusted with the task of guiding our emotional fields. To emphasise the point once more, the consciousness of elemental beings operates on the emotional plane.

If one senses the presence of an elemental being, wherever it may be, one can reach out with the subtle feelers of one's solar plexus and 'palpate' that being. The information so gained streams into one's consciousness and can create an image of the relevant being or declare its nature through the feelings in one's body.

One can imagine such feelers as similar to the antennae of certain insects. Imagine that they attach to your back behind the solar plexus (and thus at the height of one's stomach) and rise to palpate the space in front of you, to be sensed in the solar plexus.

While palpating these invisible phenomena, we should pay attention to any change in our usual feelings, and at the same time confirm that our rational mind is far distant, quietly observing from the edge of the event. It can only involve itself when our perceptions are ready for interpretation. Have fun!

. . . .

I would like to illustrate how this separation between people and elementals can be disastrous. During a workshop on landscape healing I had another musical experience at Svetinje near Jeruzalem (Slovenia) in August 1993. We invited along two young men from Maribor who had been studying classical music in India and they gave an open-air concert one evening using some beautiful old instruments. They also brought a digital sound system because they were afraid that the subtle tones of these instruments would not be audible. They combined the true tone of the instruments with the resonance of the speaker system. This caused great confusion for the elemental 'on duty'. I was able to perceive how the elemental was torn between the sounding body of the instruments and the sound source in the speakers—it kept rushing back and forth with great speed. Intuitively I recognised that this confusion was caused by the digital system which works by logically splitting notes into plus and minus segments. The original sound of the notes is then lost. I assume that human beings are able to bridge this loss mentally, but elementals cannot do so.

A clairvoyant student sat next to me. Since her experience was similar to mine, I asked her to go to the musicians during the interval and tell them about our disquiet. They readily agreed to switch off their electronic equipment for the second half of the concert, and we gladly watched the gnome settling down at the instruments to fulfil his task with great tranquillity and relief.

In spite of the many disasters which we humans inflict on the elementals I have received a feeling during our communications that they love humanity, that they respect our ways of learning and that they try to follow us in our ways of creative activity if the slightest opportunity is offered to them. For instance, simple pixies ensoul rock strata. To my eye they appear as sparks of light, like star formations which are evenly distributed throughout the rock. On their path of service they developed into the so-called mountain dwarfs, as they contribute to the making of mineral veins. As goblins they continued to help in the techniques and craft of melting and forging. When the methods of metal working were moved into industrial factories, this line of elemental spirits tried to follow even along this difficult route. For instance, in a car I cannot perceive them in the complex engine, but they are still present in the relatively simple construction of the wheels. They showed me how they adjust their vibrational form to the shape of the joints and axles.

At the end of October 1993, I came into contact for the first time with yet another type of elemental at Döllach in the Moll Valley, Carinthia. I intended to prepare for a workshop there on the Grossglockner mountain. In the evening, on arrival at the guest house where I would be staying, big logs of wood were blazing in the fireplace in the dining room. The room was furnished in a pleasant, old-fashioned way. According to the old traditions there must be an earth elemental in such a room, the name of which in the German language is 'Kobold'.[10] As I carefully looked around I did indeed perceive one of these little guys. He was sitting cross-legged by the fireplace right in front of the store of stacked firewood. He looked like he had stepped out of the pages of a fairy-tale book with his tasselled hat hanging down below his shoulder. I did not take this episode seriously enough to include it in my research on elemental beings, and so I went to bed.

The following morning I was to have breakfast in the same room. The fire had just been lit and the flames were dancing brightly. I could not help but notice the little goblin again. This time I saw him spinning with his fingers all the time, just like the musical goblin at the feet of the violinist.[11] This coincidence made me stop and think, and so I said hello to him telepathically while

---

[10] Derived from *Kobe* (Middle High German) which means room, hut or house, and *Bald* (Ancient Nordic)— manager or ruler. The goblin is the ruling elemental in the house.

I was chewing my bread, and I asked him about the purpose of his spinning. Without interrupting his work he sent me a thought wave which contained a lot of information.

His first message was that we humans wrongly believe that the material world in which we live and learn is a fixed commodity and that we can make use of it indefinitely by changing it according to our egocentric whims. To effect such a change a huge crowd of all types of elemental beings must take action, for within each split second each must make sure that the dynamic shaping of the world remains in unison with its cosmic blueprint. His task was to spin the quality of the living space inside a human dwelling.

I asked him how it was that the earth elementals had entered human homes in the first place. He replied proudly that his line of descent had been accompanying human development ever since we became cave dwellers. In fact, throughout most of our history we had spent our time living in caves right in the middle of the dwarf kingdom. The dining room of the inn where we were sitting just then could be imagined as a kind of manufactured cave. This is the reason why it is not difficult for the mountain dwarfs to follow our development even into the cities. They will always try to fulfil their task, even in such different circumstances.

However, I have never met an elemental in a 'high-tech' living space where there are no natural building materials and where there is a dry, cold and very mentally ordered atmosphere. Apparently there are limits to the ability of nature intelligences to follow humanity's will. Beyond these limits a desolate space is created which is devoid of elemental life, and where there is no room for experiences of the soul. Instead, it is a somewhat ghostly, unreal world. If one is obliged to live in such an environment, it is only with great conscious effort that an atmosphere can be created where elementals will settle, perhaps by arranging rocks or roots in the space. In a too formal garden one could solve the problem by leaving a small patch of wilderness. Within a 'concrete jungle' it would be the so-called weeds that would offer hope for the elementals.

One of the great remaining qualities of the elementals is their optimism Their positive attitudes and their intuitive understanding testify that help is available from the most highly developed teachers in their ranks. They are still willing to support our learning processes to the best of their ability, and often they seem to understand why humanity is so wrapped up in egocentric illusions, and why

---

[11] Interestingly enough there is a German idiom that somebody is said to be 'spinning' if they are looking too deeply into the hidden dimensions of life.

we abuse nature so violently. The world of elementals is just as important an evolution as ours; they are striving for continuous development and perfection, although their world is created and organised differently from that of human evolution. People have put cruel obstacles in the path of the elementals, but it makes sense in the end: they challenge the courageous elementals to face hitherto unknown difficulties and so enhance the speed of their growth. In spite of human energies which flow contrary to theirs, they are always able to maintain their fundamental vibration, which is one of loving joy.

I have never perceived this infinite happiness as clearly as I did in the summer of 1993 when I was revisiting the grounds of Türnich castle, near Cologne. One sunny day at about noon I went to an oval-shaped clearing that contains a large, flat rock which I call the 'Black Madonna' because it carries the energy of transformation. I was allowing my eyes to wander freely across the wild, unmown meadow when I suddenly noticed a great number of tiny elementals working on each blade of grass. I would classify them as elves. All around me there was an apparent frenzy of dancing, working and singing which I took in with a sense of great wonder. Suddenly I was reminded of Walt Disney's three dancing musical piglets. I felt indescribable joy.

When I looked for the source of this inspiring vision, I noticed that I had unconsciously been watching the meadow from the level of my solar plexus, and not in my usual manner with my 'third eye' which is connected to my heart centre. To test this newly discovered level of perception, I went to a nearby tree, as I often do when I want to communicate with a faun. I tend to get very close to a tree trunk to lean against it with both my hands, and my nose almost touches the bark.

This time my perception and consciousness was concentrated and centred at the level of my stomach, and I was almost knocked over by the immense joy of life which emanated from the faun. His bubbling laughter was like the staccato of a rolling thunderstorm and I could not bear it for very long. When I set off to experience some other trees in the same way, I met a faun near four oak trees (I call it 'the oak gate'). The oak gate is situated between two big meadows. This faun sang incessantly in a powerful voice, just like a tenor in an Italian opera.

These events again caused me to question what kind of form was most suitable for visualising the elementals. In my opinion it is not right to force the world of dwarfs, nixies (water elementals) and fairies into visible forms related to our physical reality. Many people believe it would only need a refinement of our sense of vision to be able to see the ethereal forces of the elemental world,

A goblin by the fireside at the inn at Dölach, Carinthia.

as if normal sight could be upgraded to clairvoyance. Unfortunately, there are not so many clairvoyant people, and therefore only a few people would be privileged enough to communicate with the elemental world.

In my experience, this idea of clairvoyance is based on unfounded preconceptions. It rests on the assumption that the human viewpoint is the reference point for all of creation, without giving any consideration to the unique differences in the elemental world. Human beings have developed a very definite, refined outer physique, but we display to only a tiny extent how our inner thoughts and feelings operate. In contrast, the elementals are free of any predetermined form. They can change their appearance to show what is happening inside themselves, which is very different from our human ways. Whatever form we perceive them in, it is either a mirror which reflects our stored archetypal memory of how we imagine them to be, or it derives from the language of pictures used by the elementals themselves to draw our attention to a certain message they want to deliver. They are without any definite form unless we project our archetypal or imagined forms on them. One of these imposed makeshift images is the little gnome with his red pointed cap, his long white beard and leather trousers. Lovers of nature superimpose this picture onto the being of earth spirits. In turn, this picture influences clairvoyants, who then claim it as the definite, indubitable truth.

. . . .

22. COMMENTARY: Environmental Spirits in the Context of other Continents and Cultures

With the exception of those events that occurred in the Canary Islands, nearly all my experiences of the elemental world, which originally happened during the years 1992-93, took place on European soil. In later years, I have often worked geomantically or in earth healing on other continents where local cultures have constructed their own images of nature spirits and elemental beings.

These experiences of the ambience of other cultures wore two different faces. On one hand, I was amazed at the unique languages that the elemental world had developed to communicate with humans in other parts of the earth. On the other, I could easily distinguish the commonalities that identified the elemental world as a global system.

When I visited the other continents, I found the elemental beings making real use of the language of the local culture in order to show themselves to me. They clothed themselves in the grammatical forms of their particular language and in these I recognised the characteristic art forms of the relevant culture.

For example, the gnomes of South America showed themselves in forms resembling the script of the Mayan or Inca cultures. My intuition tells me that, to make contact with me, they use the language of the last culture that communicated with them. The Spaniards or Portuguese who have conquered the land were certainly never interested in the language of South American gnomes. In consequence, the elemental beings of the conquered lands could never learn the medieval forms of speech that at that time was still occasionally used to converse with nature spirits in Europe.

After making contact with me, their traditional forms of communication faded away. I could now put the elemental beings of foreign lands in their rightful place within the usual pattern of the elemental world, and for this I looked at their function in their respective landscapes. These are similar world-wide, or nearly.

As a result of these experiences, I stopped using the old names like 'faun' or 'Pan' for elemental beings. I sense that over time they have become too linked to the traditions of Western culture. As long as we are not in a position to invent new names, I propose to name individual kinds of elemental beings and environmental spirits by their functions. These are the same worldwide. They are essential functions without which the web of life on the terrestrial eco-sphere cannot survive.

. . . .

This confusion in the matter of perception is common and is reflected in my own experiences before I contacted a particular type of fairy being. At the beginning of my communication with elemental beings I could only determine their presence through feelings in my body. I encountered a vibrational pattern, which until then had been unknown to me. This happened very close to our house in a forest at Sempas. Four oak trees grow on a stony hill and form a square. (This is the hill where I had first entered the underworld in my consciousness to visit my heart—see Chapter One). I could sense an unknown presence right at the centre of the square.

When Erika, one of our collaborators, came to visit I asked her to meditate on this phenomenon. She has been clairvoyant from childhood. After a while she returned and reported that she had seen a beautiful fairy at the spot, with a white horse at her side. The fairy's white magic horse is an image which is well known from fairy tales. When I returned to the place I was able to verify with the sensitivity of my hands that there was a twofold vibration. It appeared to relate to two beings: the fairy and her white horse. On the one side my hand was moving in a horizontal lemniscate (8-shaped pattern) as I had experienced it at other fairy focal points; on the other side, where the horse was supposed to be, my hand was moving vertically up and down in spiralling rotations. However, what my perception told me did not help me understand the real purpose of this enigmatic duality in a fairy being.

Therefore I asked my invisible teacher for clarification through a dream. A dream image followed where a white-bearded World Creator showed me round his workshop. There were many figures as in a sculptor's studio. A small figure of pure silver caught my eye. Its posture was like someone braced against the wind, and it gave an impression of great dynamism. On awakening I immediately realised that it was the figure of the unknown fairy, and I was sure that the horse was an expression of her dynamic character. I was unable to understand more of this dream at the time, but when I talk about the realm of fairies I often point out that there are other kinds of fairies besides those of place. I would like to call them 'yang fairies'.

A short time afterwards this particular 'yang fairy' made a tragi-comic attempt to enter my consciousness in her real form. When I was preparing a workshop on the townscape of Graz with my friend Erwin, we visited a park which is a part of the local psychiatric hospital. A little later we returned to Erwin's home where I discovered with horror that there was something terribly wrong with my eyesight. I thought I must be over-tired and went to sleep for half an hour. When I was called for lunch, I was feeling worse. I thought I would go mad. I was only partly present; it felt like the other half of me was a shadow. I had to leave the table and I sat down to meditate. While concentrating on the disturbance, I suddenly realised without a doubt that an elemental had attached itself to my aura and was now casting a shadow over me. When my hand began to make the typical spiralling, vertical rotations I became convinced that this was the 'yang fairy' which I had not fully understood. Instead of taking the opportunity to find out more about the unusual presence of this particular fairy, I could only concentrate on trying to get rid of it as fast as possible, because I was frightened, and I had no previous experience with the humorous side of elemental beings. With the consent of my host I went to a wild corner of his garden and implored the fairy to settle there. My wish was granted instantly, and I felt healed and clear. But I had not discovered anything new about the function of the mysterious fairy.

Eventually there was to be a turning point in autumn 1993, when I was leading a seminar in the grounds of Türnich castle. There is a circle of seven linden trees which were planted around an energy centre about 120 years ago. Eight earth acupuncture meridians (ley lines) emerge at this point. The root of the ley lines at the centre of the circle is energised by a cosmic source via a pillar of light. On October 2nd I took the workshop participants to this place to let them experience the rich vibrations around the seven linden trees. I also wanted to draw the attention of the group to the presence of the fairies which I had first discovered here after I became sensitive to the level of elemental vibrations in the landscape. I showed the participants a visible sign of the elementals' activity where two branches had grown together in the form of a cross. This had been sculpted into the crown of the last of the three trees (it has a forked trunk) by its faun. These crossed branches formed a cosmogram in the shape of the infinity sign (a lemniscate). I often find such cross-branching in trees where there is a focus point for fairies nearby, and the cross-branches often take the approximate shape of the sign of infinity.

To prepare the workshop participants for the vibrations of the fairy dance, I told them about my observations of fairies of place at Venus Hill on the Isle of Srakane. Afterwards we remained in the silence for a while to experience the different dimensions of energy in the circle of linden trees. As soon as I had closed my eyes I saw a woman's face (larger than life-size) looking at me from the direction of the fairy cosmogram. Her gaze radiated infinite love towards me, but also had an element of cheekiness and criticism. It was as if she wanted to convey to me that I was not meeting a host of fairies but a single fairy being, as yet unfamiliar to me.

Excited by this friendly criticism, I rushed out to the linden circle after the workshop had ended in the evening. I wanted to find out whether I had really gone wrong in my investigations of the elemental realm. Inwardly I probed into this level with much greater care. Next to the central linden tree, to the right of the one with the cosmogram, I used my hand to discover vibrations that were running vertically along the trunk, and which I associated with the so-called 'yang fairy'. The tree faun had marked this special spot with a club-like growth on the trunk. Although I had noticed this formation before, I had not been able to find a meaningful reason for it. Again I had contacted a fairy with a white magic horse. Unfortunately there was not enough time for me to find out more about her being, because I had to leave for my home in Slovenia the following morning. The first thing I did on arrival was to visit the stony hill where I used to descend into the underworld. I wanted to thank the fairies for the good care they had taken of my home while I was away. As soon as I entered the silence, an enormous face of a woman from the realm of 'fairy and the white horse' beamed at me. I recognised her from the circle of seven linden trees. This time I gladly accepted her invitation to climb the hill and to open my consciousness in a new way to the mysterious fairy.

At first I felt an unpleasantly strong pressure on my crown chakra, as if a message wanted to carve its way into my consciousness. In order to try and overcome my fixed ideas, I first visualised the colour violet for transformation. Only then was I able to become aware of a female figure at the site. She appeared to me in such completeness and seemed so real that I was reminded of Paracelsus's stories of elementals who present themselves as if they were human and are hardly distinguishable from our own human appearance.

At that moment, although a deep silence filled the forest, a tiny bird became very excited, so much so that it rushed away chirping loudly. Suddenly I knew beyond doubt that the role of this woodland fairy had to do with guiding the animals. To clarify her function, she had been using an image of the Goddess Diana, who roamed through the forests hunting wild animals. But this ancient image needs to be turned around. The fairy made it explicitly clear to me that it was her task to guide animal species within a certain landscape by giving energy impulses towards a harmonious pattern of movement within the chosen area. Our idea of her hunting wild animals had put her into a rather passive role; instead, she has a truly creative role in the forest.

She told me that plants can only sprout from the earth when they are strongly rooted in the soil. This leads to the logical conclusion that earth elementals are active during the plant's manifestation on the material plane. But animals are independent of the grip of the soil. Because of their quality of movement, they are accompanied during their life cycle by elemental beings of the air element. The white horse is a symbol of the mobility of the animal kingdom, and this kingdom is cared for by her kind of fairy. She wanted to be called a woodland fairy so that she would be clearly recognisable as an individual being, distinguishable from the fairies of place which always appear in groups.

These numerous different pictures, inspirations and experiences were necessary for me to get to know the pure beings of the elemental world. It shows how demanding it is to regain knowledge of the elemental realms. It is not sufficient to send out clairvoyant people in order to be able to extract from their reports 'objective' pictures of individual representatives of an evolutionary stream which runs parallel to our human evolution. Elementals deal with a network of definite qualities of power and intelligence which are not expressed through form but through the task which these beings fulfil within the wholeness of cosmic-earthly creation.' [12]

---

[12] In esoteric terms elementals are a synthesis of a certain energy structure on the etheric level which represents the body and more or less individualised intelligences who have their consciousness on the astral level.

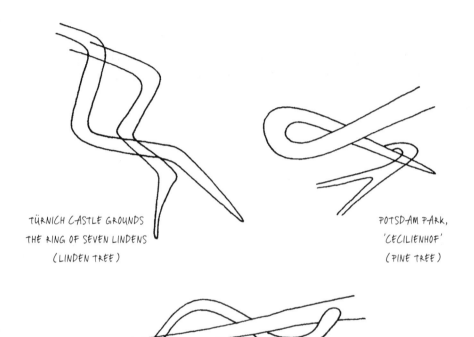

TÜRNICH CASTLE GROUNDS
THE RING OF SEVEN LINDENS
(LINDEN TREE)

POTSDAM PARK,
'CECILIENHOF'
(PINE TREE)

KENSINGTON GARDENS, LONDON
(PLANE TREE)

Fairy cosmograms in some tree branches.

A human being who works in a garden or landscape with an awareness of the busy elementals all around may not need to know about such pictures. It is enough to listen to inner impulses and signs while working, and to include the beings of the elemental realms in what we do. If we send out waves of love and acknowledgement while at work, we will get good feedback from the world which exists parallel to ours. There is a spectrum of feedback all the way from highly spiritual intuitions down to the physical experiences which sometimes appear to be 'miracles'. This spectrum is identical to the areas of activity of the elementals, and it embraces the archetypal dimensions of the spiritual world as well as the manifest forms of the physical space-time dimension.

The woodland fairy took on the form of a huge head of a woman.

THREE

The Goddess and
the Seven Dwarfs

AFTER MY SERIES OF REVELATIONS about the elemental realm had got off to a good start, as I have described, another process of discovery in my consciousness began in spring 1993. Step by step, I became aware of the definite role the elementals play in maintaining and rejuvenating the ancient landscape temples. What I call a landscape temple is an invisible energetic fabric penetrating a landscape, thus expressing its divine being. I could only comprehend this spiritual-soul dimension of a landscape after reorienting my world view to the female aspect of creation. This happened through the Goddess experience I had in 1991-92.

In previous years I had tried to put together a coherent model to demonstrate the invisible dimensions of a landscape. In my German book *Die Erde heilen* (Healing the Earth) I had wanted to introduce for consideration a system which would give an overview of the various vital-energetic aspects in the geology of a landscape. Within that model all energetic phenomena at a site can be put into systems that we can detect using radiaesthetic means. Thus I am able to explain reasonably well how a landscape with its hills and valleys, rivers and towns relates to its vitality-giving power points and energy lines. Today I would say this is only one level of being within a landscape; there are others. It is the dimension most closely connected with the material level, and I call it the vital-energetic dimension.

I have already mentioned the spiritual-soul dimension where landscape temples are found; it is a higher level than the vital-energetic dimension, and similar to the energetic structure of the human soul, which is higher than the system of acupuncture meridians (energy lines) and chakras. It is the task of energy lines and centres in the human body to pass on the soul's guiding and rejuvenating impulses to the organs of the body. We can assume that energy lines and centres in a landscape would have an analogous function.[1] They impart impulses of cosmic life power and spiritual-soul development to the physical landscape and its manifold life structure. These impulses find their source in landscape temples which are an expression of the spiritual-soul configuration in a certain landscape area.

To understand the geometric structure of a landscape temple we must first of all rid ourselves of images of the human soul as a spiritual object floating somewhere above the body. On the contrary, I perceive the soul as a highly sensitive power system containing energy vortexes and fields of the highest potency out of which it manifests the individual human I. In the same way, the landscape temple as the soul of a region shows itself as a kind of power structure, pulsating at rates beyond those measurable by divining instruments. Through my investigations I have verified that a landscape temple manifests itself in geometric triads, thus connecting it with the three aspects of the Goddess. I call these the *aspect of wholeness*, the *aspect of creativity* and the *aspect of transformation*. The axis of this triangular formation of the landscape temple creates a further system of inbreath and outbreath. It nourishes the soul structure of the landscape with cosmic power.

In my book *Die Göttin der Landschaft* (The Goddess of the Landscape) I have given several examples to demonstrate how this model of a landscape temple works—for instance, in Venice, in the grounds of Türnich castle, on the border of Derry/Donegal in Northern Ireland, and in the macro-landscape of Slovenia. I also refer to other indications which show that because of the increasingly patriarchal development of our civilisation over the past five thousand years the landscape temple's key role has been obscured by one veil after another until it has been completely forgotten. By suppressing the female aspect of the divine, all memory of landscape temples as an expression of the tangible presence of the Goddess has also been extinguished. Knowledge of individual sites was preserved a little longer and can be glimpsed when we look at places which were chosen for churches and castles in the Middle Ages. But our awareness of the holistic interconnections has been lost. The last culture in our part of the world which carried this awareness was the neolithic-megalithic culture of the Goddess.

---

[1] People often ask how to classify the radiaesthetically perceptible orthogenic networks (Hartmann, Curry etc) or how to understand the so-called stimuli patterns within this school of thought. I believe it has to do with projecting perceptible energetic phenomena in a landscape onto an existing system of coordinates. This system has its roots in thousands of years of Western mental development, but it is of an illusory nature. It has its place as a kind of artificial language to help locate energy structures within a landscape, and to give an approximate estimation of the landscape's quality.

23. QUESTION: **Who is the Goddess, Really?**

Rather than attach a mythical distance to the word 'Goddess', I should like to explain precisely what I mean by the expression.

It is not hard for me to accept the concept of God as the Christian culture has defined it. The idea of the loving and compassionate God includes the masculine and feminine view points of the Whole. They are both united in its universal embrace.

The concept of Goddess is not competitive with the concept of God. Rather, one should say that there is an aspect of the divine that should have a feminine name to honour its true Presence. In the figure of the Goddess, the all-embracing quality of divinity rightly comes nearest to earth, nature and incarnate humanity.

The Presence of the Goddess is tightly bound with the ensoulment of the endless universe, and the ensoulment of each individual aspect of creation, each individual being.

In this sense the concept of the Goddess can be placed on a par with the Earth Soul, in that she is recognised as the Mother of the whole spectrum of terrestrial creation. In Greek mythology she is named Gea or Gaia, which are the names that today we give to the Earth Soul. After Hesiod, she was honoured not only as Earth Mother, but also as Mother of all the gods and goddesses of the Greek Pantheon.

This means that we should not only connect the Goddess closely with our earth, but we should also remember her cosmic aspect. In the biblical tradition, this is called Sophia, the Wisdom of the First Beginnings. In the theology of Hildegard von Bingen, she is placed on a par with Christ, as his feminine complement.

The Goddess' presence in the landscape is expressed through landscape temples. Our individual souls too, each as an atom of creation, represent an expression of her wisdom, love and spiritual dedication. And among animals she is present as the group soul of the different species.

. . . .

At Easter 1993 I received an invitation to conduct a four-day seminar to work with the landscape of Wendland, near Hanover. In planning the schedule for the seminar, I wanted the group to begin their work by becoming familiar with some of the power points in the landscape, and the specific problems in the area. After that, through our deepened connection with the selected places and their problems, we would go on to recognise their different functions as part of the Wendland landscape temple. In this way, our work on the vital-energetic level would flow organically into an exploration of the spiritual-soul level.

Until recently Wendland was strongly shaped by its waterways. It was connected to the flood plain of the river Elbe and its feeder streams. Only a few hillocks used to raise their heads above the water in times of flood, but these hillocks have developed into strong, yang-polarised power centres with an ability to balance tremendous amounts of watery yin power. I believe that this has not been an entirely natural development, the result of a striving for balance by the nature forces, but that the ancient cultures played a conscious part in it—they strengthened it through the placement of stones and through rituals. Only in one other place have I found a similarly strong structure of yang points in a landscape: on the islands in the Venice lagoon.[2]

Halfway through our century, land reallocation and artificial drainage systems led to a regrettable loss of the watery nature of this unique landscape. Now it was the opposite of its former state. Because of the drainage systems, yang became the predominant energy, but nobody considered that the already strongly represented yang power points would need to be damped down. As they were completely out of balance, the former yang power points must have drawn immense blockages to themselves. They became the victims of a wide range of crippling distortions. Another contributing factor was the separation of one of the valleys in the wider region of Salzwedel and Arendsee from the rest of the landscape because of the 'iron curtain'. The border was erected with such vigour during the German/German confrontation that we found that the east-west energy lines along the frontier had no power. The landscape was split in two on the vital-energetic level.

Our seminar began at the education centre in Königshorst near Wustrow. In the 19th century this house had served as the administrative centre for this domain of the King of Hanover. In 1843, this part of the domain was granted the exceptional honour of bearing the name Königshorst (King's Eyrie), as proclaimed by the King's bailiff in Hanover. Such a great honour would be surprising, if it were not hiding a secret which I was about to discover during my stay at Königshorst.

My examination of the Wendland landscape temple brought to light the fact that the nearby towns of Wustrow and Königshorst formed one of the main centres of the landscape temple, the creative aspect of the Goddess. In ancient cultures this was celebrated in a ritual of holy marriage. It was therefore Königshorst's role to be the centre for a sacred union between yin and yang. In terms of the distribution of power, it is a place where the whole of

---

[2] The similarity between the names 'Wendland' and 'Venice' is no coincidence. Probably the same people settled in both countries—the ancient Venetes were most likely of Slav origin.

creation begins. In a strange way a connection was made between the long-forgotten sacred role of the place and its given name, 'Königshorst'.

The mysterious relationship between the royal family of Hanover and the Wendland landscape temple added to my feelings of wonder as I leafed through a report which gave an account of a ceremonial procession through Wendland in 1865 by the blind King George V and his twenty-year-old son, Crown Prince Ernst August. The photos documenting this festive parade show the people giving their King and his escort an overwhelmingly splendid and emotional reception in all the towns and villages. This unusual intensity of feeling in the people only seemed plausible to me when I sensed that the King's triumphal procession was in resonance with the ancient pilgrims' route. In the time of the Goddess culture, the people of Wendland would each year walk along the landscape temple of their country in ceremonial procession to renew the sacred relationship with their land and to invoke nourishing powers for the temple.

A topographical map on which the royal procession of 1865 is clearly marked shows that it connected three main centres of the landscape temple and that King George V and Prince Ernst August took exactly this route linking the three centres on their fifth, sixth and seventh days. Hitza-cker is the centre of the Virgin Goddess (aspect of wholeness), Königshorst/Wustrow is the seat of the Mother Goddess (aspect of creativity) and Gorleben/Höhbeck/Schnackenburg is the area of the Black Goddess (aspect of transformation).

This was as far as we had been able to get in the unveiling of the secrets of the Hanoverian kings when we went to Höhbeck, the area of the Goddess of Transformation, on April 13, where we visited an ancient fortification. It has the misleading name of Schwedenschanze (Swedish entrenchment). According to my findings this spiralling rampart is one of the original holy places and was only much later rebuilt for defence purposes. It is situated on an imposing hill with a steep descent on one side to the majestic river Elbe.

After World War II this part of the river Elbe was declared the border between the Eastern and Western parts of Germany. For this reason it was spared the fate suffered by most of the other rivers in Wendland, and was allowed to flow freely through the landscape instead of being straightened out. I thought this would provide an excellent opportunity to observe the nixies living their undisturbed life, and I walked down the slope to the river. To prove to the water elementals that I was an initiated visitor to their world I carried a small stone in my outstretched hand on which a little fairy from Slovenia had put her focal point before I had left for Germany. She was given to me for my journey as an envoy of her kingdom and to help me with my training.

24. COMMENTARY: **Fantasy and Playful Creativity**

'Reasonable' people will question how I come by such quaint ideas, for example, carrying a tiny fairy about with me on my travels. Is this all a fantasy?

In the first place, fantasy is nothing inferior. As a culture we produce an un-broken stream of various fantasies, be they novels, fabulous types of vehicles or embellished, post-modern opera houses. Fantasy is a creative tool which we use continually, whether we know it or not. If we are attempting to communicate with the invisible world of elemental beings, the wisdom of fantasy is indispensable. It renders the almost unimaginably strange phenomena of that world accessible to our logical consciousness.

Secondly, fantasy's tool is a plaything of our own inner child. Without this tool its life within our psyche would be unbearable.

The concept of the inner child is the name given by modern psychology to that aspect of our being which is not subject to the forceful imperative of linear time. However old a person may appear, they carry in their inner being a fragment of eternity that is not affected by the process of aging. This relates not only to the so-called spark of divinity which is present in our hearts, but also to our ability to revive the holographic fragment of eternity within us and let it participate in our everyday lives.

As adult men and women we are too bound up in our time-conditioned, social and psychological roles to offer living space to the infinity within us. It follows that we tend to forget the constant presence of eternity within us.

The inner child's imagination links us to the picture of the Fool in the Tarot pack and encourages us, in every moment, to shuffle from our shoulders the whole burden of ever-rolling time, and dance instead with eternity. Only a simple change of consciousness is needed to achieve this, and then we can find ways to lead the inner child into the bustle of everyday life. For this, fantasy can be a helpful tool.

. . . .

My trick worked. When I arrived at a side branch of the river it was teeming with water beings—all staring at my fairy. Then from their midst a tall nymph with royal insignia approached me. To my surprise and quite innocently she offered to grant me a wish. This was such an enchanting fairy-tale situation that my first spontaneous thought was to ask for a lump of gold. But I realised immediately that avarice in fairy tales always brings misfortune. Very quickly I went for a different wish. I asked to be told the story of Crown Prince Ernst August and the young wife of the bailiff. According to the prevailing gossip, something had happened when the Prince and his blind father were staying overnight at Königshorst on the sixth day of their procession through Wendland.

Compared to a lump of gold my wish might be considered trivial, but I was so deeply involved in the question of how to re-energise the Wendland landscape temples that unlocking the door to this piece of gossip meant finding out more about the cause of the blockages and the paralysis of Wendland's creative centres. The royal nymph was unable to answer my question, to my regret. But she felt I could find out more from the dwarfs. I was to climb the steep slope again, and there on the path find a crippled oak tree. I would see the entrance to the underworld underneath the oak. I thanked her and climbed all the way back up. I readily found the oak on the spot she had described and also saw the small archway. Kneeling below the oak I followed the subterranean path in my consciousness.

Soon the tunnel ended in a huge hall, so large that my eyes could not see the far wall. This sacred hill was completely hollow. The walls of the cave-like structures were covered with rough rubies. The dark red colouring gave me a sensation of being quite literally enclosed in the womb of the earth. There was a huge crowd of miners in the hall. From the entrance I was taken straight through the crowd to a place where the king and queen of the dwarfs were sitting on an elevated throne. But when I came close to the throne I found to my surprise that the queen had vanished from sight. I could sense her presence but I perceived her as absent.

At the throne I felt an immense sadness emanating from the king. When I looked deeply into his sorrowful eyes I completely forgot why I had come. I asked him why he was so sad. He indicated that the queen of the dwarfs had been 'ill' ever since the people on the earth had banished the Goddess from their world. The illness was manifest in the fact that the queen of the dwarfs could only be 'present in her absence' down below, analogous to the Goddess in the upper world. This allusion to the vanished landscape temple of the Goddess reminded me why I was here in the first place. Again I posed my original question: Did the Crown Prince and his father, King George V, stay overnight at Königshorst in those days, and if so, what happened between the young prince and the bailiff's wife?

The king of the dwarfs nodded his head and indicated that I needed to consult his wise men, who were seated to his left. So I went over to the sages and repeated my question. And this time I was rewarded with an answer. The dwarfs had tried everything to heal their queen, so they said. They had made tremendous efforts to revitalise the neglected landscape temple of Wendland. First of all, in 1843, they had inspired the old King Ernst August to give the heart chakra of the landscape temple its proper name, Königshorst. Next, in 1865, they had motivated the blind King George V to visit Wendland with his son. To make the ceremonial procession resonant with the ancient tradition of pilgrimage they had inspired the king's officers, who planned the procession, to route it exactly so that they would visit the three landscape temple centres on the fifth, sixth and seventh days.

But the ritual of a holy wedding at the creative centre of Königshorst was needed to get the Goddess and also the queen of the dwarfs to manifest once again during the secret revival of the landscape temple. Therefore the dwarfs had tried their utmost to kindle love in the hearts of the crown prince and the bailiff's young wife. Unfortunately this plan did not work because the young woman resisted strongly. She did not want to cross the line between herself and the future king, and suppressed her feelings of love to such an extent that she preferred to suffer sorrow and grief rather than submit to the secretly planned ritual. Consequently, the dwarf queen stayed away and the landscape temple had waited until now for its revitalisation.

· · · · · · · · · · · · · · ·

25. COMMENTARY: **Rituals as Creative Tools**

Work is much reverenced in our human world. We create through our work. For this we use hands, tools which we manipulate with our hands, automatic devices or even robots. Through work we are creative. People even work with their heads or their calculators.

The elemental world does not know work in this sense. From our point of view, elemental beings are creative through their laziness. Our fantasy perceives their 'work' to consist of constant laughter, dance and song. To some extent this is true, but it has nothing to do with laziness. They have another role to fulfil in creation, and therefore their work looks quite different from our own. To be creative, they perform definite rituals.

To be ritually active does not mean working with materials, but rather to be guiding various forces, changing them around, focusing them, etc. One can understand rituals as empowered imaginations which move the forces that rule behind the scenes of the physical world.

The forces on which we depend for our survival and the quality of our daily life cannot be gripped and moved by our hands or other tools. However, rituals can be performed which move them in natural ways. That is what elemental beings

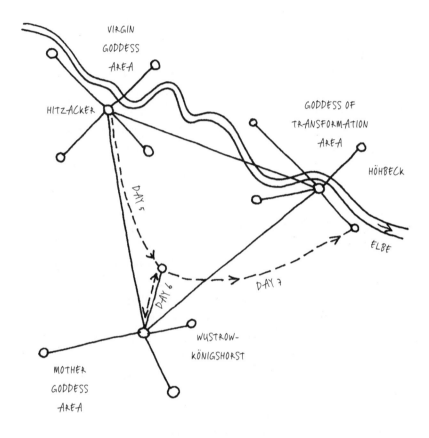

The landscape temple of Wendland and the route of the royal
procession through the countryside on days 5, 6 and 7.

are doing when they dance, laugh, sing and do much that is similar. We observe the fruits of their rituals all around us, and call it the wonder of life.

The peoples of the original cultures learned and practiced the art of creative rituals from the nature spirits, in order to take an imaginative part in the creative process. The 'idea of the rite' became an indispensable part of their lives. Without the ritual element in their healings, consecrations, agricultural and craftwork, their life went off the rails.

People today see rituals as no more than formal traditions that can be exploited to increase the happy coincidence of holidays and tourist revenues.

Woe to us! We are unaware that by devaluing ritual we have gambled away our share in the universal creation. Our activities now turn more and more within the narrow circles of the manifested world, and we are ignorant of the cosmic consequences.

. . . .

Before I was granted these experiences in Wendland I had merely been aware of the relationship between the elemental world and the vital-energetic dimension of the landscape, and of the role different elementals have taken to maintain our physical experience of reality. Although the Wendland message was partly obscured by its fairy-tale character, nevertheless it pointed to a deeply rooted relationship between the elemental world and the 'higher' spiritual-soul level of the landscape. Now at least I knew of the downside of this relationship. My experience told me that the merciless destruction of a whole landscape and the suppression of the structure of a landscape temple would cause great suffering among the elementals. If their relationship with the spiritual fabric of the landscape temples is disturbed, then for obvious reasons their whole evolution is at stake. They can no longer serve freely as mediators between the soul level, energy level and physical level of the landscape.

A few days later I would experience a more hopeful aspect of this relationship between the elemental world and the spiritual-soul level when I travelled to North Friesland to facilitate another seminar on earth healing in Bohmstedt near Husum. On April 29th we visited Heidenberg near Enge, with our host Elke, to look for a fairly large research area for our group project. Heidenberg hill, 45 metres (146 ft) high, is the highest point in the landscape, and for this reason it has in the past been subject to a misuse of power. A burial mound had been placed on top of it, which is protected as an archaeological monument, although my feeling is that it was erected only recently. It hides the true function of the hill within the landscape temple of North Friesland. On

The dwarf king of Höhbeck and his vanishing queen.

approaching Heidenberg we stopped in surprise at the foot of the hill: a pair of oak trees formed a perfect polarised enactment of a love scene. One oak, with a female-polarised faun, was growing straight up towards the sky, which is rare for an oak. Her neighbour, on the other hand, branched out in all directions, her trunk shaped like a ballerina in motion. Her faun was a male type, but on the form level she embodied the female of the lovers. The first oak tree showed the same reversal of physical and energetic polarities. It was not a coincidence that we found here such a system of role division and a tree sculpture with such striking polarised features.

To safeguard myself against forming wrong impressions of the burial mound, I asked the local elementals to guide me towards it and allow me to experience its true nature. Avoiding the common tourist trail, they led me through the forest to the left of the mound, where it was completely covered with undergrowth. They showed me a lilac bush which had one of its branches low down near the ground. I thought this would again be an entrance into the underworld, but on attempting to use this 'entrance' I was stopped by a very clear impulse, and in this way I began a dialogue with an old sage of the dwarf family, who was sitting by the entrance thus preventing me from descending into the underworld.

He very proudly told me that elementals had been trying for hundreds of years to signal to human beings the true spiritual significance of this place. As a reminder, he pointed out the two dancing oak trees. He also asked me to look behind me to see the last remnants of a ramp in the shape of a vulva. Originally, this place had been dedicated to the Virgin Goddess. It was one of the main functions of the Virgin Goddess, whose vibrations were anchored here, to embody the quality of love. For that reason, his family had built the 'sculpture' of the two oaks entwined in love-making as a main feature or cosmogram on the hill. The two fauns of the oak trees had participated consciously in the work.

· · · · · · · · · · · · · ·

26. COMMENTARY: **The Language of Cosmograms**

The fascinating thing about cosmograms is that they are visible indicators which communicate with the invisible planes of reality. It was at the beginning of the 1980s that I discovered the language of cosmograms. It happened when I was searching for a means to convey my plans for an environmental healing to the intelligence of the place concerned.

Some towns had invited me to carry out lithopuncture projects to dissolve the blocking patterns that hindered the free flow of life force within this particular

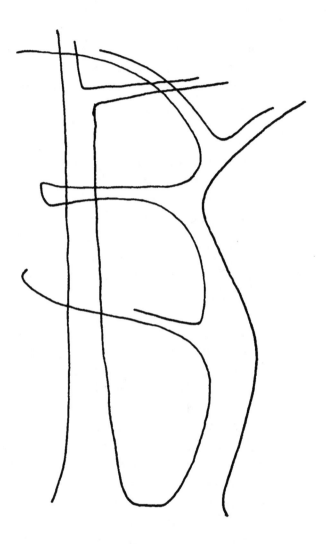

Love scene of an oak couple at the foot
of Heidenberg at Enge, North Friesland.

place. I knew however that I could not heal the place by myself; no one can. Apart from that, one may not simply involve oneself in an autonomous world. However, it is permitted to activate a place's self-healing potential, but this can only be done if one can communicate with the elemental beings which administer the place's potential power.

In answer to my search, I came time and again across certain symbols, signs or patterns which showed themselves pricked out with a faint light. It was obvious that these functioned not only on the physical plane but also in the invisible realm and could be perceived by environmental spirits as well as by people. I began to call them 'cosmograms'.

Cosmograms are multi-dimensional signs. One cannot shape them in a purely logical way. That demands the collaboration of the elemental beings of the designated place, together with the cosmic intelligence of the relevant quality, which works together with the powers of your own soul. For the ritual process of forming cosmograms, the prerequisites are the clarity of your inner dedication, your ethically sound intention and your expertise in the relevant craft. The result is a pictorial sign language that is related to the language of fairy tales. We have already heard why this language can transmit complex messages that can be understood by elementals and other invisible beings.

· · · · · · · · · · · · · · ·

The old sage suggested that I re-read the fairy tale 'Snow White' in the light of what he had told me, to gain a better understanding of the role the elemental world has taken on to preserve landscape temples with their old structures. Snow White was born in the three colours of the Goddess: white, red and black. As the Goddess she was banned from human consciousness by an aggressive patriarchal culture. Where else but with the seven dwarfs would she have found a safe haven? In a practical sense this meant that the elementals were looking after every place where a landscape temple could be found, and where the Goddess and her temple structures had been driven from consciousness and from the surface of the earth. On a cultural level the Goddess had indeed disappeared, but not on the level of the nature intelligences. The dwarfs and their collaborators have done this work, which used to be a human responsibility, ever since. By shaping trees and branches, the elementals have created suitable cosmograms to maintain the sacred quality of certain energy centres. They have also ensured that the ancient rituals have been continued.

I felt deeply ashamed of our human failure and infinitely grateful towards the brave dwarfs, nixies, fairies and all the beings of the elemental world. They have preserved with love what we human beings in our self-centredness have tried to destroy. Through Irish folk tradition we are told that at the time of the Goddess Danu the Tuatha Danann people marked the landscape with their stone circles. After the Celts took over the country, they continued to live, transforming themselves into fairy folk. Even to this day they care for the sacred places and perform the forgotten rituals there. This transformation from neolithic into elemental lineage, according to the old sage of Heidenberg, can be seen as a kind of transfer of functions to the nature intelligences which are now looking after the landscape temples.

. . . .

27. COMMENTARY: The Heart of Monte Verita

I have recently been involved in an emotional situation which revealed how elemental beings not only watch over the sacred level of the landscape but also care for the health of its vital functions.

This story is about a sacred place near Ascona in the district of Ticino in Switzerland. It is called Monte Verita, the Mountain of Truth. In October 2006 I was leading a seminar there on the theme 'Inner Change and the Language of the Landscape'. The place's state of health was not the subject of the seminar, which was directed more at enabling the participants to experience the place's transforming potential.

It was early morning and I was getting ready for the seminar, busy looking for places that would facilitate transformational experiences, when I came across a roughly hewn stone that had obviously been put there on purpose. The place was pervaded by a strong sense of the presence of elemental beings. For a long time I leaned on the stone, engrossed in its secret without progressing in my efforts to decipher it.

The seminar was intensive and ran its course through the whole day. Finally in the evening I gave a very complicated lecture. When I went to bed, I simply could not get to sleep. I began to suffer serious heart trouble. None of my self-help exercises were any good. I reproached myself for allowing my ambition to overstrain my strength. Towards morning I was already thinking it would be necessary to cancel the second day of the seminar and go to a hospital.

Dawn brought a little respite and I resolved to keep up my courage and finish the seminar, even if I died doing it. My heart troubles were bearable so I was able to hold out till the midday break. During the break I went to the above-mentioned stone to ask for help from my friends, the elemental spirits.

I had scarcely leaned against the stone when I saw a dwarf approaching. He reached into my heart muscle and drew out a thick thorn. Then he calmly let it fall into the etheric depths of the mountain. I followed the thorn with my inner sight and perceived a huge heart muscle, frozen within the inner parts of the mountain. By the look of things, the district's heart centre had been sunk in sleep for centuries. I realised at once that the dwarves had purposely slipped the thorn into my heart when, sunk in abstraction, I was leaning on the stone the day before. They had wanted to draw my attention to the forgotten heart centre within Mount Verita and persuade me to perform an Earth Healing exercise that I had certainly not planned. Obviously the time had now come to awaken the sleeping heart centre and lead it back to its nurturing role in the landscape.

The break was now over and I got back to the seminar group at the last minute. I told the group about my night-time troubles and the dwarf's message. By general consent, the seminar's programme was immediately altered and we dedicated ourselves to awakening the heart centre. We could not have achieved this if the time had not been ripe, but neither could it have happened if the environmental spirits had not used that drastic way to draw my attention to the deplorable defect.

. . . .

In between the two workshops I also visited Türnich. On the way I had to spend an hour in Cologne while waiting for my train connection. Since the main train station is conveniently situated next to the cathedral, I took the opportunity to admire this Gothic masterpiece. The moment I entered the awe-inspiring church interior, it occurred to me to ask whether there were possibly any elemental beings present in the cathedral. In response, I was guided by my feelings to a place between the third and fourth columns on the left of the nave. To my surprise I could sense different kinds of elementals through the sensitivity in my hands. The focal points of dwarfs, fairies, fire spirits and so on were closely connected in the church. But there was no more time, and I had to go back to the station.

Three months later I was in Cologne again, at the south end of the cathedral square. I had just missed my train connection to Türnich. Attempting to make good use of this spare hour I decided to buy myself a pair of sandals. There is a fountain dedicated to the 'Dwarfs of Cologne' in the street leading to the shoe shop (I mentioned these dwarfs earlier). I soon found the right pair of sandals and returning to the fountain passed the time exploring the various dwarf carvings with my hand to see whether they actually held any elemental life.

Indeed, I did find them present in the last carving on the right. These dwarfs were busily engaged in tailoring. I felt magnetically drawn to one of the carved dwarfs whose face was in profile, and I headed straight for its tiny earhole. To my great surprise I was able to slip into the opening with my consciousness, and I soon found myself in a different dimension behind the dwarf's head. I had hardly had time to reorient myself when I perceived a dwarf sitting there dressed in a Renaissance costume of ruby red colour. In human terms I would say he was about 60 cm (24 inches) in height.

. . . .

28. COMMENTARY: Snow White and her Relationship to the Elemental World

At this point I should like to return to the theme of 'The Goddess and the Seven Dwarfs'. The story of Snow White, which is the origin of the theme, has an even deeper meaning for the understanding of the elemental world than at first thought. It concerns not only the maintenance of the sacred extensions of the landscape but the soul and spiritual backgrounds of the elemental world itself, and its relationship to human beings. It was not by chance that Snow White found her new home among the dwarfs.

In the celebrated story that the Brothers Grimm have brought to us, their descendants, from the folk tradition, Snow White symbolises the human soul. The three colours, white, red and black, are signs of her descent from the lap of the Goddess. The stepmother, to the contrary, represents the alienated, egocentric world, dominated by cold rationalization, into which the human soul is born. The stepmother cannot stand the natural beauty and integrity of the indwelling soul. To suppress the voice of the soul once and for all, the Ego orders the huntsman to lead the maiden into the forest and there kill her. The dark forest symbolises the soul's suppression in the subconscious.

The huntsman is merciful and allows Snow White to vanish in the forest. There she finds refuge in the house of the seven dwarfs. In other words, the suppressed soul joins itself to the elemental foundations of creation. To put it the other way, the elemental beings become the guardians of the spiritual and soul dimensions of earth, landscape and humans, in which our rationally oriented civilisation has no interest: or worse than no interest; the stepmother 'descends' three times into the elemental world to poison Snow White! I compare her murderous attempts with modern technology's invasion of the worlds of atoms and genetic codes. These are worlds that are under the care of the elemental beings, and they involve original creative forces that the nature of elemental beings knows how to handle.

However, the fairytale ends on an optimistic note with the return of the soul to her home, and her marriage to her loving partner, the awakened human Self.

This encounter was a big surprise to me. At first, I felt unable to ask any questions at all. But I remembered that I was involved in a process of revelation where it was very important not to miss any opportunity for learning that the elemental world might offer me. So I took a chance and asked him whereabouts in Cologne I would find the creative aspect of the Goddess.

I must give some background to my question. During my healing work in recent years in the grounds of Türnich castle near Cologne and at Cappenberg near Dortmund, I have become more and more aware of a vast landscape temple which on a macroscopic level is connected to the whole of Western Germany. This landscape temple has three main centres in the areas of Cologne, Cappenberg and Extern-steine; their inbreath is energised from the Munich region. Since each of the three main centres also contains all three aspects of the Goddess, there must exist a complete and unique structure for the Cologne area.[3] From working at Türnich for many years, I knew that the aspect of wholeness for the Cologne area was to be found there. The creative aspect corresponding to this would have its focal point somewhere in the city. It was questionable whether this point would have maintained its vital power in the face of urban development. Therefore, I asked the dwarf this particular question. Without hesitation he answered that he was unable to tell me. But I did not give up so easily and I asked again, this time requesting that he show me the place. Very clearly he consented, so I took a beautiful stone from my pocket and held it against the tiny earhole, so that the goblin was able to transfer its focal point onto it. With my right hand I carried this stone in front of me, while I used my left hand to receive the guiding impulses.

To start with, he led me to Hohe Strasse, and then along this main shopping street towards the central station. As we crossed the extended axis of the cathedral I was instructed to follow this axis into the cathedral itself. Finally, I was guided exactly to the point between the third and fourth columns on the left of the nave where I had previously experienced a dense population of elementals. From there I had to turn my face towards the beautiful Renaissance window on the north side.

Suddenly it became crystal clear. Surrounded by the familiar Christian forms was the hidden figure of the threefold Goddess. I found her creative aspect depicted in the adoration of the three magi, and also in a picture of the Queen of Sheba visiting King Solomon. She is accompanied by two other

---

[3] Analogous to the principle of a doll within a doll within a doll…

The profile of a dwarf with his inviting earhole, and another dwarf behind him.
(The Fountain of Dwarfs in Cologne).

royal women. The three kings and the 'three queens' alternate in the glass window, and so seem to reflect the holy female/male polarity and interaction as we know it from the examples of the ancient ritual of enthronement of the annual king by the priestesses of the Goddess culture, or the ritual of the holy wedding. There is a complementary representation in the lower part of the window. Here the Virgin Goddess is depicted as the Virgin Mary with a lily in her hand, and the Goddess of Transformation is shown as St Elizabeth with a crown on her head and a crown in front of her heart chakra, as well as a golden chalice which she holds in front of her lap.

. . . .

29. COMMENTARY: **Holes in Space and Time**

Twelve years later there was an interesting epilogue to the story of the 'ear-hole jump'. Repeated experiences had taught me that 'black holes' exist not only in galactic space but also in terrestrial space. These appear to be inter-dimensional portals, i.e., 'holes' leading into other dimensions of being.

The ear-hole opening to which I had been magically drawn had proved to be a micro-interdimensional portal. When I went through the 'black hole' on the wings of my imagination, I landed in another dimension of space. For me this is the fifth dimension that vibrates beyond those of time and space. It exists simultaneously with our day-to-day reality but beyond its four dimensions (the three dimensions of space plus time).

At the moment in question, my consciousness had automatically switched from a logical to a pictorial language to adjust to the new dimension. From that moment on I existed simultaneously on two levels. There I stood, just like any of the other sightseers around the stone dwarves, and at the same time I was 'within' another dimension where, as the continuation of the story shows, I could move without any problem.

In the years 2005-06 I discovered inter-dimensional portals in the landscape which I, like every one else, had previously passed by without noticing. One can say that there are places and landscapes that can lead a human being, or even entire cultures, over to the fifth dimension, reason enough to reverence them as sacred. I am thinking of Hallstatt in Austria, Geneva, Manhattan... There are an unexpected number of places and landscapes equipped with a specific geomantic system that makes possible our translation into the fifth dimension – without our having to say goodbye to our material body, as otherwise occurs at the moment of death.

As the example of the tiny ear-hole demonstrates, the inter-dimensional portals offer the possibility of raising us from the narrow, right-angled structure of rationality and initiating us into the freedom of the multidimensional world. Because of this, they may play an important role in the near future.

. . . .

I meditated deeply on the hidden Goddess symbolism of the north window and became aware that it had been the work of busy elementals who took care that the artists were appropriately directed and inspired while making the glass windows. But I was also interested to find out why it was exactly this spot where the Goddess temple had to be built, since the cathedral had been dedicated to entirely different purposes. For an answer I was guided towards the fourth column to look inside. I saw a dark, vertical shaft leading deep down into the earth underneath the cathedral. As a precaution and to make sure that there was no mistake, I went to a few of the other columns. But they rejected me on an energetic level and did not allow a glimpse into their interior.

Suddenly, I was able to understand. It is known that the cathedral was built on a former sacred hill where Celts and Germans erected their holy shrines; presumably it had been used for the same purpose by the earlier Goddess culture of pre-Indo-Germanic Europe. Under Roman rule a Jupiter temple was erected on the same spot. This temple was transformed into an early Christian basilica, and on the ruins of this were built first a Merovingian and later a Carolingian cathedral. Then, on top of this, the largest Romanesque church of the West was constructed, and it is on the ruins of this that the present cathedral stands. In order to protect the original power point of the Goddess, the elementals had followed as each layer was built higher and higher up.

Today the cathedral is situated quite a few metres above the original hill, and the elementals have settled into what must be a very strange environment for them—a Gothic cathedral. The shaft which I had seen inside the fourth column was a kind of umbilical cord and power line to the sacred hill of the Goddess. This shows that in spite of all adversity and the constant reconstruction the nature intelligences of this sacred hill of the Goddess were still present and gladly fulfilling their task.

Meanwhile my train connection was due, leaving me with just enough time to say 'thank you' and to return my friendly travel guide back to the earhole at the dwarfs' fountain.

My experiences at Heidenberg and Cologne cathedral showed me how elementals have been caring for the focal points of landscape temples ever since the spirit-soul dimension was removed from human consciousness. As these places have been left to nature, they have developed cosmograms[4] designed by the appropriate shaping of trees or rocks. The elementals wanted to make sure that the original power and potential stayed there anchored and alive. In other places where there were superimposed structures or in urbanised areas, designers, craftspeople and artists were inspired to weave appropriate cosmograms or symbols into their pieces of art. In this way, knowledge of the true essence of a place was handed down covertly through the ages. Most of the present elemental tasks and activities became necessary when holistic consciousness became more and more clouded. But what was the function originally assigned to the nature intelligences within the landscape temples?

I had to wait for another month before I was given the opportunity during an earth healing seminar in Svetinje/Jeruzalem to observe a host of temple goblins at their original job. This gift was given to me after I had been working periodically at this place for the previous two years, carrying out healing and harmonizing work. The Pilgrims' church at Jeruzalem in Eastern Slovenia was built in a square shape by the Knights Templar in the 13th century. In the middle of the church there was an extraordinary icon representing the Black Madonna, brought back by the Templars from Jerusalem in the Holy Land. Today, only a good baroque copy exists, but it is not in its original position. With the placing of the icon above the present-day altar, the vertical power shaft has lost its focus. It used to descend through the icon in the centre of the square room, nourishing it with cosmic energy.

First of all I worked with my seminar group on restoring the room's sacredness by strengthening and centring the original power shaft in the middle of the chapel, mainly through our harmonious singing. In a follow-up meditation in the chapel in June 1993, I was able to see how the power flow descended from heaven and now, once again, touched the earth. What was missing entirely was the response of the earth centre to the cosmic impulse. Without this, an energetic dialogue between earth and heaven cannot begin. This response would revive the sacredness of the place.

The one-sided connection of the place to the sphere of heaven can be explained by the Templars being a Christian Order. Primarily they were interested in the cosmic relationship and regarded the opposite pole—the earthly one—as inferior. In other words, the awkward Christian scheme of division into good and evil played its part. Finally, during a meditation in the chapel

---

[4]   As far as I can tell, cosmograms in crop fields also belong in this category. These have been discovered over the past few years in England and other places.

in August 1993 I was able to observe how a vortex from the Goddess presence, which I perceived as sweet, ascended from the central point. Suddenly, in front of my eyes the floor burst open and an almighty stream of power started to bubble up from the earth—like a dirty pool of water. It became increasingly clearer and calmer, connecting more and more with the descending column of power. It seemed to climb up the column.

. . . .

30. COMMENTARY: **Environmental Healing**

The modern concept of earth healing starts from the premise that the earth and its locations are fundamentally sound. No earth healers are needed to care for her health. However, this does not mean that we human beings have no responsibility for the wellbeing of earth and her landscapes. Earth has made available to us her surface together with plants, beasts and elemental beings so that we can develop ourselves as an evolution and as individuals.

For humans to develop as beings with free will, it is necessary that we are allowed to make mistakes so that from them we can learn what is right. Beings of the parallel evolutions often suffer under the weight of our faulty decisions. They are sacrifices to our ill-treatment and suffer in huge numbers. That is also true of places and landscapes.

At this point it is timely to begin the environmental healing practices. To redress our karmic responsibilities, we must develop ways to balance humanity's wrongdoings. This is not a call for us to intervene in the wellbeing of the landscape, but rather to tackle blockages that hinder earth from breathing and developing itself as a healthy organism. Above all, it calls for awakening and supporting the self-healing powers of earth in the places that have been damaged, so that the natural healing processes can unfold.

. . . .

I could assume that the relationship between the chapel and the original temple of the Goddess on this spot had begun to flow again. It had been blocked for centuries. I asked my daughter Ana to consult her Angel teacher about the form of the long-vanished temple structure, because I wanted to get a spatial image of this relationship. He revealed a picture of a clockwise spiral on top of the hill. This spiral was an old ritual pathway. The pilgrims of the ancient Goddess culture followed it from station to station, experiencing inner cleansing, transformation and renewal. The power point, which today is located in the presbytery of the Pilgrims' church, which used to be the Templar chapel, represented the second station on the spiral path. Originally there was a hollow space dug into the earth with a stone circle in the centre. The pilgrims used to go down into the hollow to experience the Earth Goddess directly.

In light of this revelation, during a further meditation in the chapel on this same site I tried to look at the ascending vortex of power very closely. I perceived it as a slightly open rosebud, woven from fine silver threads. With a sense of wonder I saw how the power bud turned evenly around its own axis while it began slowly to open. Then I tried to look deeper into the earth to find the source of the turning motion. This took me into an underground dimension of the chapel where to my delight I saw a whole host of temple goblins. They were deeply engaged in their activity of turning the wheel clockwise around the vertical axis of an imaginary platform where the power bud was fixed.

Their concentrated effort on turning the platform very slowly and precisely took me by surprise. I finally grasped the significance of this work of precision when at a certain point the power bud became aligned and in resonance with the power of the Mother Goddess. Immediately the goblins stopped pushing. In the ensuing stillness I could see how a radiant Goddess figure descended along the column of power in the middle of the room. Her presence gave a blessing to the room. When through further turning another alignment of the bud took place it manifested as a blue colour filling the room. After a short break which allowed the colour to fade away, the platform was turned again until the Black Goddess of Transformation manifested. During this phase the room was filled with a golden yellow colour.

When the platform was turned into its next position, the white figure of the Virgin Goddess appeared, as I had expected. Now I became curious as to which colour would come next. But there was none. The wonderful dance seemed to have run into an obstacle. I also noticed that the outer contours of the white Goddess appeared darkened. Obviously there was a blockage in this phase of the original function of the temple. I began to sing quite loudly, hoping to release the block through the proven method of harmonizing sound. The group immediately joined in and beautiful harmonies began to fill the room. After a while the shadows around the Virgin disappeared and the platform could be turned again. The last phase produced a violet colour after which the mother figure reappeared. The whole cycle could start anew.

According to my observations, I was able to reconstruct the role the temple goblins originally played in pilgrimages here, although the rituals which the elementals performed underneath the chapel appeared like something from a fairy tale. They worked underground in a spot comparable to the

The temple goblins of Jeruzalem (Slovenia) turn an imaginary platform.
It causes a rotating 'energy blossom' to unfold, periodically manifesting
the Goddess in her three forms.

hollow which was mentioned by Ana's Angel. The stone circle would represent the platform which the goblins were turning into different alignments to attract the diversity of life powers through colours and divine qualities. We can vividly imagine how the pilgrims sat in silence in the stone circle to receive the various vibrations which resulted from the elementals' spiritual ring-o'-roses.

. . . .

31. COMMENTARY: **The Paradisiacal Underworld of Sarajevo**

Certain holy places have the good fortune of maintaining their original sacred space intact in their subconscious. I experienced a further example at Sarajevo in Bosnia. In this case too, the indefatigable assistance of the elemental beings was of decisive importance.

After the war in Bosnia I led a few city healing workshops in Sarajevo and while doing so, discovered that the old city centre was built over the site of a former grove sacred to the water nymphs. It was situated on the water meadows where the River Miljacka crawled out of its ravine and poured itself over the level plain. The water meadows were later drained by the Osmanic Turks for the construction of Sarajevo.

The draining of the meadows forced the water nymphs and their whole realm into the place's subconscious. After I had found the etheric entry to their underworld on the opposite bank of the Miljacka, I was able to move in spirit underneath the old city and enjoy the silvery liquid beauty of the sub-terrestrial sacred grove.

While I was contemplating the phenomenon in 2004, I noticed that there was sadly no apparent connection between the human city above and the fairylike world below.

Two years later I was once again in Sarajevo, travelling through the Balkans with a group of geomantically inclined colleagues. To my surprise, I perceived that this time there was a somewhat hesitant but nonetheless lively exchange between the worlds 'above' and 'below'. With my inner eye I saw the nymphs' gifts rising up as etheric jewel drops to the human city above. Going the other way, specific powers of the human world directed to transformation and regeneration travelled downward. Perhaps my contribution to this positive change had consisted simply in my having mentioned, in my lecture after the first experience, how the two worlds along the Miljacka were separate, so there were now a few human beings who were aware of the two parallel realities.

. . . .

The following experiences came to me at the pilgrims' church of Heiligenblut at the foot of the Grossglockner. They were to add to my previous insights because this time different kinds of elemental beings were involved.

The massive, majestic rock of the Grossglockner sits at the end of the Moll Valley and at 3798 metres (12460ft) is the highest mountain in Austria. On seeing the snow-covered peak for the first time from the high mountain road, I realised immediately that it resembled a bird with outstretched wings, with its beak pointing straight up to the cosmos. In it I perceived quite naturally the figure of the neolithic bird goddess which represents the holistic aspect of the Virgin Goddess. One has to consider that the symbolic bird goddess is a bird in flight, connecting the earthly with the cosmic sphere. It therefore re-states the original unity of heaven and earth. The Goddess in her virgin aspect represents this unity.

We know from several examples that the holy places which were used for ritualistic contact with high mountains or their emanating powers were lo-cated at the foot of the mountain rather than the top, at a strategic point that resonates with the focal point of power at the top. Heiligenblut, a steep hill with a famous Gothic pilgrims' church, is such a contact point. There is a legend about the founding of the church which reveals the relationship of this ancient sacred place with the mountain and the early Goddess cult.

The story tells us that St Briccius received a vial containing Christ's blood as a present from the Byzantine emperor in Constantinople. Shortly afterwards, the emperor asked him to give back the precious gift. But St Briccius escaped with it on an ass across the Balkans until he reached the foot of the Gross-glockner where he was buried under an avalanche of snow. Earlier on he had sewn the vial inside the calf of his leg to protect it from discovery. His body and the vial were found one day when three ears of corn grew out of the snow. Where the ass had stopped with the corpse of the sage, a pilgrims' church was erected. The vial with the blood and the three ears of corn have been kept in the relic shrine of the church unto this day.

To my mind, life-giving blood with the power to make ears of corn sprout from the sterile snow is a symbol for the menstrual blood of the Goddess. The ancient cultures saw this as a covenant for the eternal cyclical process of re-newed life. In the Eleusinian Mysteries the life-renewing power of the female cycle was celebrated annually. This cult was of great social and political signifi-cance for 2500 years, lasting in the Mediterranean until the 5th century AD. The central symbol for these mysteries was the three ears of corn tied together in exactly the same way as the relics in the shrine of Heiligenblut. In addition, there is also the fact that the place was revealed by an ass. Symbolically the ass can be compared to the ancient satyrs, which were to that period what the dwarfs are to our epoch. This means the presence of the elementals was essential in the decision about where to erect the pilgrims' church.

But there was something I could not understand. Why would the vial be hidden of all places in the tissue of the leg? Another factor was that when I entered the church, I felt irresistibly drawn to the Gothic Madonna to the right of the main altar. As is common, Mary is holding her son by the hand. But, surprisingly, he is touching his right foot with his left hand. This gesture seems so unnatural that Mary has to hold this overbalancing Jesus child with a firm grip on his bottom, lest he slip from her hand. Again, the foot!

I went down into the crypt to find out more about this secret because I assumed that there the elementals would be close. And so it was. I saw an invisible opening in the middle of the room, leading into the underworld, and a great number of gnomes were running back and forth. Relying on my previous experiences I climbed down in my consciousness to ask in a loud voice what was the meaning of the foot. Nobody had time to listen. I should have carried a token of my connection to the elemental world, as I had at Höhbeck in Wendland.

Therefore I looked for another source of information in the crypt. An old sage of the dwarf lineage was sitting on the staircase which leads to the tomb of St Briccius. After I had repeated my question about the foot several times he posed a question of his own: "Are you not at the foot of the mountain?" Suddenly it dawned on me that all these signs were pointing to the law of resonance which allows certain places at the foot of the mountain to participate directly in the power of the Grossglockner. The first of these sacred places is marked by the church of Heiligenblut. Jakob Lorber mentions in his revelations about the Grossglockner that such special places can be found over a wide area. Even the castle hill in Graz is part of the system. Just as the acupuncture points on the sole of the foot are connected to all the organs in the body, so are the power places at the foot of this holy mountain connected to different sources and power points. This explains why Heiligenblut has been worshipped as a holy place of pilgrimage throughout the history of many cultures. The uninterrupted chain of veneration reaches back to the Virgin culture of the early stone age.

I noticed another elemental in the main church when I came up from the crypt and faced towards the main altar. I perceived a charred figure which appeared as if it had been burned. Only the upper part of an eight-metre-tall

The Grossglockner with the 'Heiligenblut'
pilgrims' church at the foot of the mountain.

(26ft) figure was visible. Again I descended into the crypt to see whether the figure would continue in the lower part. And in fact there was a deva figure who had held her focal point at this place for thousands of years. In her highly evolved position she is responsible for the interplay of all forces which combine to make this place a power point. I call this kind of deva a deva of place. In the church of Heiligenblut the steps down to the crypt were arranged in such a way that they led directly to the focus of the deva of place.[5] There the people could receive the highest blessing of the power point.

It must have been a sad period in the history of the pilgrims' church when the invisible presence of the deva was no longer tolerated. Somebody must have been sensitive enough to feel that there was a strong radiation at the altar which was in competition with the light from the celebration of mass. The church has the wrong proportions for the height of the deva figure. She reaches with the upper part of her energy body beyond the crypt into the area in front of the altar. I assume that they tried to control this power using rituals of exorcism, which caused a darkening of all the parts of the deva's energy structure that extended into the main church. This is how I perceived it. However, they never succeeded in driving out the deva entirely because her focal point down in the crypt continued to pulsate untouched in its original position. The deva had to be saved from her torture so that she could once again be a blessing for the place and its visitors.

. . . .

32. COMMENTARY: **The Elemental Beings Cry for Help**

It is not only critical situations out of the past that need healing. This is illustrated by my experience with the motorway in Slovenia. This is the motorway from Barcelona to Kiev which is under construction and is to run though our Vipava Valley.

A few years earlier the mayor of the Borough of Vipava had asked me to examine the planned motorway, which affected his community, to determine whether it would present geomantic problems. I found only one spot likely to be problematic. It was at the end of a deep valley, and there I discovered a group of elevated beings who had something important to tell me. But at that moment I had insufficient time to attend to their business. Because it was thought that road construction would not begin for some years, I asked to be informed in good time before construction began so that I could discuss the problem further.

---

[5] I want to replace the term 'spirit of place' (Latin: *genius loci*) with 'deva of place' because I consider the former term as deriving from old patriarchal images.

Unfortunately, we all forgot about it. Then one day, as I was driving by the neighbourhood, I saw to my horror that cranes were already standing on the critical spot and work was going on around them. But once again I could spare no time to go in and see what the elemental spirits had to tell me.

A few days later my wife and I were once again driving by – and once again we were in a hurry. This time, there was an accident: a young man decided to overtake a truck, just as we were already overtaking it. There was a slight collision. We waited for an hour by the side of the road for the police to arrive. After about half-an-hour I finally got it! The collision had happened at the exact point where the road turned off to lead to the construction site.

After this cry for help, I took the time to find out why I was being called to the site so urgently. Workmen were starting to erect a bridge support pillar on an extremely sensitive place, actually the site of the etheric opening to an inter-dimensional portal through which earth's archetypical powers must be allowed to flow freely. These are of the greatest importance for the maintenance of the valley's power centres.

. . . .

It is unbelievable how little understanding and how much panic and rejection the Christian religion showed towards the highly developed elementals which take care of ritual sites. This attitude developed when the culture began to spread. I found the saddest example of this on the hill of Gradišca near Črnotiči in the Slovenian Kras when I visited this sacred site together with Hanna Moog, the editor of my books, and my wife Marika in August 1993. I had described in the last chapter of my book *Die Landschaft der Göttin* how the stone walls in the Kras landscape temple provided the manifestation of yin power in the absence of water on the surface of the dry Kras. Modern archaeologists say that these are ramparts for defence purposes. But this example demonstrates that in fact it was a purely sacred site, and completely useless for defence because the walls enclose the hill like a horseshoe only on one side.

The high stone wall begins at a rock formation on the west side where there is a focal point for cosmic powers, then goes around the northern part of the hill and ends in a construction of three oblong underground chambers to the east. There used to be another sacred site in the centre of the whole structure, enclosed by a round wall. In this place now is the pilgrims' church of 'Maria im Schnee' (Mary in the Snow). Even during my first visit, the three chambers to the east particularly attracted me. I felt that they had been dug into the earth and that they were the remains of three initiation chambers, each with a different energy focus. In the first chamber I experienced a focal point for so-lar energy, in the second an incoming radiation from Planet Venus and in the third an angelic energy focus. I assume that there was a step-by-step initiation procedure in the same order as these three forces.

When we visited Gradišca this time I felt drawn to a mighty pine tree which spread its branches across the first of the three chambers. A cosmogram in the shape of a lem-niscate led me to the conclusion that it was a fairy tree. As I was standing close to the trunk, trying to build up a loving relationship with the faun of the tree, he sent me a very ugly picture. I could see a pitch black creature wrapped in flames and writhing with pain on the ground as he tried to extinguish them. Every time the creature tried to stand up the fire flared up again. Again he writhed painfully on the earth to quench the fire, and again it restarted as soon as he got up. It seemed to go on eternally. The torture of this being was never-ending.

I was very moved by it and I asked the faun to give me some clues as to the cause of this drama. I could guess that the memory of a terrible death was involved. The faun had stored it in his memory to pass it on to the first human being who approached him with love. He led me to the edge of a thicket, a few steps outside the range of the overhanging branches of the pine tree. This shows that a faun can actually reach in his consciousness beyond the edge of his own tree. From this spot I was able again to perceive the tragic event. It re-minded me of a torture system dating from the time of the witch hunts where the victim was rolled in tar and feathers to be burned afterwards.

I called my two companions to try visualisation and singing as a way of cleansing the place and to release the being from its torture. For a long time our efforts were absorbed by the darkness of the creature and were in vain. But then I could see how a white veil of grace descended onto the scene, and finally a work of transformation began. Out of the misty power structure a fairy fig-ure developed. She wore a crown on her immensely beautiful head as a sign that she belonged to the highest rank in the evolutionary chain. Otherwise, she almost resembled a human being.

She explained this resemblance through an intuitive dialogue between us. For centuries she had been serving at the rituals to initiate people into the se-crets of life on earth, together with the priestesses of the sacred site at Gradišca. She herself belonged to the lineage of fairies but through a very long time-span of development she had reached the highest grade of unfoldment within her species. Therefore she was allowed to serve as the ritual deva together with the human priestesses. It was her task to sensitise the people who came to the

The ritual deva of Gradišca tortured and in great pain.

shrine to the powers and beings of nature. At the time her place was at the centre of the first of the three chambers which I have mentioned.

The ritual deva was still closely connected to the last priestess who presumably had cared for the ritual site in secret at the beginning of our modern age. When this priestess was tortured to death as a 'witch' by the methods described, the ritual deva had unconsciously attached the suffering of this woman to herself, and had carried the pain until now because, unlike us, she knows no death, which of course would have released her.

Then I asked her where she would want to settle after her liberation. Contrary to my expectations she expressed a desire to be carried back to her original place where she had fulfilled her duties, although today only a hollow reminds us of the old sacred place. I could feel in her determination a great faith in humanity, that we would soon undergo a fundamental shift and would appreciate her services once again.

. . . .

33. COMMENTARY: Ouspensky Cathedral, Helsinki

The threshold of the third millennium found me leading a workshop in Helsinki. After that had ended, I still had some time left before the return flight took off for Ljubljana and I decided to visit the celebrated Ouspensky Cathedral of the Russian Orthodox Church. I had hardly passed through the door of this holy place when the eyes of my soul were opened! I saw an unimaginably large throng of tiny elemental beings, all busy and eagerly engaged in keeping the individual stones and construction elements of the giant building in their allotted places.

We humans take for granted that the stones of a building stay in the arch or cupola where they have been placed, provided there is static equilibrium and no earthquake. Now I had an opportunity to look behind the scenes. I saw how stones are permanently on the point of slipping but at the last moment are pushed back into their allotted place...I saw the keen vigour of a million folk at work.

My consciousness was ready to put the vision in a logical perspective. I understood it as a pictorial representation of the role played by simple elemental beings of the earth element to maintain the world of form. What reason sees as a long-term static form must at every moment be brought into accord with the form's original plan. The whole universe is in constant motion as its electrons circle wildly along their chaotic paths. It is only the eye of our reason that is too slow to perceive the constant flow of renewal.

The millions of gnomish folk were not left to themselves to do their tasks. I saw a pellucid veil of light descend through the cupola and arches of the cathedral. I interpreted it as the presence of an exalted being of light, a Deva of the cathedral. I could sense that this veil of light was constantly and reverentially touched by the elemental beings, as if the plan was there encoded from which each could read the instructions for their immediate task.

. . . .

FOUR

The Classification of
the Elemental World

THE MIDDLE AGES was the last epoch in history which accepted the existence of elemental beings in its world view—for instance, the 'Green Man' and other grotesque creatures which often support the arched buttresses in Gothic cathedrals. These figures have very striking countenances and exist in many variations, and quite often one can see plant growth flowing from their mouths. Symbolically, we can identify the mouth with the creative word, and this means that the spiritual task of such a being is to help manifest plant growth in the physical world; in other words it represents an elemental who serves the unfoldment of nature. In a very natural way these nature beings share the spaces between the ribs of church vaults with other types of being from the invisible world—the ones we call angels. This inspiring unity between nature and the spiritual world was deeply rooted in the images of art and folklore, but not in the dominant theological teachings. There should be no illusions about this, nor about the fact that artistic unity collapsed with the dawn of the age of 'Enlightenment'. In 1487, witch hunting was initiated by the papal bull of Pope Innocent VIII, leading to a wave of terror which lasted for three centuries. The invisible worlds were split into two poles: a demonic pole and a light pole. Clairvoyant people who had any connection with elemental or nature beings were now persecuted as representatives of the demonised pole in the Christian dualistic world view.

A systematic attempt to reintegrate the world of elementals into an all-embracing world view was made at the turn of the 20th century, first by the Theosophical movement, and then on another line of development by Rudolf Steiner's Anthroposophy. In his ten lectures on 'the spiritual beings in the heavenly bodies and kingdoms of nature',[1] given at Helsingfors in 1912, he introduced a sevenfold hierarchical model which incorporated nature spirits as well as angelic beings. The various elemental beings which I have described so far are given their place according to their level of unfoldment in the three lower ranks of the hierarchy.

According to Steiner, the first (and lowest) hierarchic level comprises the nature spirits. They serve as builders in the dense, liquid and gaseous forms of nature. Above them, on the second level of hierarchical order, stand the spirits of cyclic time which 'command and orchestrate the rhythmic flow and repetition in nature'. For instance, from my description of a tree faun, he would be placed on the first level, for it is his duty to dedicate himself to the unfoldment of an individual tree. The host of fairies I was able to watch on Venus Hill on the Isle of Srakane would belong to the second level. They look after the coordination of all processes of unfoldment within a given area. The overlighting being of the fennel deva would be classified in the third and highest level of the nature realms. She revealed herself to me as a fairy queen, and therefore in the realm of air elementals she represents the highest possible level of development. According to Steiner, it is the role of the beings of the third hierarchic level to instil their sense of purpose into the worlds of nature. If they moved up to the fourth level of hierarchy they would join the realm of angels, also called the spirits of Will, or Thrones in the esoteric tradition.

This model of three levels of hierarchy in the world of nature spirits corresponds exactly to what I have experienced myself, although personally I prefer to talk about three levels of unfoldment of elemental beings, because it paints a picture of a dynamic interconnectedness between one level and the next, whereas the word 'hierarchy' suggests a kind of static arrangement. In order to give a clear impression of the three levels of unfoldment in the realm of elementals, I have organised my perceptions of the earth elemental beings within the following structure:

In the first and second chapters I have described only the first level of unfoldment of the earth elementals. I mentioned the gnomes in the legend of the sleeping King Mathias. They represent the most simple aspect of the earth spirits, who with their static presence in the crust of the earth enliven planetary matter. When I was talking about the cultivated landscape and the polarising effect of hedges the dwarfs came into play. It is their task to maintain the fertility in the earth. They are more developed than the gnomes. The further unfoldment of the earth elementals works in two directions. One direction leads to working with plants, the other to supporting human beings.

---

[1]   Rudolf Steiner: *The Spiritual Beings in Planetary Bodies and in the Realms of Nature* (in German). Published by R. Steiner Nachlassverwaltung, Dornach, 1960.

The oak spirit serving as a bracket in the
Church of Elisabeth, Marburg, Germany.

I contacted such beings in the grounds of Türnich castle where they look after single plants. They are elves, and to me they are reminiscent of the 'dancing musical piglets' in the Walt Disney story (see Chapter Two). A higher development in this direction is shown by the fauns, who are the intelligences of individual trees. They are mentioned in Chapter One.

The second line of development is directed towards the formative processes in nature, and furthermore to accompanying human beings during their incarnation, because every form is an expression of the earth element. I also described the modelling of musical forms by the gnome at the feet of the violinist, and the formative function of the gnome in one of the guest houses in Möll Valley (see Chapter Two). In Chapter One I also touched upon the work of the earth elementals in taking care of the human physical form. I say more about this in Chapter Seven.

The second level of unfoldment of the earth elementals was first mentioned in Chapter Three in connection with the subject of landscape temples. I described my talks with the old sage of Heidenberg in Norm Friesland, and with another one in the crypt of the pilgrims' church at Heiligenblut. In addition, the dwarf who guided me to Cologne cathedral belongs to the second level of unfoldment of nature spirits who work in the earth element. In theory the function of these highly developed beings is to direct and coordinate. But every time I communicated with them I had the feeling that they were just sitting there, detached from all activity. Most of all I was deeply touched by the infinite wisdom which surrounds them. Therefore I found it easy to ask them questions about all kinds of matters concerning the secrets of life which I had failed to understand. But it never occurred to me that I had not asked them about their own real function in the territory which they administer. Similarly, I had a long discussion with an old sage who resides under a white magnolia tree beside a brook at Türnich castle, and this conversation went in many directions. On that spot, next to an arched gate, there stood in the Middle Ages a chapel dedicated to St Michael. It was moved in the 19th century, to be re-erected in a different place, thirty paces further into the courtyard. The old sage rejoiced in this decision to move the chapel. He indicated to me that it was a conscious choice by the people to free his focal point.

As was the custom in the early Middle Ages, the old St Michael's chapel was built directly above the centre of the location which had the strongest contact with earth energy, so that the earthly dimensions of the place were kept in check. The picture of St Michael battling with the dragon was seen as a symbol of the fight against the dark forces of the earth and nature, and these forces were labelled as evil. Therefore the chapel was purposely built above the spot where the old sage of the earth elemental lineage had his throne. In the dualistic world view he was perceived as a dangerous dragon. Building the chapel exactly above his spot vividly expressed the misconceived Michaelic fight with the dragon, and this forced the old sage to withdraw into the depths of the earth. From there, he told me, he often disturbed the holy mass with his loud whining.

It was a great breakthrough for the old sage that his throne was liberated by the moving of the chapel. At the dawn of the 20th century (the chapel was reconsecrated in 1893) people had given a very clear sign of reconciliation with the kingdom of the elementals. As a visible manifestation of this a picture of the Archangel Michael was created in the central window of the nave of the new chapel, showing the features of the old sage on Michael's armour. The countenance of the old sage appears on the archangel's right arm which is holding his flaming sword, ready for battle. This is a depiction of the dragon fighter pointing forwards to a future where he is not mobilised against the forces of nature and the earth, but rather includes the elementals as allies in his symbolic fight for the divine truth.

Then I acted as if I were ignorant and asked the old sage what was his part in the divine truth. As is normal in conversations with the elementals, he answered with a cloud of feelings which I quickly tried to translate into logical sentences. If I understand it rightly, he has unhindered access to the wisdom of life, symbolised by the legendary treasures which are guarded by his kind. All wisdom is a result of the life experiences of countless beings of the earth, and it is stored in the 'bones' of the earth, the rocks. This is the true treasure of the earth, which he guards. His throne is always located at an important focal point of power within the landscape. There he concentrates the patterns of wisdom of a place. And so a resource is created from which the elementals of the region can draw the exact formative patterns necessary for their work.

My insight is that the opposite pole of the old sage is the crone, the ugly but loving and kind old woman who often forms the basis for ideas of the witch. In my opinion she has been more severely suppressed in human consciousness than her male counterpart, because I discovered her only in the late autumn of 1993, after I had been communicating with the old sage for many months. The reason for this might be found in her connection to the Black Goddess who filled the patriarchal culture with horror. I first met her in the depths of the grounds of the castle at Murska Sobota in Eastern Slovenia. In 1993-94

I was commissioned by the local authority there to work on a lithopuncture project.

The loving crone sits under an acacia tree which appears to be involved in a playful love-making with a hornbeam. When I asked her about her function compared to that of the old sage she pointed to this beautiful tree composition as an example that her task was to concentrate the power of love rather than the power of wisdom. This means that the love of Earth (the Goddess Gaia) is available to every creature on the planet without exception. The source of love is maintained through the connection with the crone, and it remains constantly ready to strengthen the efforts of every elemental being with a distinct duty in the kingdoms of nature. In fairy tales, this source appears as the witch's cauldron where the crone brews a magic potion.

The old woman of Murska Sobota indicated to me that I would be able to recognise her crooked form in the bark formations of 'her' acacia. And indeed, I had often noticed previously that the beings of the second level of unfoldment, because they are advanced in their individuation, would engrave their personal features or body into the material of their immediate surroundings. I have mentioned the old sage whose features were visible on the right arm of the Archangel Michael at Türnich. Another old sage on Venus Hill on the Isle of Srakane has engraved his features in the stone he sits on. Since I had been communicating with the old sage of Venus Hill daily for two weeks, we had developed a trusting relationship, and one day I dared to ask him what his name was. He answered, "Julius—just like Julius Caesar." Bearing a name is an expression of the highly developed individuality of the elementals of the second level of unfoldment. Beings on the first level, apart from the fauns of old trees, have no comparable signs of individuality.

Now and again we can meet an individual representative of the second level of unfoldment whose name has passed into history. For the years 1584 to 1588 at Castle Hudemühlen in Lüneburg there are records of the presence of a gnome whose family name was Hintzelmann. He would sometimes show 'a small hand like a boy or girl's', otherwise he could only be observed by children or mad people. He also told that he had a wife called Hille Bingels. She was probably his female counterpart, the loving old crone. Hintzelmann was said to oversee the whole of the castle during his time there. This corresponds with the higher role played by beings of the second level of unfoldment.

Another feature of the nature spirits of the earth element is the badly proportioned, sometimes unsettling or even ugly form which they present to us.

The old sage of Türnich — his features are
reflected on the armour of St Michael.

For example, our standard picture of an ordinary dwarf includes comparatively short legs and a head that is too large. This 'malformation' is puzzling, and it is even more poignant with beings of the second level. In my view this reflects the true proportions of earth matter, which we experience as strange and inaccessible, for we humans are spiritual beings. Consequently we can only perceive earthly aesthetics as an aberration from our sense of beauty, a deviation which our minds register as ugliness.

I was finally able to make contact with an earth elemental on the third level of unfoldment after I had broken down my resistance to the word 'Pan'. For a long time I resisted accepting Pan as the God of Nature because I saw it as a patriarchal thought pattern forced upon the female essence of earth nature. Therefore I was very surprised, when visiting the Findhorn Community in the North of Scotland in 1993, to perceive the presence of Pan on a low hillock in the so-called 'Pan's corner'. I recognised him from a description by R. Ogilvie Crombie, called Roc (see page 61). Pan's upper body was human-like. He sat in a squatting position and his furry-haired goat's legs were folded.

He gave me the impulse to go to an oak tree which marks the central power point of the eastern part of community land, called Pineridge. This tree was planted 17 years ago and I have always felt a deep connection to it. As I was standing in silence close to the trunk, Pan tried hard to melt my resistance. First of all a memory of an old sage was recalled in my mind, and Pan was shown to me as a further development of the lineage of gnome-dwarf-elf-faun-old sage. Secondly, I was able to understand that Pan indeed embodies the highest representation of the earth element beings, but he is not responsible for the whole of nature, only for the sum total of natural life within a certain area.

I had plenty of opportunities to converse with Pan in the early mornings, since I was leading a week-long earth healing seminar at the Findhorn Community. Because my inner barriers had dissolved, communication flowed between us without difficulty. The lower parts of his body, especially his hairy legs, form a picture which is repellent to us humans, but they indicate that Pan is connected to the dwarf family. A wave of shame hit me when the sight of his legs momentarily reminded me of the legs of a lizard. It was clear to me that the traditional picture of Pan fits only with the aesthetics of olden times. His upper body reveals a refined spirit which makes him the equal of the angelic beings. Clearly his form is a true expression of the third level of elemental unfoldment, forming a bridge to the more highly developed world of the angels.

The loving crone reveals herself in the bark of 'her' acacia.

To give me an idea of his role in the nature kingdoms, he opened up to me in such a way that I was able to see all aspects of 'his' landscape, one after the other. Now I could understand that he upholds perfect consciousness in each particle of life in his entrusted area. An infinite number of insights into the different levels of the landscape opened up before my inner eye. Not only did I feel that he is holding all the different aspects of the landscape in his consciousness, but that Pan himself is present simultaneously in all its entire existence. His quiet, conscious presence in the life processes within his area gives nature its fulfilling sense of being.

Third level of unfoldment	Pan
Second level of unfoldment	The loving old crone The wise old sage
First level of unfoldment	Fauns Elementals of animals and humans Goblins, dwarfs Elves, gnomes

Classification of earth elementals.

Pan's ability to be present at every place and in each particle of the landscape makes him distinctly different from the beings of the second level of unfoldment. They also participate in the common work of forming and modelling the processes in nature but they are bound to one territory or task. Pan's universal quality comes out even more strongly in the sensation that the different Pan aspects of different areas cannot be separated. United they represent an integral Pan, Pan of Planet Earth. Now it becomes clearer why Pan was the God of Nature in ancient Greece, although he was not one of the twelve gods of Olympia.

Concern about a one-sided patriarchal idea can be dispelled once we realise that Pan shares his higher spiritual duties with female forms of equal rank. Usually he shares these duties with a deva of place who is the most highly evolved being of the air element, and also with a queen of the nymphs who is in a similar position for the watery element.

A balanced spiritual leadership pattern exists in the nature realms. I want to use the grounds of Türnich castle, which are so familiar to me, as an example. According to my research, Pan of the park has taken residence under an old maple tree, right next to the large oval area where I perceived the dancing and music-making elves. The oval clearing represents the heart of the park on a vital-energetic level. Therefore it is not surprising to find Pan residing there.

It is easy to find the place when we take the path around the oval, looking outwards towards the outer boundary of the grounds. Not far from the path is the maple tree, and its tall trunk displays creative animal-like formations in flowing lines. At the top of the trunk you can discover Pan's face with a long beard. Exactly opposite, two or three steps on the other side of the path, we find the noble landscape nymph of pasture where she is anchored within a row of yew trees. It is possible to recognise the place from the extremely long branch of another maple tree which points sideways across the path. The branch looks as if it is coming out of the trunk quite arbitrarily. It makes a sudden turn close to the trunk, and then purposefully runs in a big curve eleven metres long to spread its wings exactly above the focal point of the landscape nymph. I saw the nymph herself as a beautiful maiden, about five metres (16ft) tall, made of clouds and waves of power.[2]

Later on, when I looked at the park in connection with the larger area of Türnich castle grounds, I realised that each section of the castle grounds has its own focus for Pan: in each of the three parts of the orchard,[3] in the castle area and in the deer park behind the castle. Within the next few years I would like to mark Pan's seat in the three parts of the orchard with stone sculptures. Pan's focus in the deer park goes back to ancient times, and it seems to me that here the Celtic people had a holy grove. The Pan here is still filled with the spirit of the epoch which last honoured him, and so his figure in the deer park is a Celtic Cernunnos with antlers, sitting in a characteristic cross-legged position, the way he is depicted on the famous cauldron of Gundestrup.

---

[2]   The grounds of Türnich castle were originally wet pasture, although today it is dry land. Pan's rich flora was strongly interwoven with the watery element of the nymph. This special character of the landscape finds its reflection nowadays in the twin positioning of Pan and the pasture nymph.

[3]   The orchard was started in 1989 over an area of 25 acres and is maintained by biodynamic agriculture. The design was created during the restoration of the castle grounds, in harmony with the vital-energetic principles we came to know.

34. EXERCISE: **Perceiving the Elemental Beings of Earth**

The world of earth elementals resonates in human consciousness through a chakra (power centre) that is classified with the earth element and is situated between our knees. If we still had a lovely long tail, this chakra would vibrate at the end of it. To communicate with the world of the earth elementals, one can use this chakra as the starting point.

Take a few moments to be present where the power centre vibrates between your knees. Imagine the centre to be like a little sphere. Now there are two possibilities:

- You can move vertically downwards with the sphere so that you arrive in the underworld. Now open the sphere, just as you would open one eye. Look around with your eye and pay attention to your subtle perceptions. You are now in contact with the subterranean world of elemental beings.
- The second possibility is to let the sphere rise vertically upwards till it reaches the region between your hips. At that height open the sphere as you would open an eye and you are in contact with the elemental beings in your environment.

During the process you should remain inwardly free and have no expectations.

. . . .

I was able to perceive the deva of place at a region above the central pond by the castle chapel. When we look from the castle into the sky above the trees towards the French garden on the other side of the pond, we can imagine in the rounded, convex lines of the treetops the imprint of an invisible pulsating sphere high up in space. We can further imagine that this sphere of light complements a visible sphere, made up of the unified tops of two huge sycamore trees. These are located to the left, beneath the invisible sphere of the deva of this area. The deva of place is one of the air elementals, and therefore she reigns over the area from the air.

To be able to understand the structure of the elemental kingdom we must imagine that the respective representatives of all four elements have their own threefold path, not just the earth elementals. In this way, the following basic pattern is a product of all three levels of unfoldment, multiplied by the four elements—earth, air, water and fire: 3 x 4=12.

So far we have met and systematised the three levels of unfoldment of the earth element. Some beings of the air element have also been mentioned; they are from the highest level of unfoldment, like the master fennel deva, the ritual deva of the holy shrine of Gradisca and the deva of place (which I have just

Pan in the grounds of Türnich castle.

described in connection with Türnich). I have also mentioned some of the air beings on the second level of unfoldment. Fairies of place care for the coordinating processes within a region. Plant devas embody the group soul of a plant species, and woodland fairies work as companions to the animals. Only the basic first level has been omitted so far.

In my experience the first level air elementals comprise a variety of fairies and sylphs. Fairies are connected to the expansion of life in an area, while sylphs have to do with movement in space, for instance with modelling and directing the wind. Once I was able to watch the elf of a rose working together with a tiny fairy to give birth to a rose bud.[4] It really was like a birthing process. The elf was pushing from the inside of the plant outwards, while the fairy was hovering outside in space to play the midwife. Very carefully she pulled the single petals out and helped to unfold them according to the archetypal pattern of the rose. In this case the fairy was involved with the rose as a manifestation in space. There would be numerous fairies of her kind in any living garden.

Third level of unfoldment		Master deva
		Deva of place
		Ritual deva
Second level of unfoldment	Fairies of place	
	Plant deva	
	Woodland fairy	
First level of unfoldment	Sylphs	
	Fairies	

Classification of air elementals.

Once, while flying from London to Belfast, I watched some sylphs who accompanied the plane, and in my opinion it was they who made it possible for the plane to move through space at all. They were flying alongside it, moving rhythmically back and forwards. They were able partly to enter the plane, since

---

4   Elves appear as male and female.

Pan of the deer park at Türnich revealing
himself to me as the Celtic 'Cernunnos'.

walls are not an obstacle for them. From time to time some of them turned their heads in surprise and looked back when they felt that they were being watched by one of the passengers. It must have been a rare event for them.[5]

. . . .

35. EXERCISE: **Just Like a Bee**

To experience two different developmental planes of the beings of the air element, the best exercise involves bees. I developed this over a lengthy period. The idea was born when I was observing bees creeping into an amazingly beautiful bell flower to get nectar. It reminded me of a book of fairy tales that had pictures of little fairies engaged in painting flowers. I truly believe that the quality of colour in a flower is maintained by the fairy world – and therefore by the consciousness of the air element. In this respect, flowers represent the smallest possible fairy space. However, since this fairy space vibrates outside the limitations of time and space, it can really stretch endlessly far and wide. It would be interesting to follow a bee and experience for oneself the tiny-huge space of fairyland!

In fact, I began to discover all manner of colour spaces after I had learned to let myself, in my imagination, fall into the flower space. While I was immersing myself once again in the breathtaking beauty of a flower space and in very high spirits, I was led to make a somersault. Unbelievable! In the next instant I found myself on a higher plane of the fairy consciousness, on the plane of the archetype of the plant concerned, the space of its Deva. This is a cosmic space that cannot really be logically presented in our consciousness. But it is worth taking the trouble to experience its vibration. This is the exercise:

- Seek out a flower that is in bloom.
- Incline yourself towards the chosen flower and look at it attentively and lovingly.
- When the moment feels right, slip into the flower, just as a bee does when it is gathering nectar.
- At the same moment, look around you and sense how the quality of a flower's inward space feels. Be aware that you are presently on the plane of fairy consciousness which is responsible for the colour quality of the flower.
- Immediately afterwards, in your imagination, make a forward somersault and find yourself on a higher plane. It is the plane of the archetypical con-

---

[5] To complement my observations of different elemental beings I recommend the perceptions of other seers, such as Geoffrey Hodson's *The Kingdom of the Gods*.

The deva of place at the central pond at Türnich.
The castle chapel is to the left.

sciousness of the flower species concerned, the world of the Devas.
- Afterwards, you should become conscious once again of the flower and its outward beauty, by which means you return to everyday consciousness.

The exercise should be performed with a variety of different sorts of flowers to give yourself practice in the power of discrimination.

. . . .

Next, the beings of the watery element deserve our attention. Two types on the first level of unfoldment have been mentioned before, the elementals in underground waters who look after the balance inside the earth's crust. They showed themselves to me in the form of the world fish Faronika (see Chapter One, pages 26-29). I have also mentioned nixies in connection with the destroyed spring behind our home. Traditionally, nixies enliven rivers, springs, lakes and marshes. To human beings they reveal themselves as beautiful maidens, in sharp contrast to the earth elementals. In cases where they are equipped with a fish tail it is a symbolic representation of their affinity with the water element, but this is not necessarily a feature of their bodies.

In the summer of 1993, I was able to watch a group of nixies on the slope of Venus Hill on the Isle of Srakane as they went about performing their duties in the landscape. I was surprised to find them dancing in such a completely dry place—there is no visible water on the naked rock of the island. Even though the island is surrounded by water, the sea is energised by a different kind of being with different tasks—the undines.

Later on, when I investigated this place with my instruments, I discovered that the dance of the nixies took place above an underground source of water. For them the physical presence of water is of less importance than the radiation of water energy, which was abundant in this particular spot.

Originally I did not see it as a dance; it appeared as if horizontal layers of round disks of light were rotating clockwise around a central water spout. Only after I had asked a faun from a neighbouring pine tree to confirm my perceptions was I able to recognise the rhythmic dancing of the nixies within the rotating movements. Their purpose was to distribute the life force of the water which wells up from their centre. Their circular movements took them ever back to the centre and out again, and never further than forty steps away from the centre. When I asked how they could supply the whole landscape with the life force of water by this method, the faun impressed an image of 'power through resonance' on me. My interpretation of their work is that they had responsibility for and were acting for the entire area through their dancing on this highly energised spot. For instance, when nixies serve a river or lake, they do their dancing by the river bank but never further than forty steps inland. From this centre the effects then spread out in waves.

. . . .

36. COMMENTARY: How Environmental Spirits Operate on the Basis of Resonance

Over the last few years, geomantic work on brooks and rivers has shed more light on how the dance of the nixies can have such an enlivening effect on the surrounding landscape.

River water is rich in the power of watery ether, and thus with the power of accelerating life. However, this power would remain bound in the physical molecules if it were not brought forth and distributed through the landscape by the nixies' ritual activity described above.

To translate the 'Dance of the Nixies' from fairytale language, you should imagine a wave of consciousness accompanying the stream of a river or brook. This 'standing wave' of nixie consciousness moves in the opposite direction to the stream, i.e., from the mouth to the source. This creates a stimulating polarisation. The rhythm of the water's flow is to a certain extent reversed in the ritual 'Dance of the Nixies'.

So it happens that, along its entire length, a river maintains a system of Yin-Yang polarisation that supports points in the landscape. This creates a highly energised landscape space along the river, which serves as resonance space for the nixies' dance.

This also explains why the nixies' ritual activity does not take place in the water itself, but is dependent on the quality of the riverside region. It is the interaction between the flow of the river and the power system of the surrounding landscape that enables the enlivening quality of the water to be distributed. The two river banks represent the intersection of the two spatial expanses. There the nixies' life-giving ritual dance is carried on ceaselessly to 'soften' the landscape in specific ways so that it can wholly absorb the living power and paradisiacal quality of the water element.

But woe if the riverbank is straightened and mutilated by technical protective devices! Then it becomes nearly impossible for human beings and landscapes to take part in the abundant life of the rivers and streams.

. . . .

So far, I have described the work of the water beings as a distribution of the feminine qualities of water. Since the nature realms are always evenly balanced, there are also male figures among the water elementals. I have often met a waterman whose figure reminds me of a crab's shell or a big toad. He can be recognised by his dark brown colours, and he gives the impression of a lonely being who has withdrawn far into the depths of the water with no other task but to maintain its yang pole. Only once have I seen a whole group of watermen at a yang power point by the river Ljubljanica near Ljubljana. They were singing in a choir with deep, solemn voices. There was snow on the ground and thick layers of fog on the river—water upon water.

The second level of unfoldment of water elementals is composed of nymphs, who give individuality to a river, lake or water meadow. The nymphs of wells are particularly beautiful, as they accompany the birth of water from inside the earth. Often they develop their place into a source of healing and blessing; human beings are drawn there for worship. I found one example in Ljubljana where a Lady chapel had been built in the shape of an artificial grotto at a tiny well, and many ill and despairing people visit it. While I was standing among the praying people I saw the beautiful figure of the well nymph. Her vibration was pulsating through the chapel and a few metres beyond it. She appeared in the form of Our Lady of Lourdes, and she is worshipped here as such. A whole host of beings surround her: several nixies, a waterman in the form of a huge toad, and a well gnome. They had all anchored their focal points around the area of the well in the chapel.

Here at 'Our Lady of Lourdes' chapel in the suburbs of Ljubljana, and in many other similar chapels throughout Europe, the worshippers do not have the slightest trace of awareness that a highly evolved nature being from the family of well nymphs is giving them the divine blessing. Obviously there are no clairvoyants who could tell the truth to those who seek consolation. Or maybe the clairvoyants do not think that people would accept the idea of consolation, healing and blessing flowing from an elemental being.

In olden times a well nymph would have had a very different experience. On 18th November 1993, circumstances developed where their role in the old culture was shown to me among the artefacts in a museum during a visit to the Glyptothek in Munich. In the very first hall of the museum I felt drawn to an otherwise unremarkable marble female head resting on a tall, slim pedestal. It was labelled with a question mark as an unfinished head of a sphinx from the Aegean Islands, dating from the period 570-560 BC.

In my view, the head was definitely completed, although not carved by an expert hand. I was able to perceive that it had originally had a ritualis-

A rhythmic dance of the nixies observed on the Isle of Srakane.

tic function. I imagined its top fixed to a wooden bell-shaped frame, which was covered with colourful pieces of cloth. I was reminded of the holy well of Dungiven (Northern Ireland) which I had visited during my lithopuncture work. In the Celtic tradition, rags are still, even now, tied to the branches of surrounding bushes. Those who seek healing dip a piece of cloth into the holy water of the well and tie it to a branch, while inwardly praying for their wishes to be fulfilled. It is said that healing will occur as quickly as the piece of cloth is dried by the wind. We can assume that the marble head is the figure of a well nymph. Well nymphs were made visible in stone or wood for the believers at the place of worship, since even in ancient times the ability to see clairvoyantly was given only to a few people. [6]

The head in the Munich museum helped to create an image of the individual consciousness of the beloved well nymph, whereas her vital-energetic body with the bell-like structure and the coloured rags had long since disintegrated. I was not sure why the powerful presence of the well nymph could be felt here in the museum, while the well she should be protecting is far away in Greece.

I suddenly had an idea to ask the nymph whether she would open her colourful garment and show her naked body. While I was contemplating her breathtaking beauty I noticed that in some way she was deformed. When I began to look for a cause I noticed a severely darkened spot on 'her' marble head at the point of the third eye. It seemed that the vital body of the nymph had been 'nailed' to the marble head through the use of some magic rite, maybe to draw her light-filled radiant form deeper into matter for some ritual purpose. Later on, when her cult was long forgotten, she was unable to free herself from her image in stone. Something that has been fixed by human beings through magic can only be released by a human being with sufficient knowledge.

In the 19th century, when many ancient statues were removed from Greece for the king of Bavaria, the well nymph was carried along like a slave, without being recognised. Aghast at her fate, I asked her whether I could do something to liberate her. No, she said. In the meantime she had adjusted herself to her situation in the museum, and this now provided her true function, as she was happy to be able to bless each visitor to the Glyptothek. Moreover, she was not alone in the museum because next door lived a satyr—a dwarf in my classification. And indeed, I was able to find him in a badly damaged stone relief,

---

[6]   One can assume that the clairvoyant abilities of the average person have been almost extinct since neolithic and classical times due to a stronger development of intellectual thinking. But some clairvoyant individuals remained in olden times who played a special role as seers.

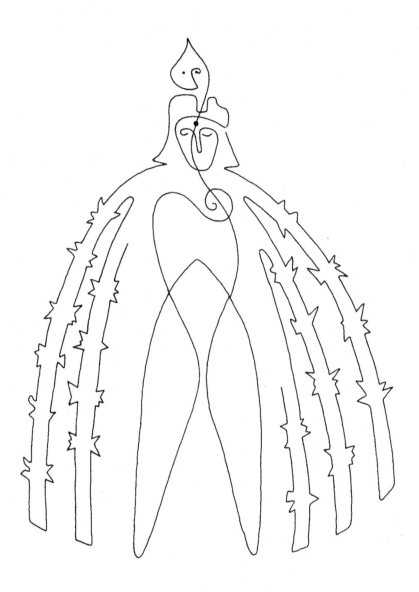

The well nymph 'nailed' to an ancient marble
head opens her multicoloured garment.

in the form of a radiating spark of light. This relief is called 'Seated God' or 'Heros under a Tree'. The artist had freed the elemental from the stone and through the power of his visualisation had pinned it to the carved tree where it was destined to shine on the head of Heros.

. . . .

37. COMMENTARY: **The Sublime Beings of Fox Basin**

To introduce the third developmental plane of the beings of the water element, I should like to relate an experience I had during a flight from London to Vancouver. It took place on the 31st of May, 2006. The flight path led in a wide arc over northern Canada. After we had been flying for several hours, I got a sudden feeling of enormous warmth in my heart region. It did not disappear but went on and on. Where was it coming from? I had to find out!

First, I took a quick look at the screen in front of me, to see where we were at that moment. We were flying over Fox Basin, north of Hudson Bay. Then I quickly took the map of Canada out of its pocket and spread it out between the narrow rows of seats to try to ground the overwhelming experience. Once I knew where we were, I concentrated again on the heartfelt warmth that I had just experienced. I became conscious that we were just then flying through the auric power field of a group of sublime beings that float above Fox Basin. I should like to identify them as Devas of the North American continent. They had a strong, basic, watery quality, but still more marked was their hearts' power that poured out from the north over the whole continent. I got a feeling of caregiving, sublime and very motherly, in which the landscape of North America was the child.

I immediately transferred the experience to the map in order to understand the interaction between the landscapes of America and the Deva group vibrating at the crest of the continent. I found that it is through the underworld and not through the space of air that subtle threads of power spread out from Fox Basin. They lead below ground to different places that serve as effusion points for the outgoing impulse of the Devas of Fox Basin. I could feel beneath my fingers how the same quality that I could sense above Fox Basin was distributed, much attenuated, across the North American continent.

. . . .

To complete the picture of the water elementals, I must finally talk about the third level of unfoldment. I have already introduced in detail one being from this level when I told the story of Vida, the beautiful queen of the water element (see Chapter One). But I really must describe my meeting with the queen of the nymphs, whom I met on Mönchsberg near Salzburg. Communication with her started during a seminar on the townscape of Salzburg in October 1993. It was my intention to introduce to the students all three invisible dimensions of a townscape. Therefore, during my preparations I searched for a place where elementals have their focus as carriers of the emotional dimension. I found an appropriate place on Mönchsberg which is right above the centre of Salzburg, in a narrow paved street leading up to the casino. There is a wooded hill, and a small spring rises half-way down the hill. It has a stone wall built all around it. I found all kinds of different elementals gathered around the well, and therefore I would call it a nature temple for Salzburg. Sadly, this precious place has had a road cut through it and is disturbed by traffic noise at night.

Third level of unfoldment		Nymph queen
		Landscape nymph
Second level of unfoldment	Nymphs	
	Well nymph	
	Pasture nymph	
First level of unfoldment	Nixies	
	Undines	
	Watermen	
	Spirit of balance	

Classification of water elementals.

So during the seminar I took the group to this place. The participants had about 20 minutes to familiarise themselves with some of the focal points of individual elementals. I felt drawn to the well and I noticed that the overhanging rock to the left of the well showed features like a frog, with characteristic bulging eyes. When I was standing on top of the 'vital-energetic, the emotional and the spiritual-soul dimensions frog', using it as a platform, I saw the tall figure of a nymph queen of indescribable beauty. She radiated white light in every possible tone of white. By the crown on her head, with its rounded silvery precious stone in the centre like a cosmogram, I recognised that she was on the highest level of unfoldment within the water element. For a moment she appeared to me like a madonna who enfolded the whole of humanity in her garment. But instead of humans the nymph queen had gathered all kinds of elementals under her robe. Then she said to me, "For me and my people, it is our duty to maintain the nature temple. You humans are destroying much, but we will stay with our duties." Horrified I said, "The people won't stop doing this." Her reply was straightforward: "They will feel the power of the elements."

. . . .

38. COMMENTARY: **Guardians of the Future Space**

While in Prague during the summer of 2006, I received a message from a group of elemental beings that also impressed me profoundly. It happened in the course of a workshop that I was holding on both sides of the River Moldau near the Charles Bridge. In preliminary research I had discovered a richly ordered underworld space beneath the river in the area between the two banks of the Moldau, that is to say, in the middle of Prague. From its quality, I would say that this etheric space beneath the Moldau was like the seed of a space that did not yet exist on the earth's surface. In my opinion, I saw the seed of a future space.

I was reminded of the 'Golden Prague' in the 16th century when the city was esteemed an incarnation of the New Jerusalem. The concept of a New Jerusalem means a space of universal peace and perfection that will be made possible in the future after a great transformation. One can also compare the New Jerusalem to a seed that will first germinate in the future.

In the workshop next day I led the group in perception exercises on both banks of the Moldau to come closer to the experience of this new space and its meaning as seed. It was especially valuable to touch into a group of elemental beings on the river island called Kampa. During the exchange following the perception phase, members of the workshop group identified the elemental beings several times as 'Guardians of the Seed'. We were obviously dealing with a group of water elementals that is entrusted with the secret of the seed of the new space. Such types of elemental being were further discussed in the last chapter.

As I listened to the reports of the workshop participants, there emerged in my consciousness the clear voice of the elemental beings, in whose sacred space we were sitting. The voice rang out: "You will survive the collapse of the old earth space. For forty days confusion will rule. In that time we will create the new earth space from seeds such as these. Be comforted, life goes on."

. . . .

Last but not least I must introduce the elemental beings of fire. So far I have described them only as spirits of transformation, as demonstrated by my experience with the compost pile in Kiel. Since then I have found the vibration of their focal points in various places but they have never shown themselves. Fire is indeed a particularly mysterious element. In August 1993 I found a place which was enlivened by fire spirits at the foot of the oft-mentioned Venus Hill on Srakane Island. For a moment I thought I was seeing a host of dancing fire spirits, not unlike the nordic trolls. I only knew trolls from certain books where they are described as unbelievably stupid and mean beings. Satisfied that I had been able to identify the fire spirits, and that I could put them in a nice pigeonhole, I was about to go home and to write down my experiences when a voice shouted at me: "For you humans we are nothing but a nuisance." Now I felt ashamed because I realised that I had enslaved the fire spirits with my false ideas.

From then on I often returned to their place and tried to perceive them in meditation without my human prejudices. It was extremely difficult to release my fixed ideas. Nevertheless I felt that I received help from the other side through pictures which brought new images to the surface. Again and again the picture of streaming light was sent to me until I was able to understand that fire is not only flames and combustion but also radiating light, and it also has to do with enlightenment and with the world made visible through light.

Suddenly I was able to understand the immense depth of the role of the fire spirits as creators of 'the world made visible'. This role has been attributed to God Almighty alone, without consideration that somebody must fulfil it here and now in each moment, in order that we may enjoy the world as manifest reality. I became aware that the three elements of earth, air and water, which are so easily noticed and greatly valued by us, can only exist in close relationship with the thin crust of the planet, and it has been a relatively short span of time since the beginning of their unfoldment. The element of fire with its mighty life force—or to be more exact, with its unconditional will to be—determines what Earth is in its deepest sense of being. Having said this, it does not feel right to begin with the fire beings who exist on the surface of the earth. At their deepest level of evolution there are the spirits at the centre of the earth who preside over the fate of our planet. Only at their second level of unfoldment do they involve themselves in performing other tasks in nature. Then they become beings who take life processes to maturity, and finally, through the processes of decomposition and transformation, they take them to the threshold of a new birth. For the nature spirits, in between life and rebirth there is a period of regeneration in the blazing life force of fire.[7]

On their third level of unfoldment, equivalent to the second level of earth, air and water beings, we find the spirits of light and of light creation, as I have already mentioned. At my request, Pan at Findhorn has shown me such a being in St Barbe Baker's woods at Pineridge. I saw a light body, radiating almost unbearably brightly, sending out light in spheres of different tones. I was deeply moved when I saw this divine being.[8]

On their fourth level of unfoldment we find spirits of inspiration. They embody the spiritual role of the fiery element in art and in life in general, and they are mediators between intuitions flowing from the angelic world and the patterns from the cosmic blueprint; out of these images works of art are created. In olden times these beings were called the muses. I was given an insight into their important function in the creation of music when I saw the muses dancing above Ljubljana cathedral during the violin concert (see Chapter Two).

During my visit to the Glyptothek in Munich I perceived two royal muses in addition to the well nymph and the satyr which I have already mentioned. The muses' task is to ensoul two marble statues of the Goddess Athena in rooms VII and IX. These sculptures are from the east and west pediments of the Temple of Aegina, dated 510-480 BC. First I recognised the muse within the sculpture from the western pediment. Through its vibrations I was able to realise that the muse was in fact slightly taller than but identical to the sculpture. I used my hand to verify this on a feeling level, confirming that this was a fire spirit. My outstretched arm began to lift up and to the left, which is my code for the presence of fire elementals.

I took my perceptions as an opportunity to meditate more deeply on the relationship between the two sculptures of Athena and the two muses. I came to the conclusion that when the temple was consecrated, the two most highly evolved fire beings had been invoked in a special ritual, and then were focused and anchored in the sacred figures, so that inspiration from the Goddess Athena would be transmitted to the visitors to the temple. From that moment onwards the sculptures were not just replicas of the Goddess; rather, the temple was a real source of her inspiration and blessing through the two

---

[7] In this context, the idea of 'hell fire' and hell itself seems to be a distorted perception of the life-enhancing primeval realm of fire spirits in the centre of the earth.

[8] I found it helpful to read Geoffrey Hodson's description of fire spirits in his book *The Kingdom of the Gods* (with colour drawings by Ethel-wynne M. Quail)

muses.[9] Even though today they are only preserved as fragments in a museum (which means 'a temple of the muses'!), they radiate power as before.

Of course their strength has diminished considerably because the underlying unity of the temple design is missing. Moreover, the third figure of Athena from the temple, which would have made the trinity complete, has disappeared. Each of the three sculptures was given a different role. The sculpture to the east embodies a fire spirit which inspires visitors with a feeling of ecstasy and certainty. It embodies the power of Athena in her virgin aspect. The statue from the west pediment is an expression of the power of transformation through the Black Goddess, and it was meant to give worshippers courage for personal transformation through their own indwelling fire spirits. The long-lost sculpture of Athena from inside the temple probably embodied the creative aspect of the Goddess. In this way Athena would have been alive and present in all three aspects within the temple compound, supported by the service of the muses.

After examining the fire elementals, it is necessary to correct my numeric system which classifies the elemental world: there are four levels of unfoldment of fire beings. We will discover that the total number resulting from the classification is thirteen instead of twelve: $3 \times 3 = 9 + (1 \times 4) = 13$.

. . . .

39. COMMENTARY: Elemental Beings in the Light of Publicity

At this point I must ask my readers' forgiveness for my previous efforts to present the world of elemental beings scientifically. When I wrote the original book, I was hoping that the account of my experiences and their systematic exposition, as near perfect as possible, would bring about the public recognition of nature spirits.

It was clear to me that in a culture guided by reason, reality was only what reason could digest and fit into its world system. Therefore, I thought, if I could detail a system as precise as that achieved for the plant world by the botanists, my friends from the world of elemental beings would be recognised as valuable components of nature and freed from their exile in the subconscious.

. . . .

It was soon apparent that this was a delusion. My reports were read worldwide in a number of languages, but the arbiters of public opinion remained

---

[9] I now see so-called idol worship in a new light. It is an example of how the sacred sculptures of ancient cultures became a source of divine blessing, and how their worship helped to build a solid foundation for a realistic spirituality.

untouched. Over the following years the absence of appropriate public reaction has to some extent irritated me, and I reproached myself for having wrongly conceived how to fulfil the task that the elemental beings had entrusted to me. They had invited me to roam for nine months in their realm, and by my reports win over humanity and have their existence recognised.

However, I realised that despite the apparent lack of success, the door was not shut in my face. I was continually coming into communication with the environmental spirits and my knowledge of their evolution grew greater with time, although more slowly than in those first nine months.

With time my trust grew and with it the conviction that the real priority was not to gain public interest, but to get human individuals, one after another, to open their hearts to the soul of nature and its consciousness. Lasting relations can grow between humanity and nature from this awareness. When there is a sufficiency of human beings who are inwardly and emotionally touched by the world of elemental beings, or even have personally experienced its existence, then the road to public awareness will open of itself.

Fourth level of unfoldment	Muses
Third level of unfoldment	Spirits of light
Second level of unfoldment	Spirits of maturity and transformation
First level of unfoldment	Spirits of the centre of the earth

Classification of fire elementals.

Thus we can differentiate thirteen main groups within the elemental kingdoms, and within each group there are further divisions. But in reality these are not separate from each other; rather they are interconnected and interwoven in various ways. For a moment, let us look at this work of cooperation by taking a tree as an example. In October 1993, the master deva whom I met through the fennel deva in our garden, explained to me how the networking in nature takes place. On this occasion she described the beings who participate in the unfoldment of the oak tree. My example is a young oak which we had transplanted to our meadow twenty years previously from a cold frame where it had seeded itself.

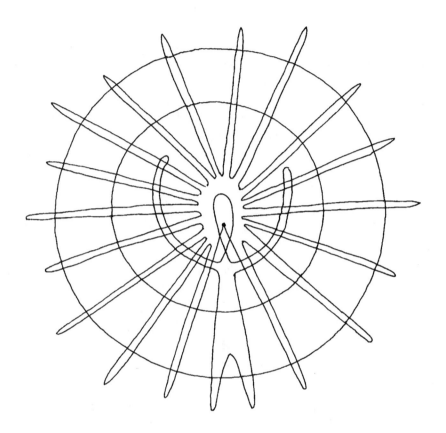

Spirit of light creation observed at Pineridge.

Our examination of the tree began with the focal point of the faun. From a central node there is a relationship 'downwards' into matter as well as 'upwards' to the spiritual levels. In Chapter One I have described the role of a faun. I would like to mention a further important factor which is based on my later experiences: the faun has a relatively highly developed individuality for a being on the first level of unfoldment. He is able to materialise his vital-energetic body and to move around and near the tree in relative freedom, although he is usually bound into the structure of roots and tree-tops. When he does this, his quite well-proportioned body becomes visible. The dynamic way in which he cares for developments in and around the tree for which he is responsible is characteristic of earth elementals.

The faun's (level 1)[10] incredible dynamism is needed because he can extend his attention in at least five different directions. First, he communicates with the deva (level 2) of the oak tree. Her function is that of a group soul for all the oak trees within her area where she maintains the blueprint of this particular species. Next, he is connected to the Pan of the landscape (level 3) who is his master and spiritual teacher.

In his relationship with matter the faun is tightly bound to the currents and centres of the vital-energetic structure of the tree, in other words with the 'etheric' tree, and in this way he is able to influence the physical body of the tree. To do this he cooperates with the elementals of water, air and fire on their first level of unfoldment. The elementals initiate different phases of growth within the annual cycle of vegetation. Water spirits rule over the budding plants in spring, air elementals help blossoms to unfold in early summer and fire spirits make the fruit ripen in autumn. They themselves are guided by the fairies of place (level 2) who are spirits of cyclical time and who take care that the right elementals do their work at the right time within the yearly cycle.

The 'etheric' tree is directed in its development by the faun and the elementals on the first level of unfoldment who assist him in the correct season. The etheric tree is also connected to the biophysical processes of the tree which is a plant embodied in matter. All in all, I visualise the tree with aspects in three dimensions. The lowest level is the physical embodiment, which together with the vital-energetic organism forms the plant itself. The second level represents the consciousness of the plant with the faun at its centre, with the Pan of the area as the master intelligence, and with the rhythmically contributing ele-

---

[10] Numbers in brackets indicate the level of unfoldment of each of the elemental beings.

mentals of water, air and fire. Above it, on a soul level, is the deva of this particular species of oak tree.[11]

At this point, I would like us to remember the fact that the plant which we see merely represents the level of embodiment in matter. If we want to look at levels comparable with the spiritual levels of a human being, i.e. the levels of consciousness and soul, then we discover that even these levels are taken care of by elemental beings. Above these there is an even higher level, perhaps the highest level for a tree. I would call it the level of Higher Self or God Self. In the case of our oak tree the beingness of the God Self is represented by an angel of the oak blueprint, guarding the source of spiritual qualities out of which all types of oak trees have developed. This archetype was shown to me as a vibrational pattern, with only a few of its aspects manifested in the oak tree. Other aspects are realised in different cosmic dimensions in forms which I cannot perceive. I can only suspect that all these forms are connected through a common quality which is anchored in the heart of this angel. This interconnectedness makes us realise how a tree can radiate qualities connected with certain planets or forces, and that their connection is determined by the angel of the blueprint.

· · · · · · · · · · · · · · · ·

40. EXERCISE: Experience the Organism of a Wood

The analytic manner in which I discussed the cosmos of trees has led me to omit something which is of basic importance for the being of a tree: its integration within the holistic organism of the landscape. The exact relationships between a tree's different nature spirits were never perceived as being separate from it or from each other, but rather experienced as tender or even powerful contacts, which blew through the tree in rhythmic sequence, sometimes penetrating it powerfully.

This is true of trees standing by themselves in a landscape or in a garden. Trees that grow in a forested neighbourhood are even more intimately integrated in the holistic organism of nature consciousness. The orchestration of a wood can scarcely be described. Here is a proposal how you may experience for yourself the holistic consciousness of a wood:

- Imagine that the wood is a glass full of water and that you are a lump of sugar.
- Throw the lump of sugar into the glass of water and let yourself dissolve.

In this exercise, pictorial imagination is of less importance than a right under-

---

[11] Two kinds of beings of the air element should be added in connection with a plant deva: the fairies of place (level 2) and the master deva (level 3). See Chapter Two.

standing of the proportion between the human being and the wood. I too have puzzled over how to carry out the exercise after it had been proposed to me by a woodland community of nature spirits.

After I had put aside my brooding rationalism and simply let myself fall in full trust and holistic emotion into the wood's wholeness, I was surprised at how lovingly the organism of the wood embraced me. It is worth testing that leap of trust as often as is necessary until one has mastered the process of dissolution. The trees are ready to teach us how to free ourselves from the control of reason.

. . . .

Within this context I would like to mention the so-called 'fairy trees'. Apart from exhibiting the normal pantheon of elementals they act as a link between certain beings with special tasks in the wider area. As I have already mentioned, they can often be recognised by a fairy cosmogram. I discovered a great big copper beech on the north bank of the river Rhine at Konstanz. Its branches bend down close to the earth, thus generating a specific vortex of forms in space. If one enters this space consciously, then there is contact with elementals of different levels. From their living quarters they serve the surrounding area. Under all circumstances we must protect such royal trees as they are also called.

. . . .

41. COMMENTARY: A Fairy Tree in the Philippines

Introducing another fairy tree, I will tell of my meeting with a celebrated ficus tree on the Philippine island of Panay. It stands in the midst of rice fields not far from the town of Santa Barbara and its fame dates from more than 80 years ago when German engineers were planning a railroad in the district. They agreed the tree should make way for the railroad. However, it proved impossible to fell it. They even tried to blow it up with dynamite – all in vain. In the end, they had to survey another route.

I went straight to that tree and knelt my upright body before its many-limbed trunk – the position I favour when I wish to perceive a place's invisible extensions. Hardly ever before had I sensed so unequivocally the presence of the Archetypical Earth Mother. "Why not say simply, Mother Earth?" I asked. "It is 'Archetypical Mother' because the connection maintained by the sacred tree leads directly to the archetype in which the Soul of the Earthly Cosmos is rooted. When we speak of Mother Earth or Mother Nature, we are speaking of her daughter." Such was the answer to my question.

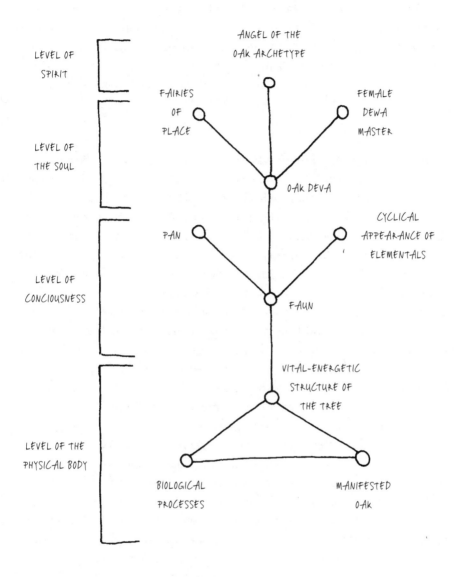

Cooperation on all levels as demonstrated in an oak tree.

When I looked at the tree from afar, I saw innumerable fairy-like elemental beings swarming around its crown and bathing in its light. This light was created by the power which arose from the fairy tree's intimate connection with the archetypical mother and it fully illuminated the elemental beings. I caught a sense of the attraction that the sacred ficus tree had for them. They swarmed around it spellbound, as if the tree was an incarnation of the Tree of Life that was the bud of all earthly creation.

. . . .

Around a tree the main activity takes place through beings of the earth element and the air element. Therefore I would also like to illustrate the networking among the elemental realm with an example from a landscape where all four elements are equally represented. I was shown an example of this in the landscape of Bled in Slovenia. It is the area of the Virgin Goddess within theTriglav[12] landscape temple, and this is also the landscape temple and inbreath point for the whole of Slovenia. The significance of Bled for the whole of the country becomes clearer when one looks at the role of the island on lake Bled. Even before Christian times it was the most important place of pilgrimage in Slovenia. The power and beauty of the place originate from its strong polarities. There is the contrast between the horizontal surface of the lake and the rocky island with its pilgrims' church on top of a hill. The watery pole of the landscape is also balanced by a solid rock cliff above the lake, which is crowned by a castle and chapel. On its north side this rock castle makes a steep descent to the parish church on a plateau.

This parish church, the chapel and the pilgrims' church on the lake are the three most important sacred sites in Bled's landscape temple. The castle chapel on the highest point of the cliffs represents the Virgin aspect of the Goddess where human beings can realise the unity between cosmos and earth. The pilgrims' chapel on the island in the middle of the lake stands for the creative aspect of the Mother Goddess. In ancient times this was celebrated through the ritual of the sacred wedding. The parish church on the plateau plus several cave openings in the rock face above are part of the area of the Black Goddess of Transformation.

During the IDRIART Festival[13] at Bled in summer 1993 when I was preparing for a seminar on the sacred dimensions of landscape, I climbed into the biggest of the caves to see whether I could discover new perspectives on the

---

[12] Triglav is the highest mountain of the Slovenian Alps.

transformative area of Bled. It was a steep climb up to reach the cave. Inside, after about ten metres (32ft) the path ended at a vertical wall. I put both my hands against the wall in order to penetrate it with my mind and see whether the path continued on the invisible level. At that moment the wall opened up. Before me was a being like a guardian of the threshold.

I soon felt at ease and asked him about the function of this cave within the landscape of Bled. Through feelings he indicated that I should turn around and look down onto the plateau in front of the church. There was an important connection between cave and plateau but I was unable to understand. In my consciousness there was no terminology to translate into linear thinking the complexity of feelings which he sent across to me as a reply, however often I repeated my question. Therefore I asked him to explain to me the entire context in which the elementals cooperate within the three sacred areas of Bled. I felt that in this would lie the answer to my first question.

Without further reply, the guardian of the threshold stepped aside. The tunnel opened in front of me, showing a passage leading deep into the castle rock. Inwardly I let myself enter and I saw that the entire rock had been hollowed out. The inside of the gigantic vault was covered with black velvet. Now I was in the realm of the dwarfs. They were going rapidly to and fro in large numbers, attending to their tasks. As I looked closer I noticed that the cave had three entrances:

1. Vertically towards the top of the rock there was an opening where nowadays we find the nave of the castle chapel. It was my feeling that through this opening the cosmic forces would flow into the inner cave, just as they flow through the crown chakra of the human being.
2. To the left and downwards a tunnel led underneath the bottom of the lake to the centre of the island—more precisely to a point between the church building and the bell tower which is separate. It seemed that the power of the cave was flowing out through this tunnel.
3. Another opening, the hole by which I had entered the underworld, led to the plateau in front of the parish church. I had the feeling that this passage was another source of incoming power.

Afterwards I was shown how these halls and passages were connected with the corresponding functions of the elementals of all four elements. I could see that the multitude of dwarfs transformed the streams of energy which approached

---

[13] DRIART is a Foundation for Intercultural Relationships through Art, initiated by Miha Pogačnik.

vertically from the castle chapel and sideways from the parish church. They actively 'spun' the energy to transform it into a life-enhancing power, which was then directed down the tunnel to the island.

Next, I became aware of a host of fairies of place above the centre of the island. They were doing their dance right at the top of a column of light, similar to the one I saw at Venus Hill on the Isle of Srakane. Simultaneously I saw a dance of the nixies on the shores of the round island, which served to spread the blessings of water. The two dancing circles were organised symmetrically one above the other, centred around one point—the opening where the life energy from the chamber beneath the castle flows out. Obviously the purpose of these dances is to distribute life energy, which comes from the realm of the dwarfs and is channelled through the airy realm and through the element of water in such a way that the whole of the surrounding landscape can share in it.

Finally, my attention was drawn to the plateau in front of the parish church. There I saw a mighty glow, as if countless fires were burning. I asked myself what this could mean in connection with the rest of the process. Then I noticed a strong suction at this particular point. It meant that all of the used life energy from all over the country was brought to this place for transformation. The glow was an indication of the activity of the fire spirits who were busy cleansing the used energies. The renewed energies were sent down the passage from the cave to the hall of the dwarfs where I was presently standing. There the energy was revitalised, mixed with a fresh flow of cosmic power and then sent on to the focal point of the dancing fairies and nixies. This is a ceaseless, circular flow.

Perhaps physically there is no chamber underneath the castle and no tunnel leading to the island. There is a possibility that it merely served my consciousness as a model to convey a spatial impression of the orchestrated coordination between the elementals of the four elements within a landscape. They do not necessarily need to manifest on the level of matter, since elementals can move free of physical restrictions in the etheric-astral spaces.

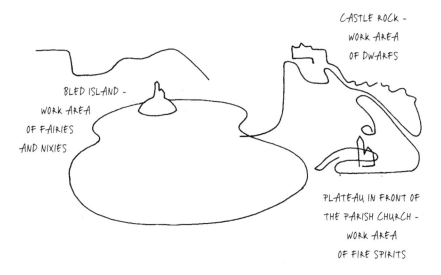

Areas of elemental activity at Lake Bled, Slovenia.

FIVE

Evolution in the
Elemental Realms

THERE CAN BE NO DOUBT that the evolution of elemental beings takes place in a dimension parallel to our own reality. However, they are not tied to the same laws of time and space that rule our own existence. In my experience there is some order in the world of elementals which resembles our rhythm of time. In Chapter One I described a threefold cycle in the life of an elemental. But this still leaves a major question unanswered—is there a much greater evolutionary cycle similar to the evolution of our Planet Earth?

It was at Traunstein, in the Waldviertel, Austria, that I first became aware that there must be different evolutionary epochs in the elemental realms. With some friends I had been visiting a collection of huge granite blocks near the town, which seemed to be randomly stacked on top of each other. I was guided into a cleft between the rocks in order to find out more about the origins of this huge stone composition. All of a sudden, in response to my question, a giant stood before me. At the same time I received an explanation that it was actually the giants who had built these strange granite blocks—an idea which is also mentioned in local legends. The giants belong to an earlier epoch of the Earth's development. They disappeared long ago, leaving only one representative to guard the place, whom I had happened to encounter.

This experience seemed somewhat strange to me. It unsettled me because I was not able to fit the idea of a giant into my existing, fairly logical system of the elemental realms. In the back of my mind I thought that it might be an illusion which I had created and that the giant did not really exist.

This denial of my own experience proved to be wrong, and later on I read that Paracelsus too had believed in the existence of giants. Eventually, in summer 1993, I was busily working at Venus Hill, the nature temple for elementals on the Isle of Srakane, when I took a further step in unlocking this secret. As you may already have realised, there is a large number of different kinds of elementals in this place—and one day there was also a giant.

In my desire to find out more about the fire spirits which were a great puzzle to me, I asked Julius, the old sage, to show me yet another unknown aspect of the fire spirits. Telepathically I was guided to the southern slope of the hill where I observed a giant. In our measurements he was at least forty metres (130 ft) tall, and his naked muscular body had the ideal proportions of an ancient Greek athlete. He was completely motionless, staring far off into the distance. When I entered his form with my consciousness I discovered that the giant was entirely composed of thin vertical lines of fire. Julius commented on my experience that giants are a relic of the oldest evolutionary cycle on earth, when the civilisation of the fire element covered our planet. When this epoch ended, some giants were left behind in the landscape but at present they have no real function. They are more or less like fossils, reminding us of an epoch of the Earth's development in the far distant past.

Shortly before leaving the Isle of Srakane I went early one morning to see the old sage again. I asked him to introduce to me any elementals which I might not have encountered in the previous two weeks due to my lack of awareness. He led me towards the top of the hill and asked me to immerse myself in the atmosphere of a certain spot. There I perceived a silvery mist which had a 'fish scale' patterning. As the mist thickened, a being like a nixie appeared with a fish tail entirely covered in silvery shining scales. This being almost reminded me of pictures of the mermaid of medieval legends. But its appearance was nothing like any water elemental that I had so far experienced, and again I had the feeling that it was a being from a different epoch. According to Julius it was a remnant from the watery age of earth development, in the same way that the giant was left over from the fiery epoch.

. . . .

42. COMMENTARY: **The Earth Looking Outwards from her Centre**

When I originally wrote this book, my world view was still heliocentric. Since then I have become convinced that our ancestral cultures had it right when they reverenced the earth as the mid-point of the universe. I am again a believer in a geocentric system.

In my opinion, our rational mind let itself be led astray in the era of so-called enlightenment. The real question is not whether the earth revolves round the sun or vice-versa. Much more important is the loss of the earth's true identity, ever

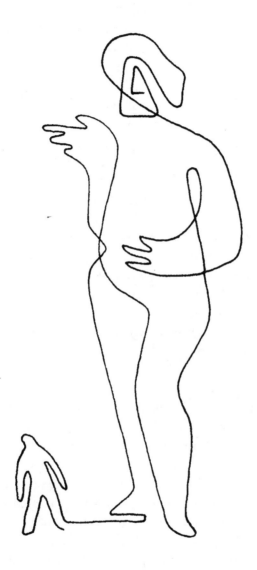

My encounter with the giant on the Isle of Srakane.

since it came to be considered as no more than a dull ball of rock that had the sun's rays to thank for its whole life potential.

Obviously, the sun is unarguably the midpoint of the solar system. However, one should not jettison the intuition of countless generations of earth worshippers who, independent of the astronomical reality, saw the earth anchored in her own centre. The heavenly bodies of her own universe, moon and sun included, dance around her centre and their radiation contributes to the fullness of life in the earth's surface. However, we must look inwards as well as outwards and differentiate the various dimensions of existence that are ranked towards the earth's centre. One can imagine these dimensions as strata, of which our physical earth is only one. Above is the stratum of angel consciousness, below the stratum of the so-called underworld civilisations, deeper still the plane of the earthly archetypes which we visited together in the first pages of this book. Deeper still, one reaches the earth's centre where the Earth Soul vibrates, Gaia, core of the Earth's Being.

There the evolution of the fire element, which has long disappeared from sight on the earth's surface, continues in a specific way within Earth's inner universe, and one can say the same of the civilisation of the water element, which we know by the name Atlantis. If both 'underworld civilisations' still exist in their own way, we may suspect that in some measure they are still present among us.

. . . .

These indications about earlier phases of our planetary evolution fit perfectly with the messages my daughter Ajra Miška has received from her Angel Master Christopher Tragius.[1] In her book, in the chapter about the incarnation of Planet Earth, he says that there are four stages of development on our planet in order that it may unfold according to the divine plan. This development is accompanied by the evolution of elementals and human beings.

The first epoch was a fiery one—the planet's form was that of a fire ball. Even then human beings incarnated on the planet, not in a physical body but in a fiery energy body. According to Christopher Tragius the people of that era developed a civilisation in cooperation with the beings of the fiery element. Its cosmic name is Lir.[2]

---

[1]   The angel messages of Christopher Tragius have helped me tremendously in many different ways during my earth healing work.

[2]   In the esoteric tradition it is called Mu or Lemuria. But it was not a continent which sank into the Pacific Ocean, as is commonly believed; rather, it was a civilisation of the whole planet on a particular level of being.

An elemental similar to a mermaid from
the watery epoch of Earth's development.

After an intermediate period when almost the whole planet was submerged in water and ice, the civilisation of the watery element developed, which we call Atlantis. Again, Atlantis was not just a continent now sunken in the Atlantic Ocean, but rather a civilisation spread out over the whole planet. Instead of physical matter it used a watery substance for its development.[3] The elementals of water developed in this period as an addition to the fire elementals which had evolved earlier. I had met representatives of both types at Venus Hill.

In the third phase of Earth's development the material level of our planet was finally ready to allow human beings the step-by-step unfoldment of their biophysical body. But We needed to learn the laws of a new element in order to clothe ourselves in matter. Thus, a civilisation of the earth element evolved, and we are presently in its final phase.

Almost imperceptibly the future fourth age of the air element is beginning to manifest (Christopher Tragius calls it 'Krex'), for we have just begun to witness the breakdown of the material foundations of the earth-element civilisation. In comparison to the earth element, the air element gives us total freedom from the shackles of matter and brings a new, holistic consciousness.[4] The elementals pass through the same big transformations from one civilisation to the next; they have created the structure described in the previous chapters during the development of the earth-element phase.

Such a system of step-by-step experience of the four elements within the context of different cycles of evolution sounds very logical and is hard to reject,[5] but in reality it presents its own problems. In fact, huge difficulties are created by the complicated processes of transformation from one civilisation to the next. I became aware of this in October 1993, during a seminar in Gailtal (in Carinthia, Austria), where I encountered elementals from the Atlantis epoch which are still very active in Europe.

Erika, one of the workshop participants who is clairvoyant, told me that certain beings at the rocky summit of the Reisskofel were eager to

---

[3] According to Christopher Tragius the mysterious 'sinking' of Atlantis is a symbol for the decline of the watery civilisation when seen from the perspective of our civilisation, for we cannot imagine a life or its decline in any way except on the material level.

[4] In astrological terms we call it the transition from the Age of Pisces to the Age of Aquarius.

[5] Interestingly, Christopher Tragius states that for the earliest human incarnations, the bodies of primates were used, as they were the most highly developed animal form.

pass on a message to me. A little later I managed to find enough peace and quiet to follow up on her suggestion. When I contacted the beings of the mountain top in meditation I saw huge figures which seemed separate from me because of their great pride. It was clear that they could not communicate directly with my sense of reality; nevertheless it felt like they had a great desire to influence me and my environment. I would even say that they clearly hoped to exert influence on my consciousness, and they did everything they could to connect my awareness with theirs. A small bird alerted me to the danger when, during the decisive moment in my meditation, it flew into the meditation room and immediately flew out again, jolting me out of the stillness. This was a very unsettling experience for me, and I went home as soon as I could to get advice from my friend, the old sage in the forest.

I asked him what to do about the beings who tried to entangle me in their longings, which were completely beyond my understanding. The old sage transmitted exact impressions to me so that I could understand the residual line of unfoldment of these elementals which have no relationship to the elemental world I know. Those beings are remnants of the elementals of the Atlantean epoch. They were unable to make the necessary transformation to the level of earth-element evolution. Such withered ghosts seem to have survived in great numbers, waiting for their salvation. On the one hand they have no real function in today's landscape but, on the other, they have taken on a secondary role in connection with human illusions and emotional desires. On a hidden level, which is subconscious to humans, they offer their help for the realisation of illusory dreams. Unfortunately they become more energised in this way. Human beings then tend to follow either the false spiritual guidance or the ignorance of mass culture, both of which are usually retrogressive.

To complete this explanation, the old sage dropped into my consciousness a schematic plan of the classification of the elemental world. In addition to the 3 x 3 plus 4 levels of elemental unfoldment, there are also remnants of the fire spirits from Lemurian times, like the giants I had seen. There are also the remaining elementals from the Atlantean epoch which nowadays have the secondary function of reflecting the egocentric illusions of humanity. In this way they unwittingly assist us towards self-knowledge, for when we see our own egotism manifested and mirrored by these monstrous figures, it helps us to question our belief systems and to come a little closer to the recognition of truth.

43. COMMENTARY: **Earth's Archetypical Civilisations**

I have been relating the shadow aspects of earth's archetypical civilisations whose presence here today is scarcely perceptible. I must qualify these aspects by relating the unconditionally positive experiences which I have also encountered over the past few years.

One example is the Slovenian region called 'Jesersko' (Seelandschaft). At the end of a long, narrow ravine that leads deep into the Karawanken mountain chain there is a surprisingly broad basin lying between steep cliffs. The basin was once full of water, but in the 15th century an earthquake shifted the ground and the lake disappeared. Also at that time there appeared three almost perfectly rounded hills, which together form a triangle. One of the hills stands quite imposingly in the middle of the basin, the other two lie somewhat more modestly on the line of the former lake shore.

I wished to communicate with the beings of the three hills and for this I must transfer myself in my consciousness into another world that vibrates parallel with our reality but is grounded in a quite different frequency.

First, I found myself facing a sort of lens of water that represented the portal of a strange world. After diving through it, I emerged in a broad spherical space, which exists simultaneously with the Jesersko landscape, and there I discovered something like a laboratory. My consciousness had a great deal of trouble translating what went on in this laboratory into logical images. Beings or intelligences whose quality is similar to that of our fire spirits are present there. On the other hand they also appear to be related to the bee folk. The way they are organised hierarchically, with a 'queen' at the top of the cosmic pyramid, is astonishingly similar to the bee folk. Moreover they work with the proverbial industry of bees, focusing absolute concentration on their allotted tasks.

One could best compare their laboratory to an alchemical workplace, where they apply their knowledge of how to transfer manifested forms from one state to another. I memorised in detail how the archetypal images of individual plant species were first pictured as etheric forms and then translated into their physical shapes.

Yet it was obvious that the 'workplace' had previously long remained unused. It seemed that it had become busy again only a short time earlier. Does this mean that a great change is approaching, when the archetypical spirits of change will use their knowledge to serve the Earth Soul? More on this in the new closing chapter.

. . . .

While staying on Tenerife in November 1993, I was able to learn about all three evolutionary epochs of elementals in a single living context. I had been invited to investigate the geomantic properties of the land for a project called 'Mariposa', along with the artist Mary Bauermeister and my daughter Ajra Miška.

It is hard for me to describe how confusing my first contacts were with the elementals on Tenerife. Even the fauns, my most familiar friends in Europe, seemed strange to me. When I tried to see them with my inner eye I could sense a presence, but not with its usual clear structure and form. Obviously I did not have a special key to translate the reality of these beings into the language of my consciousness. Ajra had the same experience. Once she tried to draw the faun of a palm tree, unconsciously working with forms in her usual way. No sooner had she finished and put her drawing pad aside than she received a strong protest from the faun. He demanded that she let him use her hand so that he could draw himself with her help. The end result was an endless spinning of spirals.

Fortunately, thanks to Ajra's mediumistic connection to Christopher Tragius, we were able to ask him for clarification. He confirmed that the elementals on the Canary Islands really were entirely different from the ones we had encountered before. The islands are powerful volcanoes, although inactive at present. Tenerife consists of a volcanic cone that rises three thousand metres (9750 feet) above sea level. The original elemental beings who served nature in this area were fire spirits only, in accordance with what was needed for the fiery essence of a volcano. Therefore, the beings which are working with the indigenous trees on the island or are looking after the air and water elements belong to a line of unfoldment from the fire spirits of the centre of the earth. To us, in our materialistic age, they are hardly noticeable in their spiral forms. Christopher Tragius says:

"The form of the fire elementals is the spiral. Their own nature is a vital-fiery one but they are also carriers of consciousness and so can influence different levels. One might compare them with snakes. The beings of fire are the oldest of the elementals and therefore their consciousness is the most developed. They are called the fiery sages or the guardians of fire. The ancient civilisations knew about this and therefore they were able to integrate them into their belief system."

Apart from the fiery elemental beings, I repeatedly encountered on Tenerife some grotesque-looking beings which I identified as stragglers from the Atlantean epoch, based on my experiences in Gailtal. First of all I met a sponge-like being with a face like an old leper. He had a large mushroom head growing around his waist, but he seemed to dwell in a far-off world where I was unable to reach him or ask him about his purpose in life. Suddenly a group of dwarfs appeared as if ordered there by appointment.

I must add that one can also find elementals of our present phase of evolution on the Canary Islands. In the course of hundreds of years of close connections between Europe and this group of islands they have arrived with the introduction of foreign plants and by a number of other means. Inwardly, I pointed to the little mushroom guy and asked about his original function. Laughing scornfully, the dwarfs told me that the old guy thought he was looking after the dimensions of space, but in reality the surrounding space was not supervised by him at all. From this I felt that he had taken the form of a spongy mushroom during the watery spatial conditions of Atlantis. At that time it had been his task to take care of the integrity of a spherical area in space. In the same way that a sponge is able to hold water inside it, this being had helped to maintain the humid atmospheric conditions of a certain area of watery—not physical—substance.

On another occasion I perceived an incredibly impressive being close to me during my morning meditation at Chayofa. It wanted to tell me something very important. But my deepest feelings told me that it was deceiving me. Therefore I asked the faun of a nearby laurel tree to show me this being in its true form. It appeared to me as a relatively small figure which moved constantly through the air. It looked like a wide hat with a hole in its centre. Black clouds of smoke emerged from the hole. My interpretation of this picture is that at the time of Atlantis these beings gathered astral forces and distributed them in space. (Astral forces in those days had the same function as the air element has in our time.)

Mary Bauermeister added from her own observations some reasons why these beings were in such great need of human communication. In the Atlantean epoch they had been used to daily contact with human beings—a very commonplace affair of mutual recognition and conversation.[6] But nowadays the situation was a totally different one. Christopher Tragius added some more information:

"Concerning Atlantis, I must first state that everything about this subject is very difficult to put into words. It would be easier if more people were

---

[6] A modern comparison would be the closeness that is possible between human beings and plants.

Self-portrait of a fire spirit on Tenerife
who was guiding Ajra's drawing hand.

able to remember their role during that time. In fact, every soul existed in Atlantis. It was not a planet of the chosen ones, as all people went through processes of learning. Just like our souls, all the elementals also existed in Atlantis with all of their functions. Today, these beings are found everywhere as lost elemental souls, remnants of the destruction of Atlantis. They have been unable to pass through the transformations of Earth up to the present time, and now they remain imprisoned in a non-existent world. On a vibrational level they are stuck in an illusory in-between realm which makes it almost impossible to contact them. But paying attention to them and allowing them to express themselves means giving them a chance to grow into gigantic proportions and to turn demonic. In reality they are powerless and without influence on the energetic-astral level; they only pretend to be influential. The truth is that they will have no effect because they are not anchored in today's time-space structure. Their appearance is like an imprint on the astral level, like a memory. Nobody can help them because they do not exist in the here and now. They do not really need help since they dwell quite happily within their own dream state.

"Nowadays, one needs to be very sensitive on the Canary Islands in order to be able to judge which beings are illusory and which ones are the still-active fire elemental spirits. The active fire beings are needed here, but the watery beings from Atlantis have lost their function and so must appear as an empty shell.

"In the developmental phases of elementals today are the water elementals who could make the transition between the watery and earthly civilisations, so they can experience another state which enables them to be active in the world of matter."

Our experiences on Tenerife have brought to light some of what happened in the past, in that all three evolutionary epochs of elementals co-exist with each other on Tenerife. The evolutionary cycles of the fire and water elements have been completed, and now we are in a transition from the earthly to the airy phase of planetary development. I wanted to get an image of the rapidly approaching age of the air element, so I asked Ajra to consult her Angel Master about the elementals of this future age. Since they do not exist yet, I was unable to explore them experientially, but his response was:

"The civilisation of the air element will be saturated with music, colour, rhythm and wholeness. Physical boundaries will dissolve in wholeness. In the same way that it is difficult to grasp the watery civilisation, it is equally difficult to describe the airy one. Even Nostradamus has fore-

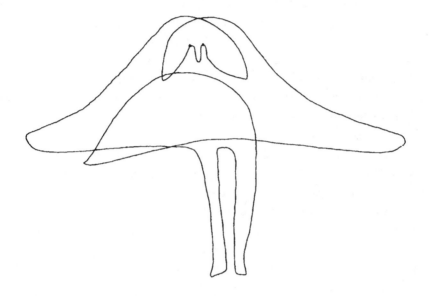

The 'mushroom dwarf' of the Atlantean epoch.

told its coming, although he prophesied that the transition to the new civilisation would be through physical destruction. But this physical destruction is not necessary, because humanity has been given enough time to decide for itself to make the transition into the era of the new element. Basically, people are already practising ways to deal with the new world of the air civilisation—you are being taught about laws in music, about intuitive perception, about comprehending energetic structures, etc. You are getting to know the world of elementals and you can again include them creatively in your work. These are the first steps.

"Wholeness is a basic feature of the air civilisation and it means that a fundamental split, which has been necessary on the material level, will now become superfluous. This is the split between positive and negative, particularly between good and bad. It is the split which makes you judgemental and creates hierarchies. When this split is overcome, then the shackles of hierarchy will not be needed any more, and they will be dissolved in an all-embracing unity. Thus, all presently existing classifications, norms and laws will crumble, because their existence is based on positive and negative. As soon as the world has found unity, your lessons in matter will be over, for the soul does not need any more experience of the physical world.

"But it is wrong to imagine that the airy civilisation will be one of rest and delight in unity. People will have to enter into the laws of the new guiding element, and within the new circumstances they will try to achieve the highest possible within such a civilisation. Afterwards, another transition period will follow, then the path will once again lead through all four elements on a higher level.

"Elementals accompany your evolution and learn much along the way that is important for them. They take what they can use for their own learning process, and they give by performing their tasks. Each epoch of civilisation brings deep changes to their tasks. Many cannot grow into these new tasks, and this is also true for some souls.

"In the present civilisation of the earth element there are already elementals of the air element, for instance fairies and sylphs. During the coming epoch of the air element these beings will actualise interconnectedness. Elementals which are presently serving with human beings will have to learn how to act in the air element. This transformation is part of their schooling. These transformations always mean a change of focus towards that element which is destined to become the leading element of a civilisation."

A spirit of the Atlantean epoch is exposed.

44. COMMENTARY: **The 'New' Elemental Beings**

Christopher Tragius' predictions were fulfilled six years later when in 1999 I met the first of the changed elemental beings that belong to the future evolutionary epoch. I have identified them here as elemental beings of the fifth element.

The first time that I came upon the 'new' elemental beings was in April of that year when I was preparing a healing workshop for the city of Amsterdam. I was looking for places in Rembrandt Park where one could feel the processes of the present earth changes. Up till then I had known only the so-called sources of archetypical power which I interpreted as providing etheric 'construction material' for the new constitution of earth space. This time I also found power sources which were enlivened by beings and which radiated rays of perfectly clear, white light. I saw them approach in procession over the earth's surface. Nearby, I perceived tiny, green, luminous beings that rose in a flock from the inner earth. I knew at once that I had never before encountered beings like these.

Indeed, it came out later that these were not a 'new' sort of elemental being, but recognisable beings of the four elements that had undergone a specific 'educational process' in the inner earth. This resembled a transformational initiation through which they became bearers of the change processes through which our Earth is trying to overcome the ecological crisis that threatens our planet.

We can imagine this process as follows: during earth's present transformation phase, the classic elemental spirits are still around us to carry out their tasks in the countryside and city spaces; in amongst them are the 'new' elemental beings which move freely and extensively, busy with the transformation of their allotted space and time structures.

This raises the question whether one can distinguish the 'new' elemental beings of the five elements from the 'classical' nature spirits. I have already mentioned the exceptionally pure, radiating light that surrounds them. A second identifying factor is their ability to enter into loving communication with people, and to interact with the human psyche. More on this later.

. . . .

Regarding the present evolution of elementals, which is controlled by the earth element, I have already described two of their time cycles in detail. One is the developmental path which the elementals take in a certain rhythm, and which they go through on all three levels of unfoldment (see the previous chapter). Then they ascend into the level of the angels, continuing their unfoldment through different stages of development in the angelic realm.

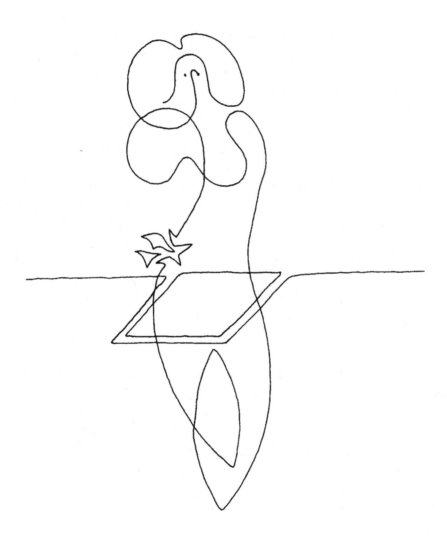

The well nymph at Derry giving birth to her two sisters.
In the centre is the iron cover of the sewage system
where her source has been suppressed.

However, we should not imagine that the stages of unfoldment of the elementals are only linear; they also have cyclic characteristics. Once I had the chance to see highly developed angels (my sense is that they were cherubim) while they were in the process of generating very simple forms of elementals. The very tiny beings are called 'rudimes' by Daphne Charters. I could see how the angel was sending its rays of consciousness down into the planetary energy body and was creating small foci of power and consciousness, from which simple elementals began to emerge.

Secondly, there is also a cyclic time rhythm within the life of each individual elemental, as I described in Chapter One. During the first phase of the threefold cycle the elemental lives on the emotional level of the planetary energy body (called the astral level in esoteric traditions). I have called it the virgin phase. During the following creative phase the being takes on a task to serve nature or humans in some way. It must get closer to the material level in order to fulfil its duty, and in this way it develops its vital-energetic body. In esoteric terms it extends its being onto the etheric level. By unfolding its energetic umbilical cord (or its focal point) it may touch the material level in order to mediate between the vital-energetic and physical realities. This is followed by a phase of regeneration within the womb of the Goddess Gaia—the Earth Goddess—before the cycle is repeated.

. . . .

45. COMMENTARY: 'Kindergartens' of Elemental Beings

In the meanwhile I have discovered that there are places, which can be confirmed geomantically, where great flocks of elemental beings spend their 'childhood phase,' as mentioned above. To be more precise, this is the last stage of their regenerative phase. One can only find such places in especially remote landscapes, for example, in the middle of moorland, in mountain ranges, or in deserts. They want to be left in peace.

A 'nursery for elemental spirits,' as the phenomenon might be called, is an astounding place. One might expect to hear gales of laughter or sounds of dance, but in fact the profoundest silence rules. They are places that seem especially old, like, for example, the mountainous wastes of Sinai or the age-old domes of Scotland's Grampian Mountains – both represent spacious 'nurseries for elemental spirits'. You find vibrating there a particular lightness in the atmosphere, which is penetrated with the exalted feeling of standing on the well of life.

In human words, this means that nurseries for elemental beings are not mere play spaces. Their purpose is much more to help the beings become accustomed anew to the vibrational structure of the earth's surface and attune to their forth-coming tasks in Nature's web of life. This is the last stage of their regenerative phase, after which the elemental beings will be born into the living world of Nature to take over the tasks allotted them by the Earth Soul and their guiding intelligences.

. . . .

From my observations there is also another 'retroactive' connection in the lives of elementals, whereby beings of the second and third levels of unfoldment can clone simple elementals of their own type. For this purpose they take a small particle of themselves, which then develops into a new individual. I was able to watch this happening with the well nymph at the three holy wells of Derry in Northern Ireland.

During my lithopuncture work on both sides of the border between Northern Ireland and the Republic of Ireland, I was also trying to help with the regeneration of the three holy wells in Derry. After I had placed three lithopuncture stones there in 1992, I visited the place again in September 1993 as part of a seminar on earth healing. This time I was able to perceive a beautiful well nymph pulsating at the only existing well, the well of St Columba. Our group had formed, a circle around it and was meditating on the presence of the nymph, mainly to honour her perseverance in a completely foreign and barren place. One of the participants, Jessica, received the clear message that three well nymphs (three sisters) had originally guarded the threefold well.

With that information we went again into meditation to find out whether we should try to reactivate the 'three sisters' aspect of the holy wells if the nymph wanted it. The response was a very clear 'yes'. I put two clear rock crystals into the nymph's area of vibration, and then the circle of people went into meditation for the third time, asking the well nymph to regenerate her two sisters. I allowed myself secretly to watch the process of creation. At the level of the stomach of her vital-energetic body the nymph secreted two beings, which were no more than two centimetres (0.75 inch) tall—according to our perspective—and she anchored their focal points on the two crystals. The atmosphere of the whole procedure was both mysterious and festive, like that surrounding the birth of a human being.

Nature Temples

IN THE SAME WAY THAT THE FLOW OF TIME is understood differently in the elemental realm compared to our world, which is defined by matter, it would also be wrong to speak of a spatial structure in the elemental realm. What we define as space is really only one of the relationships continuously created by the elementals within our spatial dimensions and maintained by them from generation to generation.

I have frequently mentioned the focal point of consciousness and power within an elemental being—a kind of umbilical cord that connects the servants of nature with the focus of their task. This connection has far-reaching consequences. For example, I have mentioned a faun who is unable to leave his assigned tree as long as there is life left in the plant. He remains bound to it and can only move within the energetic circumference of the tree.

Those spatial boundaries are more flexible for the more highly developed beings on the second and third levels of unfoldment. But the same principle is in operation: an elemental will be present within the physical coordinates of its area of responsibility and its focal point must be anchored within this region. A landscape deva can move freely through the area she is assigned to, and yet one can determine exactly the boundaries of her workplace (by radiaesthetic means), and these are limits which on the whole she is unable to cross. One can also find certain places within the area of a deva where she makes a particularly close connection. Such places are marked by a stronger radiation, and consequently they can be identified as power points in the landscape.

To describe the spatial coordinates in the elemental world I would rather talk of an ordering of space than a structure of space. 'Structure of space' defines a physical space with its three dimensions of height, width and depth.

As it is not easy for us to understand this different 'ordering of space', I would next like to give an example using the ancient Goddess Ekurna. Some very rare inscriptions from classical times were found in the marshland region south of Ljubljana.[1] Based on my inner experiences I would call Ekurna a landscape nymph who has reached the highest level of evolution for a water elemental. Her role is equivalent to that of a local deva, but a landscape nymph is the guiding intelligence of a pasture, marsh or lake area. Her role has been mentioned in connection with the old pasture around Türnich.[2]

Ekurna, in her function as a landscape nymph, is perceptible as a star-like glowing focal point pulsating high above the moor of Ljubljana and touching with her radiant glow all areas which are entrusted to her—the landscape and its atmosphere. This creates the characteristic spherical form of a landscape nymph or deva. These beings express their individuality through a specific colour combination.

The spherical shape of Ekurna is marked in the landscape by a clearly defined boundary which undulates at a fixed distance from the shore of the former lake, which turned into a marsh about two thousand years ago. Her boundary is by the old lake, formed from the strip of dry land which was once looked after by the dancing nixies. With the destruction of the marsh, the watery character of the landscape has been suppressed, and with it the nixies' dancing, but the sphere of influence of the landscape nymph remains unchanged.

In December 1993, the art dealer Taja Brejc commissioned me to make a thorough investigation of the different forms taken by this landscape nymph. (The Latin form of Ekurna is Equrna, and this is the name of Taja's art gallery.) First I asked myself if it was still possible to find points where one could contact the living presence of the nymph. I believe that beings like Ekurna actually exist for thousands of years, and perform their tasks even now. Over time, various cultures have settled in the places where landscape nymphs operate, and these beings, under different names, have been invoked and devotedly worshipped as deities.

My custom when cooperating with the elemental world is to let myself be guided initially by a gnome. I met my guide one night in the park near the

---

[1]   Five of the six Latin inscriptions which have been found so far mention the Goddess; they are from the area of two Roman towns, Emona and Nauportus. The towns were built on the edge of the moorland. The sixth was found in the Hungarian lowlands but it can be traced to emigrants from Emona. This clearly connects the Goddess Ekurna with the moorland of Ljubljana. Her name indicates that she is a pre-classical, possibly Venetian or Celtic Goddess.

[2]   As with Türnich, the marshes of Ljubljana have been completely drained by artificial means—which is another example of the conflict between the elementals who protect the landscape and the mindless deeds of human beings.

presidential palace in Ljubljana. Our meeting was the result of a touching story.

In February 1993, I had led a seminar in Ljubljana's cultural centre, and together with the participants had worked on a severely blocked acupuncture point in the above-mentioned park. Before I began my search for Ekurna's places and forms I went to the acupuncture point again to see whether our efforts had taken deep enough root. My feeling was that everything was fine and I was delighting in the good vibrations of the place when suddenly I noticed a gnome coming towards me; he was no taller than my waist.

I was even more surprised when I found that the gnome was emanating a deep sense of gratitude towards me. While I was busy trying to find outer reasons for what I had done to deserve this gratitude, my consciousness began to translate the words of thanks into the language of my mind. As a representative of the whole seminar group of over two hundred people, I received his thanks for the re-energising of the park. He said that it was now a great pleasure for all the resident beings to live there.

I took this matter seriously, and readied myself at the palace to receive his thanks with solemnity. Suddenly a thought crossed my mind: as a favour, could the gnome show me all the places where the ancient cultures had enjoyed their contacts with the landscape nymph Ekurna? Secretly I was hoping to find out more about her being, and I hoped I could first visit the places where she was honoured hundreds of years ago.

My request was easily accepted by the gnome, and soon we were on our way to the shore of the old marsh lake—I sensed very clear directions from him in my left hand; I felt a slow swinging movement. From time to time I looked at the gnome by my side to study his appearance more closely. Then I noticed something significant which related to my questions about the ordering of space in the elemental world. He was not walking by my side but was rather sitting there comfortably, with his right foot folded under him. Immediately I understood that it is only human beings who need to make bodily efforts in order to get from one point in space to another. The gnome's location is where his consciousness is focused, in this case with me. Consequently he was wherever I was.

My companion showed me three places where I could recognise three former holy groves dedicated to the landscape nymph. I feel that the oldest site is close to the ancient town centre, exactly at the spot where the gallery named after Ekurna is now located. It probably dates from the late stone age. The second place is beside a brook which has its source in the present Tivoli Park.

In former times it ran to the now-drained marsh. Much later, the brook was dammed up to form a pond, which makes it hard to sense the sacred atmosphere of the former holy grove, although the place is part of a park. I feel that this is the holy place of the Venetian and Celtic epochs. Ekurna was worshipped during classical times at a third site which is located in front of the walls of the former Roman town of Emona. Some of these ruins are still visible in Mirje.

The old consecrated place is now found at the Gradaššica stream, which probably marks the edge of the former marshland. Fortunately there is one completely untouched piece of land, fully overgrown with old weeping willows, pine trees and birches. Here, where a lucky fragment of the city's land has been spared from human activity, life in the holy grove blooms abundantly. I was able to sense many different kinds of elemental there, and among them the presence of the landscape nymph I was looking for.

In all three of Ekurna's places I was able to perceive the nymph as a being who embodies her individual qualities through form, taking a beautiful female shape. But there were remarkable differences in her presence. It seems to me that the level of development of consciousness of the particular culture which honoured her manifests itself in the quality of her presence. Within the ambience of the older cultures her presence felt much more tangible than in the world of classical antiquity where she was put on a pedestal as a local Goddess, and was thus more remote.

Two dimensions in the spatial order of the elemental world are revealed in this example of the landscape nymph Ekurna. Concerning her presence in space, I have described the first dimension (which I call the etheric dimension) as a sphere of light, radiating within her designated landscape. The second dimension—the astral—unfolds when the nymph makes contact with the material level; this level is impregnated with religious images from the old cultures. Thus the nymph developed focused images of herself at certain places in a form similar to the human body. Within the wholeness of her manifested presence she revealed the total power and beauty of her being. Thus she was not merely a thought form of the Goddess created by human rituals; she was a real being.

I used to meet this 'astral' image of Ekurna in a beautiful wooded corner of the Gradaščica stream, and I became convinced that her appearance in the astral dimension was genuine when a week later, on the 8th December 1993, I asked her to show me the power points within her sphere of influence in Ljubljana's town centre. I took a whole day wandering around the townscape of Ljubljana, and all the time I was aware of her in her materialised form at my left

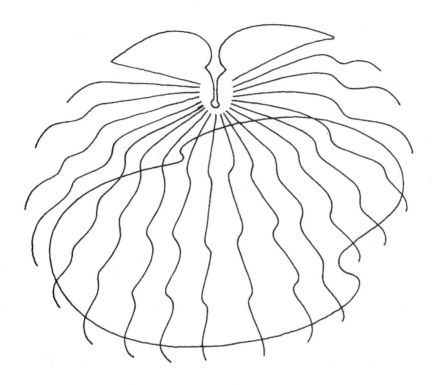

The landscape nymph Ekurna in her etheric body,
spread across the marshland of Ljubljana.

shoulder. She showed me fifteen places of power, and one of these was the 'Chapel of Our Lady of Lourdes' in Rakovnik which has a well nymph (as described in Chapter Four). I was able to mark many of these places as 'to be protected' in my report for a project by the Slovenian Urban Institute which is concerned with the quality of life in Ljubljana. In this way the landscape nymph does not just belong to a long-gone past, she also has an influence on the present.

. . . .

46. COMMENTARY: The Landscape Nymph Ekurna Today

I thought it would be interesting to check, after the space of some fourteen years, how things were going with the landscape nymph Ekurna. Even before reaching the commentary on Ekurna in the course of reworking this book, I had firmly resolved, to travel to Ljubljana and renew contact with her intelligence. However, another task superimposed itself, to be precise, the geomancy training which I was leading in Ljubljana with my daughter Ajra. Just when I reached the theme of Ekurna in this book, I was also making advance preparations for a seminar on the earth changes. I wanted the trainee group to visit certain locations where one can experience the powers and beings that are participating in our endangered planet Earth's self-healing process. I was on the look out for such places in Tivoli Park, on the edge of Ljubljana's inner city, when I unexpectedly came upon the landscape nymph Ekurna.

One of the places linked to the present earth changes, and which was shown to me in Tivoli Park by my spiritual adviser, is closely tied to the archetype of Ljubljana. It is a bronze sculpture by Stojan Batik, located precisely on the city's main axis. The subjects are a dancing woman and her partner. They are portrayed in poses that are of fundamental importance to the composition of Ljubljana's landscape temple: two intersecting triangles turned opposite to each other, like a Star of David. For the past twenty years I have on occasion used the sculpture to help explain the inner shape and uniqueness of Ljubljana.

This time, as I approached the sculpture, I saw with my inner eye that she was sitting like a crown on the head of a gigantic female being. My intuition whispered that this must be the transformed Ekurna.

To test my intuition, I telepathically transmitted the drawing of the landscape nymph Ekurna, which is in the book before you, to the female being. She refused the drawing and pointed to where it belonged, namely the Laibacher Moor. In pictorial speech she told me: "My old role as a landscape nymph belongs to the former moor. Perceive me in my present role." I now directed my inner eye to the relationship between her face and the 'crown' floating above it – and found

The gnome made himself comfortable by my side
while I went for a walk around Ljubljana.

myself in the midst of a spacious model, composed of different coloured lights, depicting the cityscape of Ljubljana.

It is Ekurna's task to saturate this ideal city model with the powers and qualities needed to actualise the relevant archetypes in its daily life. While she coordinates the city's daily reality to fit ever more precisely with her archetypes, she is also opening the city's structures to make them better channels for the new, enlivening powers of change.

In short, Ekurna in her present phase is devoting herself to the transformation of a small major city. Why a 'small major city'? Because Ljubljana, which first took on the role of a capital city sixteen years ago, must in the meantime develop all the functions that usually distinguish a metropolis.

. . . .

Ekurna clearly demonstrated to me that the elementals in the etheric dimension also touch physical space—which is where human beings exist during their incarnation. The interdependence of these two dimensions is revealed in the vital-energetic structure of a place. A good example of this occurs in Hermannsdorf, Bavaria, which I have investigated with the artist and radiaesthesia expert Peter Strauss.

Above Hermannsdorf is a small hill with an old beehive structure. During my investigations I discovered that the hill serves as a sacred place for the surrounding landscape, with a Pan focal point on one side, and the focus for a landscape deva on the other side of the beehive. The radiaesthesia expert found a high-powered energy crossing at each of the two focal points where the two beings have connected with their focus. The devic focus is found where two water lines meet which both have a clockwise quality.[3] It indicates a site of great sacredness.

One of these two water lines runs through the beehive, and then through the spot where I had perceived the Pan of this landscape. Through radiaesthesia one can confirm that Pan's focal point is at the crossing of this water line and two of the so-called 'growth bands'. These are kinds of layers of energy which (according to practitioners of radiaesthetics) considerably enhance the growth of plants, and this corresponds clearly with the role of Pan in the landscape.[4]

---

[3]   In contrast to the anti-clockwise motion of ordinary water. The classification into a clockwise or anti-clockwise quality is done by using a pendulum which is held above a landscape water line.

[4]   The example shows that radiaesthetic measurements are, as a rule, insufficient to recognise the importance of the different energetic phenomena within a landscape. It needs a heightened awareness to experience inwardly which kind of beings in particular are expressing themselves in any energy phenomenon.

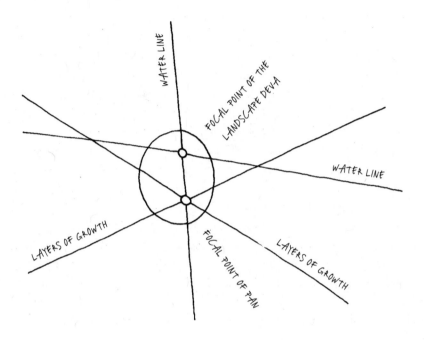

The energetic structure of the hill
above Hermannsdorf, Bavaria.

If we assert that elementals make their presence felt in a place by certain appearances in the vital-energetic structure of that spot, we must then ask how it comes about. All my stories about the infinite tasks performed by the elementals must lead us to the assumption that they are distributed randomly throughout a landscape. On the other hand, we can also imagine that their presence is felt more strongly in some places than in others because their world is hierarchically organised. Of course Pan is present everywhere within 'his' landscape, but because of his etheric nature his focal point is anchored in one or more specific spots. I have also mentioned that certain kinds of elementals perform their duties at chosen places, for example at fairy trees; from here they act upon the whole of the landscape.

My insights and practical experiences have led me to propose the concept of a 'nature temple area'. These are places in a landscape that have a high concentration of elementals. Essentially, what I call a nature temple area would in the past have been called a sacred grove.

However, I would like to distinguish between these two expressions. A sacred grove is strongly influenced by human religious beliefs and the ritualistic uses to which it is put. In contrast, a nature temple area exists because of a perfect abundance of vitality and sacredness, and also simply because of its dense concentration of elementals. Moreover, I am convinced that the nature temple areas of the old cultures were the preferred places when it came to choosing the sites for their sacred groves.

Strangely enough, I first found a nature temple area in the centre of Hamburg of all places, at the 'fairy pond' in Frauenthal. There is a small oak grove in an area where a nunnery stood between 1295 and 1530. I went there to find out whether there were still any fairies at the fairy pond. And in fact I was able to perceive the focal point of a host of fairies of place by an American copper oak where it leaned towards the centre of the park. Now I was curious as to whether there were further elemental focal points. And I found:

- nixies beneath a willow arching over the lake
- male-polarised dwarfs by a 'hairy' oak tree
- female-polarised dwarfs underneath an ancient hollow oak tree next to the road
- an angelic focus at the centre of a thousand-year-old oak which showed strong growth marks
- fire spirits at a younger oak with a low, tangled crown
- elementals of balance (see the section on the fish Faronika in Chapter One)

under an oak tree by the roadside, where the three lower branches grew in a circular pattern around the trunk, forming an open circle as a cosmo-gram of balance.

It is quite likely that there are also other beings of the second and third level of unfoldment which I was not able to perceive at that point in time.

During the following months while I was travelling through Europe to do my work, I discovered numerous nature temple areas. I have mentioned at least three of them: Venus Hill on the Isle of Srakane, the grounds of Türnich castle and the forested slope of Monchsberg above Salzburg where the nymph queen resides. A lot can be learned from the nature temple area on the for-mer holy hill in Cologne. This place has been entirely covered with buildings, but the temple area is found today right inside Cologne cathedral and is still looked after by the elementals.[5] The forgotten corner of untouched nature in Ljubljana that is the seat of the landscape nymph Ekurna shows how impor-tant it can be to leave some wild areas within a townscape.

I have commonly observed that those nature temple areas which have sur-vived within a townscape are those which became integrated (consciously or unconsciously) into parks during the 18th and 19th centuries. I have discov-ered examples of this in the park area behind Schloss Cecilien-hof in Potsdam (near Berlin), at Gaarden Volkspark in Kiel, and in Kensington Gardens in London, which is a huge, intact nature temple.

· · · · · · · · · · · · · · ·

47. COMMENTARY: Nature Temple, Nature Temple Holon

The expression 'nature temple area' now seems to me an unfortunate choice of words. It sounds rather bureaucratic! When trying to present the world of ele-mental beings just as they themselves display it, I was always looking at a world that is organised with geometric precision, although that organisation has the characteristics of a free dance. How can one present these two opposite qualities as a unity which can be grasped by the mind?

The question contains another imperative: we usually associate elemental beings only with certain places in the landscape. Between them, our conscious-ness posits giant stretches which appear to be empty of elemental beings. The intention behind my contemplation of nature temple areas was to show that the

---

5   Later on I discovered the seat of Pan: it is directly outside the cathedral behind the choir, where an extraordinarily vibrant beech tree grows.

landscapes throughout the countryside and cities are saturated with the various sorts of elemental beings. Where there are gaps in this fantastic network of environmental spirits, those places confront a health problem. We must practice earth healing there. The life-maintaining network must not be torn apart!

In the past few years I have used the expression, 'Holon' (from the Greek 'wholeness') in preference to 'area'. In geomantic practice this word carries the meaning of a rounded-off whole, within which one can discern a geomantic centre or an active being. Thus, in describing the relationship of single highly developed elemental beings to their surrounding landscape, one could speak of their Holon or activity Holon, and this would mean the energetic field of operation of an elemental being or nature temple.

So much for the concept of 'area'. As for the concept of 'nature temple', it is my experience that the uniform distribution of the various elemental beings through the landscape is basically given, but I also recognise that there are places where they occur in unusual numbers. For me, these are the 'nature temples'. One could compare them to the functions of the key organs in the human body: as, here pulsates the brain of the local Holon, here beats its heart, etc. A further essential is the sacred atmosphere of such places, which is maintained by single elevated 'individualities' that have settled there from the world of elemental beings.

· · · · · · · · · · · · · ·

In some cases, where sensitive landscaping has been carried out in the parks, the elementals have a good chance of settling in the landscaped areas. In other cases, the elementals prefer the wild areas, far away from the paths. The human tendency to try to force everything into a rational order is a great danger for the elementals. In parks great care should be taken to leave some untouched areas and to treasure trees or branches with unusual forms of growth, as these could be focal points for elementals, or cosmograms sculpted by them.

In the open landscape, nature temple areas are recognised either by their radiations and great beauty or by particularly pleasing natural formations of stones, trees, etc. They appear mostly on the vital-energetic and spiritual-soul levels, and are usually connected with power points in the landscape. They are either embedded into the energy patterns of the power point, or form a distinct nature temple nearby as a counterbalance to the powers of the central power point.

In March 1994, I carried out an investigation into the power lines in Switzerland at Seeland, north of Bern,[6] where I had the opportunity to study the distribution of nature temple areas within a landscape. In the region around Lake Bieler alone I found three elemental temple areas and was able to be relatively accurate about their spheres of influence. For the landscape south of Lake Bieler, the centre of nature intelligence is at the foot of St Jodel Hill, close to the village of Ins; for the lower part of the lake, the temple area is in the Jura mountains above Tüscherz; whereas for the upper part of the lake, the centre of intelligence is above Landeron. Another (fourth) nature temple area can be added to this list. This one plays a coordinating and integrating role for the whole of Seeland and is found on the steep rocks of the tiny island 'Chüngeliinsel' which is close to St Peter's Island in the middle of Lake Bieler.[7] Beneath a multi-trunked, supple pine tree on the island I discovered the seat of Pan for this area, and around him was a complete court of elementals.

The nature temple area above Landeron (on the slopes of the Jura Mountains) can be taken as the pattern for the temple areas in Seeland. The focal points of single guiding elemental intelligences have been marked on different rocks by glaciers during the last ice age; and the focus for the fairies of place is at the church of St Anna on a prominent hill near the village of Combes. One of the rocks in particular is covered with a great number of sculpted shallow cup marks which points to a connection with elemental beings, in particular with female-polarised dwarfs.

My feeling is that these small depressions were used for offering symbolic sacrificial gifts to ensure for the tribe or race the continuation of their relationship with the world of elementals. While I stood on the rock, a stored memory from pre-Christian times suddenly arose from it: I saw a group of people circling anti-clockwise around the rock, shaking in an ecstatic dance. In the folk-tales of dwarfs and fairies, there are numerous references to the purpose of rituals which were dedicated to the elementals. For instance, to ensure the help of the dwarfs in minding the cattle, a symbolic part of the family's meal was regularly taken out for them to the pasture or field.

Using the nature temple area at Landeron, we can also reconstruct the development of such centres of intelligence in a landscape during the course of history. Originally the earth was shaped by rocks which were left behind in this landscape by a glacier; through the awakening life processes in the landscape after the glaciers these different features were chosen by the various elementals for their focal points.

---

[6]   I was asked to do this investigation by the Central Office for the Environment, Forest and Landscape in Bern.

[7]   The islands became a peninsula in the 19th century when the water level in the lake was artificially lowered.

People of the neolithic culture were the first to settle systematically in the countryside. They could still clairvoyantly perceive the light of these particular hills or rocks, and they could then develop these further to become sacred sites. Successive cultures have worshipped at the same places with their different rituals. Even the Christian culture felt a commitment (consciously or unconsciously) to these traditional holy sites, for their first churches were built on them, even though they were often far away from the Christian villages.

An example is the church of St Theodul, which was built at the site of the nature temple area in the region of St Jodel, near Ins. Although the church fell into disuse, its history can be traced, and the tower of the church still remains at the site of the holy grove above Tüscherz. Nowadays this forms part of a worldly rifle range, which reflects the last and saddest period of humanity's separation from the nature temple areas. Even the slightest memory of the importance of the temple in the life of a landscape has been lost to the consciousness of our civilisation.

All my efforts are now directed towards a reorientation, an upswing for the process at its lowest point. I am convinced that today we understand a lot about the subtle networks in ecosystems, and from this we can comprehend with our rational minds the role of intelligent nature centres in directing all life processes. As a next step, we can imagine looking after the landscape better by taking nature temple areas out of the system of normal usage, and putting them under the protection of the law, like important re-created habitats (e.g. our Nature Reserves and National Trust properties). This would be a first step towards a new creative partnership between the elemental and human civilisations. Further steps must lead us to an even deeper soul-level relationship between the two parallel evolutions, more profound than has ever been known before.

. . . .

48. COMMENTARY: **The Nature Temple at Rafford in Scotland**

In the years since writing the above, I have been in contact with many nature temples. As one example, I will report on a hill by Rafford near Forres in Scotland. It is covered with tall pine trees and my daughter Ajra and I led educational groups there in the years 1997-99. It is a transformational nature temple where fire elementals cooperate with the fairies. The hill resonates with the planet Saturn which, coupled with the power of fire, makes the transformational function of the nature temple even more powerful.

Travelling through the place's memories, I first perceived how the hill was used ritually by ancient cultures. Groups of pilgrims came together on its summit and performed stamping dances. For the fire spirits in the hill, this was the signal to start heating the hill energetically. Finally the hill became as hot as a glowing coal and human beings thereby experienced a sort of inner transformation.

After that, I dived into the current role of Rafford Hill, which I suspect has suffered for centuries from a lack of insightful attention. I observed fire beings that transported fiery powers from the earth's centre to the surface. A fiery basin some eight meters (26ft) in height rose above the hill. Fairies and other beings of the air element were constantly at hand, diving into this fiery bowl and from thence bearing a concentrated quality of light out into the world.

A year later, we brought another study group to the hill at Rafford. Ajra and I wanted to give them a closer understanding of how to help a nature temple that is heavily burdened by its past ritual usage. Our group stood in a circle and imagined a rainbow membrane that stretched between our heart centres. The beings of the place were invited to glide through this membrane and thereby join in the ever-present 'now' that pulsates in every heart as a fractal of eternity. The process of attunement to the 'now' was supported by harmonious song.

After the ritual, I was able to perceive more precisely the nature of the interaction between the beings of fire and air. It concerned the process of change in the qualities of the light and speed of the fire from the earth's centre. Both were coordinated with the demands of life on the earth's surface before being distributed over the whole space of the landscape by the swarms of fairies.

. . . .

In general, wherever life pulsates, in such places there must be centres of nature intelligence and these I call nature temples. This is also true for the microcosm of a private garden. There are focal points for all four elements within a small garden if it is cared for with love and devotion. Often there are even representatives of the higher levels of unfold-ment. The extent to which the nature temple in a garden is saturated with the different elementals depends largely on the consciousness of the gardeners.

If the underlying attitudes to a garden are solely directed towards making a profit, or to satisfy an order imposed by the mind, then the life of the elementals is unbearably restricted. Their consciousness is rooted in the feeling level; when a garden is looked after without much feeling, then there is not a great enough power of attraction for the highly developed elementals to be drawn into that garden. This does not imply that it is sufficient only for the loving soul of a gardener to be involved. It is essential that the love of nature and of the elementals finds expression in the design of the garden.

For instance, in our garden at Sempas we have placed small stones and crystals among the garden beds; the stones are surrounded by little patches of healing plants and flowers, thus creating small areas of beauty and joy of life where the elementals can put their focus. The ancient Greek gardens all had a wild corner, a 'temenos' (holy corner), which offered a space for the elementals and their regeneration. At the Findhorn Community the elementals themselves suggested in their contact with Roc that a wild area be reintroduced.

From my own experience I can testify that the elementals need some natural spots to be left for them in the garden for their regeneration. They will settle there permanently, and will spread out from there to carry out their tasks in the cultivated garden. It is also possible that a simple private garden is in a place where once there was a nature temple area, long before people settled there. In those cases powers and presences will be operating in ways which are either good or frightening, but which are far beyond the capacity of a normal private garden.

Finally, we can imagine the landscape as one all-embracing nature temple area where elementals of all kinds and of all levels of unfoldment find their place. We should be grateful if we are the 'chosen ones' entrusted with the care of a nature temple. In such a case we must attempt to find out step by step how the focal points of different beings can best be protected and established.

It is more difficult when such a place has been built over. There may be strong reactions from the suppressed 'original inhabitants' to the effects of unbearable interference. To eliminate the interference by artificial means might result in an even greater repression of the nature intelligences. Instead, I recommend resettling the affected beings at new focal points created by gardeners or artists near the building. In Chapter One I have given the example of a destroyed well. Before taking such actions, you should contact these beings on a deep level with your feelings, and with an attitude of deepest regret apologise for the unfair treatment.

We can see the landscape as a complete nature temple area where all types of elemental beings have their place. It is really a whole dimension of the landscape in addition to its physical, vital-energetic and spiritual-soul ones. I would like to describe this as the emotional dimension of the landscape. For me, the role of this emotional dimension of the landscape is equivalent to the function of consciousness on the human level. However, the difference cannot be reiterated often enough: modern human consciousness is centred on the mental level, but in nature it is focused on the emotional level. With human beings the vehicle of consciousness is the outer self or ego, whereas in

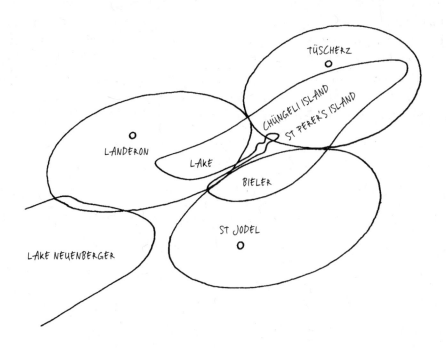

The nature temple areas of Landeron, St Jodel and Tüscherz
with their spheres of influence, and the seat of Pan on
Chüngeli Island in the centre.

the landscape the vehicle of consciousness is the all-embracing community of elementals.

Similarly, we can also represent the purpose of the emotional dimension of the landscape as directing the divine impulses which come from the spiritual-soul dimension towards manifestation in the vital-energetic dimension and finally in the material dimension. The emotional dimension builds a bridge in the landscape which helps to transfer divine impulses from the landscape temples into manifested forms in the energetic and geological/biological landscape structures. Indeed, it is the emotional dimension which opens up for us the possibility of enjoying the infinite beauty and sensual reality of the landscape, so that we can even use it to aid our own development.

DIVINE IMPULSE

LANDSCAPE TEMPLE

SPIRITUAL-SOUL DIMENSION

EMOTIONAL DIMENSION

ACTIVITIES OF THE ELEMENTAL BEINGS

NATURE TEMPLE AREAS

VITAL-ENERGETIC DIMENSION

LIFE-GIVING POWERS

POWER STRUCTURES

PHYSICAL DIMENSION

MATERIALISATION

LANDSCAPE FORMATIONS

CHARACTERISTICS   LANDSCAPE DIMENSIONS   MEANS OF EXPRESSION

My experience of the dimensions of a landscape.

SEVEN

The Personal Elemental
of Animals and Humans

TWO KINDS OF EVOLUTIONARY STREAMS, animals and human beings, have a profound impact on the landscape as they are both guests on Planet Earth. In Earth history the animals appeared first, but the expansive nature of human civilisations has meant that within a few thousand years humans have come to see animals as rivals for nature's resources, and have tried either to tame and subjugate them, to chase them from their home territory, or to eradicate them completely.

This aggressive behaviour gives rise to many confusing thought forms. One of these thought forms is the view that the animal world is inferior to humankind. Sadly this still determines our attitude towards animals but it distorts the truth. In moral terms there is no excuse for it, for if we were to give equal status to all levels of nature, then there would be no alternative but to understand the true roles of different animal species and to integrate this understanding into our picture of the landscape. Such an effort would contribute to overcoming wrong thought forms and would bring a glimmer of hope to the community of animals, which suffers greatly.

What is the true role played by animals? "Each of the numerous species has a specific function and task on the vital-energetic level in their relationship to the earth and to the landscape. Some of them take care of grounding energies, others regulate energetic tensions within an area, and others look after the connection between the earth and spiritual spheres. For instance, a mole rubs its fur against layers of earth, causing a build-up of power. As it digs through its tunnels, it distributes this power within the power structure of the earth. Thus the generated power becomes part of the earth's magnetic field. Fish, on the other hand, through their swimming balance the positive and negative charges in water, so harmonising the energetic structure of water. Birds are indispensable, because they open up channels on the physical plane which allow cosmic powers to pour in. From this perspective, it is not difficult to imagine that butterflies are quite literally flying cosmograms."[1]

I first became deeply aware of animals in May 1993 when I discovered a nature temple dedicated to animal species in the castle grounds of Rakičan. I had often visited this park in Eastern Slovenia before (it is near Murska Sobota), taking groups of people to show them the splendour of cen-turies'-old trees, which are in the front part of the grounds. But I had never ventured into the areas at the back of the park near the new local hospital. Only when a participant in one of my guided tours hit a pregnant deer while driving home, did I get a clear message to go to the area at the back of the park. As I had previously contacted the landscape deva of this particular area, I asked her now to tell me about the cause of this tragic accident, and she led me to the forgotten corner of the park in Rakičan.

There I found a large area of hornbeam woodland with a wide avenue in the centre, overgrown at the end. The trees met in a pointed arch above the avenue creating a space which resembled the nave of a Gothic cathedral. In the branches of the trees at the end of this I recognised the huge form of an owl in flight. I had a strong feeling that I should not enter this sacred space. Following my intuition, I sank on my knees instead and began to eavesdrop on what was happening. Almost immediately I could hear many voices crying and moaning. I realised that these were the voices of different animal species bemoaning the fate which humanity had inflicted upon them. I was not brave enough to face the pain of this animal sanctuary by myself, but I promised to return with a seminar group on earth healing which was planned for the summer, and then to help the animals.

In preparing myself for this work I asked my daughter Ana to contact 'Devos', the Angel of Earth Healing, regarding the significance of the animal sanctuary at Rakičan and its problems. The Angel said that the task of the place from ancient times has been to connect the world of animals with the world of human beings. Such places are a source of the purest vibrations found in the landscape, which spread out in thin strands throughout the countryside. Humankind had long ago destroyed most places like this in order to gain power over the landscape. In the case of the animal sanctuary in Rakičan, this occurred with a massive slaughter of the animals in that particular region.

---

[1] Taken from a message from the Angel of Earth Healing about the true role of animals, received by Ana Pogačnik and published in the magazine *Bio-Novice*, Ljubljana, 1993.

In August 1993, I visited the site twice with groups of more than forty people to do the work of reconciliation and redemption through guided meditations and lamentations, following the instructions given by the Angel. At the end, everybody was requested to find 'their' individual space within the animal sanctuary, to invite an animal of their choice into their meditation, to ask it to come closer, and to offer it refuge in the heart of this human. When at the end of the exercise the participants shared about their experiences, we were quite surprised to hear what the animals had to say about their true role, as is shown by the following examples.

Zdenko had invited the eagle into his meditation, and when he came Zdenko had asked him how he could help him. But the eagle replied that it was rather humans who needed *his* help. Erika met the bear who revealed his message through three spiritual qualities: *friendship, protection* and *comforting.* The female elephant who came to Slavica a introduced herself as the guardian of another trinity of spiritual qualities: *power, will* and *perseverance.* The deer I had invited embodied the qualities of *dignity, love* and *benevolence.* The message common to all these statements became clear: highly developed animal species fulfil specific spiritual tasks in the landscape, whereas the 'lower' species like the mole I mentioned have different types of energy functions.

. . . .

49. COMMENTARY: **The Eagle over Gotland**

My relationship with animals broadened into a new dimension when, on the 14th of July, 2004, an eagle landed on our few acres at Šempas in Slovenia. I was working in our garden with my wife Marika when we noticed a giant bird. It came down low over the upper end of the garden and there touched down. I cried out: 'A stork, a stork,' because no other sort of giant bird came to mind. But the colours were quite different! 'An eagle!' we both cried out together, but it was already gone.

We were quite shaken. In fact, we were later told that there were still isolated families of eagles inhabiting the mountainous rim of our valley. The second surprise occurred on the following day.

Early that next morning I was sitting in a plane flying via Munich and Sweden to Gotland, the second largest island in the Baltic Sea,. In Gotland I was to lead a weeklong workshop investigating the island's landscape. As I waited in Munich for my connecting flight, I was much exercised about my preparedness for the task. It was the first time I had been to Gotland. There were 95 Gothic churches on the island, all perfectly maintained. What meaning did they hold? How would I find my way through all the questions?

I spread out my map. The outlines of Sweden, Gotland and Europe lay on the floor of the departure hall – but I had no clue where to look for the key.

At that moment the eagle touched my heart: though invisible, he was there again. To make sure, I looked with my inner eye and saw an eagle goddess in front of me, half woman and half bird. At once she gave me her guidance. Using the map, I had no difficulty in tracing the geomantic relationships within the island and from Gotland out to the whole of Europe. Later, during the workshop, I was given help in this same way on several occasions (re Gotland, see my book *Touching the Breath of Gaia*)

Obviously, it was not the physical eagle that helped me. The eagle soul had led the giant bird to our land so that his touch might establish my relationship with the cosmic soul of the eagle family. After that, the presence of the bird itself was unnecessary, because I was communicating directly with the so-called group soul of the eagles. It is well known that, unlike humans, single animals do not represent the incarnation of an individual soul. All animals of the same species can be considered as embodiments of one and the same soul being. In the example described above I perceived this group soul as the eagle goddess.

Gotland must be deeply connected with the soul being of the eagle family. During a meditation which consciously spoke to the relationship with 'my' eagle, Gerda, one of the participants, saw an eagle bearing Christ's lance wound, the stigmata, on its right side. It flew over Gotland and as it did so, its blood dropped from the stigmata. And from every drop there arose one of the 95 churches of Gotland.

. . . .

In September, when I had the opportunity to communicate with Pan at Findhorn, I asked him whether the elementals had tasks in connection with the more highly developed animals. The reply was a clear yes. From the feeling he conveyed to me, I understood that the elementals who are associated with animals try to educate the animals in the coordination of their emotionally polarised consciousness of individuality with impulses from the group soul. This plants a seed within the animals for their future 'personality' and their path into individuation.

A few days later, in the train station at Villach during my journey home, I was given an example of how this cooperation works. I observed how a young dog had sensitive reactions to the multiplicity of stimulation provided by his environment. His consciousness was longing to follow every impulse; it was longing to experience everything and to abandon itself to the multitude of excitements. In contrast, I could perceive the group soul of dogs; it is the spir-

The elemental tries to teach 'his' dog right awareness.

itual authority which knows what is important for the unfoldment of each animal. As a third factor in the drama played out before my eyes, I was able to see the elemental being of the dog which was striving intensely to restrain the instincts of the animal and to hold the dog at an optimal level from the perspective of the group soul.

In comparison, this example clearly highlights the different role played by elementals who are connected with plants. As I have explained before, elementals are the embodiment of the consciousness of the plant. With animals, they partially withdraw from the realm of the consciousness in order to make room for the development of the 'individual F of the animal.

Their relationship to human beings is different again. Our consciousness is fairly independently active on the emotional level as well as on the mental level, so that we do not need the direct support of an elemental in this way, but that does not mean that we can do entirely without the help of the elementals while we are in a physical body on Planet Earth. The field of action of our personal elemental is on the levels of energetic and physical body structures.

In the book that Ajra wrote in cooperation with the Angel Master Christopher Tragius, she explains that the 'elemental I' is one aspect within the wholeness of the human being, and that humans are in need of some help from an elemental during the period of their incarnation. The Angel points out that the individual T of the human being, which is also called the soul and is a cosmic spiritual being, would be incapable of dealing with matter if it did not receive the support of the elemental world. In reality, the elementals are perfect in their mastery of dealing with manifested matter on Planet Earth, and they are the best equipped to direct the complicated composition of the multidimensional human body, via impulses given by the soul.

According to the message from the Angel Christopher, an agreement was reached in the far distant past between the spiritual and earth evolutions, so that the elementals committed themselves to support and assist in the incarnation of human souls, enabling them to go through the necessary experiencing of matter for the sake of their development. Since then, each incarnated soul is accompanied by an elemental which resides within the emotional/energetic structure of the human body. Christopher calls it the 'elemental P to differentiate it from the personality which is the 'outer P, and the soul which is the 'inner I'.

The 'elemental F helps the soul to experience everything it has set out to learn during its incarnation in matter. Even before conception (which the Angel calls the period of energetic pregnancy) the soul connects with a particular elemental which then manifests exactly the right conditions for the soul's incarnation, and even for the right moment of conception. Later on, the elemental also directs the formation of the body in the womb, and controls all the physical transformations throughout the person's life. There is a close lifelong partnership between the soul, the personality as its outer expression, and the elemental being.

. . . .

50. COMMENTARY: **A Landscape Temple of Incarnation**

I have discovered 'a landscape temple of incarnation' in the Immenstadt area of Oberallgau. It is one of those precious landscape areas in which human souls are prepared for their approaching incarnation. They are gradually introduced to the world of matter in order that, after their birth, they can withstand its relatively massive vibrations.

For sure, this all happens on the invisible plane but it is sufficiently close to our everyday reality for sensitive people to feel its traces. All the sacred places in this 'incarnation landscape' are either adopted as places of pilgrimage, like Buhl on Alpsee where three churches stand next to each other, or furnished with horrifying names like Teufelsee (Devil's Lake).

About the small, deep, reed-edged Teufelsee, it is said that the Devil emerges from it once a year and takes with him into its depths the first human soul he sees– a reference to the important introductory phase of incarnation which takes place deep underwater.

In my vision, I see a broad, light-filled space under the lake. Crowds of human souls who are preparing themselves for the approaching incarnation walk solemnly around the middle of the space. Running to and fro between them are smaller beings who do in fact look somewhat devilish but are far removed from being any kind of threat. They are very lovingly inclined towards the human souls and their appearance is not so much devilish as merely different from what we humans are used to. They obviously represent the elemental beings that have made themselves available to accompany this gathering of human souls on their way through their next incarnation.

I was suddenly aware that I was watching a scene of love play: at that very moment the human souls were busy choosing the elemental being/partner with which they would share their body throughout their life in the approaching incarnation. The atmosphere in the space vibrated in anticipation of the holy marriage.

In fact, when a soul and an elemental being had decided on one another, they vanished from the space. I suspect that they went on to the next station on their now common path where they will be energetically coupled with one another while life lasts. My intuition placed this station on the holy hill of Buhl, near the pilgrimage chapel of Maria Loreto.

. . . .

This partnership might turn out to be painful for both the human being and the elemental. Following the direction of the soul, the elemental sometimes must arrange pain or emotional difficulties, as we often learn our lessons more successfully through problem-solving than through harmonious circumstances. For instance, in our culture confusion has resulted because we have neglected to create conscious rituals for our transitions from one phase of life to the next. The rituals once signalled that a person was beginning a new phase in his or her development, and that the elemental should actively support this process.

Since this communication is missing today, the 'elemental F is unable to follow through with the transformations, which can lead to negativity on the emotional level. If the personality then loses its inner balance, a conflict between the 'partners' may result where the elemental will become more and more negative and may lose control over the finely tuned cooperation between the organs in the body. It is unable to maintain the perfect cohesion of the energetic and the physical body. The loss of order becomes evident first on the emotional level, then on the energetic level, and finally on the physical level of the body, possibly ending in severe illness. Christopher Tragius calls this condition an 'active block', and he recommends getting the help of a healer who can assist the sufferer in realigning the elemental being with its original state of neutral caring. The same effects on the elemental can be achieved by the ill person practising positive feeling and thinking.

On the particular day when I talked with Pan at Find-horn about the role of elementals in relation to animals, I requested that he also allow me to feel the presence of an elemental in my own body. I perceived a warm, fur-like construction which supported my body from the ground upwards. Up to my hips I felt comfortably protected within it; the 'scaffold' supported a feeling of being solidly grounded. The classical picture of Pan with his hairy lower body seems to be developed from such body experiences, especially as I also felt a connection with my elemental along my spine up to the head, where the personality is seated. In classical times this was represented by an image of goat horns.

With this picture as Pan's gift to me, I felt closer to the feeling nature of my personal elemental being. This quality is basically loving and caring as long as there is no disharmony. However, my picture of him can best be

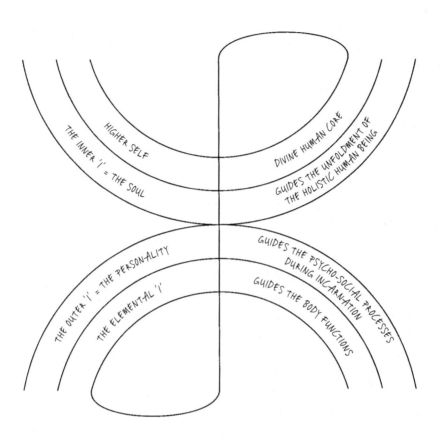

The place of the 'elemental I' within all parts of the human being.

described as a mixture of the pink panther and the devil in folk tales. There is a sense of disproportion and ugliness around the body elemental, for the aesthetics of the earth element,[2] to which the being belongs, appear strange and terrifying to us. The body elemental is a highly developed spirit being of the earth elemental line. It is comparable with a faun's level of unfoldment, for its task is quite complex. The sum total of the levels which a person inhabits during incarnation—the *emotional,* the *vital-energetic* and the *physical* levels—is taken care of by the elemental and is constantly coordinated to remain harmonious.

Some artists have identified and presented in coded forms the symbiotic communion of the human soul with a body elemental, which otherwise in our culture is kept in the dark or even demonised. I am thinking, as an example, of Titian's large painting 'Presentation of the Virgin in the Temple' (1534-1538). It covers an entire wall of the former 'Scuola della Carità' in Venice (today it is the Accademia). The Virgin Mary can be seen as representing the human soul. She is surrounded by an evanescent egg-shaped light as she ascends on her spiritual path, which is depicted as a staircase. Sitting at the foot of the stairs is an old crone who is almost completely hidden by her clothes and has horrible features. She sits between a dead hen on the ground to her right and a basket full of eggs to her left. It is said that she is a custodian of the life cycles between birth and death. In this way, the artist has pointed out the secret relationship between soul and body elemental which is a vital component of human life.[3]

I found another example of this in the pilgrim's church at Heiligenblut at the foot of the Grossglockner. Every year, a baroque wooden sculpture used to be carried three times around the church. It is a representation of a young boy who is touched by two beings. From above an angel comes down to whisper something into his ear, and from below a black devil comes up to catch his foot. I interpret the boy to be a representation of the ego, in particular the personality of someone passing through life. The ego is supposed to use the ear of the intuition to listen to the voice of the soul, represented by the angel. At the same time the relationship between personality and matter is directed by an earth elemental; in the picture it is depicted by a devil which guides the foot of the boy.

---

[2] See Chapter Four.

[3] Normal interpretations by art historians do not appreciate the relationship between the two figures. The old woman is seen as an addition to entertain the viewer.

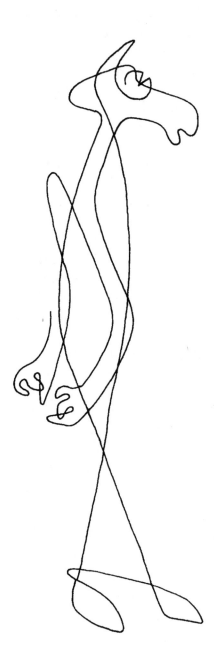

How I would draw the personal elemental of a person.

This is a surprising clairvoyant representation of how the three focal points of consciousness that constitute human life are connected—what I described earlier as the '*inner I*', the '*outer I*' and the '*elemental I*'. It is a pity that this connection cannot be accepted in the neutral manner in which I have presented it here. On the contrary, the Christian moral stance has made this idea the victim of a dualistic value system, where the '*inner I*' is revered as an angel while its elemental partner becomes the devil and adversary on the spiritual path.

The anti-life duality came to its tragic culmination at the time of the witch hunts between the 15th and 18th centuries when the Inquisition made a gigantic effort to drive 'the devil' out of human beings.[4] This moralising misinterpretation of the body elemental was taken 'dead' seriously and in an overheated way by people who were unaware of the fact that human beings would be unable to live without this 'devil' as their close companion on their earthly path. Innocent women and men died under the most cruel torture because they were accused of carrying the blessing and the goodness of an elemental inside them (as we all do). This elemental in fact makes the gift of life accessible to all people, and a body without the devotional service of a body elemental would be a body condemned to death.

. . . .

51. EXERCISE: **Make Contact with one's Personal Elemental Being**

It is much simpler to communicate with the elemental beings of our environment than with one's own elemental 'I'. The personal elemental being seems to be too close for us to perceive it clearly. The following exercise can be helpful. It is done standing up and the proposed gestures should be performed both with your body and in your imagination:

- Imagine that a bright little ball is lying on the floor between your feet. It represents a seed of life.
- Bend down towards the little ball, stretch out your hand to it and withdraw a plant from the seed of life.
- Raise the plant slowly and lovingly up to your lap. Now stand upright.
- While being lifted up the plant has developed a fruit. The fruit changes into a white-furred animal that has rolled itself up in a tight ball in your lap.

---

4   Witch hunts also demonstrate a hatred of the Goddess. The Goddess embodies the overall life forces which are manifested by the elementals.

The relationship between the 'elemental F and the soul
of a person — an interpretation based on Titian's painting
'Presentation of the Virgin in the Temple'.

> Take the time to sense its quality while you hold it in your hands and gently press it against your abdomen.

- Now raise the round ball, which is the animal, up to your heart region. Be sure that the animal is touching your body throughout.

- While you are lifting it up to your heart, the animal changes into a little child whom you embrace as it nears your heart. Finally you press it close to you.

- At this moment you can sense your personal elemental being and become aware of it through the form of the inner child.

- What are your sensations at this moment? For a while, embrace your second 'I', through whom you belong to the world of Nature. Hold it close. What feelings are now awakening in your inmost being?
Take note of the slightest stirring. When it shows itself, speak with your personal elemental being.

- Finally, give thanks for the experience.

. . . .

A conscious relationship with one's own 'elemental F is of particular relevance for the modern human being. Our culture has developed to be centred in our heads and to be ruled by a mental patterning which lifts us into an ungrounded state. We might still believe that we are constantly concerned with matter and reality, but the truth remains that we are floating above the ground, and without noticing it we have lifted ourselves into an abstract level of thinking. We urgently need to be grounded to emerge from this illusion and to develop an ability to root our soul forces within our body for personal healing and harmony. This gift of grounding is exactly what the body elemental can offer to the human being at each moment. To consciously share in this gift I use a simple form of meditation which is suitable for daily meditations to welcome the new day, as well as for any troublesome situation of the body or soul.

First of all, to make a connection with the body elemental, I bring my concentrated attention to a point a few centimetres below the bottom vertebra of the spine. I can feel the fullness of its power and its strong connection to the earth beneath my feet. The earth might be deep below a building, but it is always possible to reach it. Like the roots of a tree this unites me with the sphere of power of the Earth Mother. Afterwards, without losing the connection to the earth sphere, I gently send my attention upwards to the centre of the abdomen. This allows me to bring the quality of the elemental into the centre of my feeling level, so that it can energise the whole body/soul structure. Then, to connect with my soul force, 'the inner I', I bring my awareness to a few centimetres above my head. I seek to sense its cosmic depth and, like the branches of a tree, it spreads out to infinity. Then I direct this soul experience down into the centre of my heart, and I let it radiate out into the whole of my being.

Throughout the meditation I keep an awareness of the power of the 'elemental I', centred in the abdomen, so that both of the focal points of my being are harmoniously attuned to each other; they provide a starting point for me to begin my daily tasks with joy and balance.

. . . .

52. COMMENTARY: **The Quality of Grounding**

The qualities of grounding and inner peace are of decisive importance. They must be nourished if a person wants to come in touch, and remain in touch, with the world of elemental beings and environmental spirits. Indeed, these are decisive qualities for our own health and wellbeing.

When nature spirits try to make people conscious of their inadequate grounding, they are trying to protect modern men and women from the loss of their life's foundation. It is the personal elemental being, as guardian of life, which feels this danger most keenly.

Part of the logic of a global civilisation is the necessity to become ever more deeply involved in our rational patterns. We do not realise that, in doing so, we are severing our relationship with our own soul. This loss also weakens our connection with the flow of life power until it gets hard for the personal elemental being to take care of the normal course of our vital bodily functions. That sounds the alarm.

To avoid that sort of collapse, which usually results in illness, we should learn to permanently maintain our grounding, including our grounding to our inner earth which is embodied in the region of our abdomen. A holographic fragment of the Earth Soul pulsates at the pelvic floor of our abdomen and can guarantee our grounding with even greater certainty. A complete understanding of this power centre can be gained by consulting the Japanese tradition of the 'Hara'.

Also, in my book 'Turned Upside Down' I write of the 'lumbar energy channel'. This is the centre from which our personal elemental being orients itself in the course of its activity in our corporeal power fields. We should give continual and close attention to this centre of our personal grounding and at the same time test ourselves to establish whether we still remain anchored there.

We must also learn to permanently maintain the quality of our inner peace. Its place within us is the heart centre, and the spark of the divine presence is anchored in the middle of that. If a person is present in the middle of their heart centre, then the fountain of eternal peace, and of one's own personal peace, are both anchored there.

In the last analysis, the two qualities belong together and should be used and realised simultaneously. Through the interaction of the two centres, one will become whole again and also able to renew communication with Nature.

. . . .

Apart from a conscious or unconscious relationship with our own personal elemental during our lifetime of experiencing matter, we can also have other kinds of relationship with the elementals in our surroundings. Such relationships are only possible when we are consciously ready to communicate with the world of elementals. If this communication is pursued consistently, then we can eventually have a fruitful cooperation with the elementals. I would like to illustrate this with two examples from my own experience.

In May 1993 I was sculpting lithopuncture stones for the grounds of Murska Sobota castle with my wife. I visited the park several times to ponder on the right placement of the first nine standing stones. By 25th May I had already become clear about their placement when a co-worker phoned me from the Slovenian part of Carinthia. She had received a request in meditation that I contact the faun of a particular oak tree in the park. He would have a message for me.

I went to the mighty oak, which was at least three hundred years old, leaned against it with my hands touching its trunk and closed my eyes. I could see how at the centre of its roots the oak had formed a horn shape like the sickle of the moon, pointing in a certain direction. At the top of the horn it had developed a shining, silvery-grey pearl. I tried to understand this sign in vain. But I suddenly had the impulse to turn around quickly and look in the direction in the park where the horn pointed. I understood the message immediately.

Initially, I had intended to place one of the first lithopuncture columns on that exact spot. But my reasoning had conquered my instincts and I had created a geometric pattern for the lithopuncture plan with its starting point on the castle's axis. In order to be able to incorporate this particular stone column into the pattern, I had decided to place it on another acupuncture spot, about ten paces to the east. I would have made the very mistake which the faun wanted to warn me about: by following an abstract pattern I would have missed the real function of this lithopuncture column within the park's system. When I understood the message I immediately corrected my plans.

The second example of conscious cooperation between elementals and our human culture came from a gigantic rocking stone.[5] It is situated on a forested hill near the village of Stierberg in Austria. Together with Günther Kantilli and a group of students from the Faculty of Soil Culture in Vienna, we visited the megalithic monument during a seminar. It was snowing heavily.

The group was given half an hour for their personal experiences of the place while I crept into a cleft between the two rocks which form the monument. There I met a lively crowd of dwarfs who were very willing to tell me how the rocking stone had once served a healing purpose.

A person would approach the rocking stone and ask for their ailments to be healed. Through focusing their attention on the stone they emitted an unconscious impulse which was the signal for the dwarfs to begin to rock. They did not try to rock the physical stone, but rather its etheric complement. This is formed like a cloud of energy which fits the material form of the stone. The difference between the immobility of the physical structure and the dynamism of the etheric structure created a narrow channel through which healing powers could flow to the sick person standing in front of the rocking stone. The active involvement of the elementals together with the rocking stone therefore made healing possible.

· · · · · · · · · · · · · ·

53. COMMENTARY: **The Power of Giving**

The evidence indicates that the ancient cultures communicated with the world of nature spirits. They knew selfless giving as a ritual whose power paved the way for cooperation with the elemental beings. Today no one gives any heed to this, except maybe the children.

The elemental beings had appealed to me about this matter when I was in Basle investigating the centre of environmental spirits at the Spalenbrunnen. As I was preparing for a workshop, I had asked them how we, as a group, could be of help. At once three wishes were uttered, of which the second had to do with gifts.

This wish was made known in a characteristic manner. I received an impulse to keep my eyes focused in a certain direction. At that moment a young woman was passing by with a bag full of hazelnuts. At the precise moment that she crossed my line of vision the bag in her hand wobbled and six hazelnuts fell to the ground. I understood that the elemental beings were longing for a ritual presentation of

---

[5] Rocking stones are megalithic standing stones where one stone is placed on top of another in an unstable position, so that it 'rocks'.

gifts – a form of communication that the original cultures had practiced for many thousands of years.

At the workshop on the following day we chose three women from the group who went to the square with the six hazel nuts, and gave them, in their imagination, to the elemental beings while the group supported them by visualisation in colour.

It is important to emphasise that this was no sort of eager gift exchange as may be practiced in the West. Elemental beings have no concept of material giving. It is the conscious and loving intention that accompanies the gift that strengthens them and makes them happy. The principles of the ritual demand that the material plane is not introduced. In my experience, the presentation of a gift is just as effective if one visualises the form of the present and imagines that one is handing it over to the appropriate nature spirit. In doing so, one must listen for their answer. A ritual of this sort can easily develop into a conversation.

One can also give presents to one's personal elemental being, and in this way a plane of conversation, so to speak, can develop of itself. For example, the elemental being cannot perceive the physical beauty of nature, which we see with our eyes, unless we mediate it to them through our consciousness. When human beings experience something beautiful or meaningful, they can share it with their companion from the inner world of nature. One should intuitively translate the experience into vibrations and send it like a wave through the entire body down to the soles of the feet. Afterwards, one should be alert for possible feedback.

. . . .

A heightened perception is the decisive precondition for a conscious cooperation between humans and the beautiful realm of the elemental beings. In his lectures at Helsingfors, Rudolf Steiner talked about a threefold system of perception when we look at the invisible worlds. This is precisely what I myself have experienced.

The first step into deeper perception happens when we live in our day-to-day consciousness but in addition enter the invisible worlds through special meditative states, visualisations or trance. We must be able to remember our experiences later in order to bring to waking consciousness what we have experienced in an exceptional state. On this first level, which is often realised through shamanistic rituals, we cannot integrate our experience of the invisible worlds into our ordinary consciousness. We swing back and forth between the two worlds. My first experiences, which I described in Chapter One, were such examples of a first step into clairvoyance. I was sitting and meditating with closed eyes in our kitchen at home and mentally moved into the world of elementals.

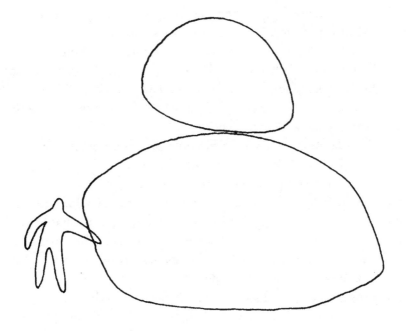

The rocking stone at Stierberg in the 'Waldviertel', Austria.

After taking the second step, we no longer need to move back and forth between two opposing levels of consciousness. It is possible to perceive the invisible world as an existence parallel to normal reality. At the same time as remaining in normal consciousness, the experiences of the 'second' reality are fully registered, examined by the mind and immediately integrated into our own world of experience. While getting these impressions of another world dimension, we are at the same time completely anchored in our own body, and we sense ourselves as fully present alongside this invisible reality. At this level the heightened perception is integrated into day-to-day consciousness. Most of my experiences with the elemental world which I have described in this book are from this second level of perception.

The third level of perception takes on a revelatory quality. If we perceive a being in this way we become inwardly one with the being and experience its reality as if it were our own. In this context I can mention, for example, my talks with Pan at Findhorn. He invited me to enter into aspects of the landscape which he has stored within himself as unique qualitative vibrations. Not only did I receive information about the subject under observation but I was allowed to experience fully the all-embracing consciousness of Pan as if I myself *were* the Pan of that landscape.

From my own experience I want to recommend to the reader of this book that they achieve the second level of heightened perception in preparation for their own communication with elemental beings. The third level is an exception, because it is only possible with the most highly developed elementals and with those elemental beings who have developed beyond the realm of elemental spirits. I would not recommend the first level of perception for our present time; it may lead one astray for the following reasons:

In an astrological sense we are in a transition time between the age of Pisces and the age of Aquarius.[6] Pisces, through its dual nature, has initiated processes of polarisation in our culture which have led to a division into good and bad, positive and negative, and so on. Therefore the first level of clairvoyant perception is based on the polarity of two opposed worlds, between which the clairvoyant person swings back and forth.

If we were to continue on this path today, the forces of the previous age could easily be drawn into our process of perception by the resonances which we create, and so our perception could be distorted without our noticing it.

---

[6] This concept is rooted in the structure of the so-called Platonic year, which is more than 24,000 Earth years. Accordingly, the Earth is under the influence of each of the twelve signs of the zodiac for about 2000 years.

On the other hand, the second level of clairvoyance is attuned to the forces of the coming age of Aquarius, an era of synthesis, where supersensible vision can be integrated into day-to-day consciousness.

I would like to advise all who have chosen the second level of perception as a goal for their own development to note that inner pictures are not necessarily essential to it. If we understand clairvoyance as an inner viewing of pictures, we put the absurd idea into our heads that this is a prerequisite for our communication with the invisible dimensions of reality. This idea may lead to a psychological block, with the result that even quite sensitive people would think they are not able to perceive the invisible worlds.

The term 'clairvoyance' points to the fact that a person's ability to perceive is extended into 'clair' (lighter) vibrational realms which are normally excluded from the range of perception even before they can reach the consciousness of the observer. These lighter vibrations were automatically excluded when the reality of their presence became taboo over the generations as our culture became completely focused on matter. Of course a spiritual tradition was passed on from one generation to the next, but we can make no excuses for the exclusion of clairvoyant perception from spirituality.

The Christian tradition is based on evaluation and on an exclusive duality whereby the consciousness of the average person cannot reach the higher worlds unless they have a secure faith. The lighter vibrational realms[7] are forbidden and are locked away from their perception because those realms are closely connected to life processes.

. . . .

54. COMMENTARY: **Mutual Perception of Two Worlds**

From now on, I am not going to use the word 'clairvoyance'. It sounds too mystical. At the time I was simply inspired by the root 'clair' or 'bright', as I have explained. My years of experience in teaching these kinds of perceptual techniques have convinced me that this kind of perception is not really clairvoyance, but a normal extension of our perceptual capabilities. Instead of clairvoyance, I will use the phrase 'extended perception'.

During this phase of evolution, now nearly over, humanity has devolved to a way of perception that is adapted to the criterion of reason. In so doing, many of our normal perceptual capabilities, which did not appear useful to the interests

---

[7] I call the 'lighter' vibrations those which directly influence the physical vibrational field but exist beyond the boundary of the visible.

of our reason, were allowed to wither away. Now it is time to reawaken them and connect them to the perceptual process. We are speaking of subtle corporeal reactions, the subtle sensitivity of our auric field and the creative potential of our imagination and intuition. Even the power centres of our etheric organism, the chakras, can operate as perceptual organs.

. . . .

I see that the best way to work through these dualistic blocks lies in gaining knowledge about the 'lighter' worlds and then turning lovingly towards their presence in the here and now. When we repeatedly face the challenges which I have mentioned, we will open the door to clairvoyant perception. The dynamics of such perception is founded on the connection between two differently structured force fields, formed by the *observing* person on one side and the *observed* being, such as an elemental being, on the other. It is really an exchange of energy between partners which makes the communication[8] possible.

When the two force fields meet, followed by an energy exchange through loving appreciation, certain feelings will emerge which will flow through the emotional level of the perceiver, and with the help of consciousness these feelings can be registered, judged and formulated. In the inner eye of consciousness, appropriate hunches, colour impressions, outlines of forms or pictorial images will appear, mirroring the perceived invisible reality of the being. In addition, impressions of sound, scent and taste are possible. When we combine these feeling perceptions and consciously formulated impressions, our mind is able to interpret the message and will integrate it into our world view.

For this process to take place successfully, it is absolutely necessary to stay grounded[9] and to achieve balanced breathing. This is a safeguard against the danger of illusion, and against losing the connection with the real framework of perception. An equally important second condition is to work on our own self and to work regularly on our psychological problems. This helps us to prevent the further danger of entanglement in illusion whereby the unrefined ego, 'the outer I', might without our noticing it project its own desires and imaginations onto the process of perception.

---

[8]   Derived from *communicate* (Latin)—to share. Communication in this sense is not merely an exchange of information but also a mutual blending of two beings.

[9]   To become grounded, it is usually sufficient always to realise that we are standing on the earth and our roots reach deep down into the earth.

A third condition for successful perception on the second level of clairvoyance is regular practice. For instance, if we go for a walk in the woods and find a place with a special ambience, we should take the time to submerge ourselves in its force field, and try to sense as precisely and in as much detail as possible the oncoming waves of vibrations, as well as observing very closely what kind of thought associations, sensations or images appear. It helps to get to know the language of one's own consciousness and to interpret the vibrational wave accordingly, and to observe carefully which symbolic forms are activated in us. But the opposite is also true: if we are in a place where we receive images we should try to see beneath them and into the underlying vibrations to recognise the type of reality they signify. In the case of pictures without vibrational waves we should disregard them as illusions. If we encounter the pain of torn, irregularly linked or chaotic patterns of vibration, then we must assume that the place is in need of healing.

EIGHT

In the Whirlpool of Change

55. COMMENTARY: The Process of Earth Change has Begun

Over the past ten years much that is new and unexpected has happened in the world of elemental beings, certainly more than in the previous thousand. I myself was surprised by the changes that happened almost daily and could hardly adjust to all the novelty. It is not just the emergence of new kinds of elemental beings, like the beings of the fifth element already mentioned, but new dimensions of the elemental world are also opening. What is going on here?

In the Fifth Chapter, 'Evolution in the Elemental Realms', we were already discussing a new age that would be ruled by the air element and subject to a wholly different set of rules and formulas than our age of the earth element. At the time, the conversation with Ajra's Angel Master on the Canary Islands seemed to indicate that the approaching change lay in the distant future. Now the signs are increasing that we humans, together with the Earth and her world of elemental beings, are already in the middle of a change process that is leading us into a new evolutionary age, although our waking consciousness knows very little about it.

What all of us could perceive over the past decade was the unusual concurrence of environmental catastrophes. They happened one after another in the framework of one of the four elements: flood (water element), earthquake (earth element), volcanic eruption (fire element) and destructive winds (air element). Add to these, waves of epidemics among farm animals.

During the devastating floods in Prague in 2002 when more than 45,000 people had to be evacuated, I had occasion for an exchange with Julius, the old sage from the race of earth elementals, who has charge of the Adriatic island of Srakane. I have already mentioned Julius in connection with his personal name, something which only the higher evolved elemental beings possess.

I asked him why many people were so deeply affected currently by natural catastrophes, as if there were some additional message bound up with them, though in all times past and present they had been seen as natural occurrences. In the next moment, his explanation surrounded me like a cloud of consciousness. He identified the catastrophes as being like a way of speaking through which the elemental world sought to warn us humans of the approaching earth change. Locked up in the armour of our perfectly developed logical thinking, we are on the point of losing our last contacts with the reality of Nature, Earth and the Cosmos. We are no longer capable of perceiving the coming turning point on Earth's evolutionary path – of which we are still part.

To ensure that we do not get lost in the confusion of the coming earth changes, our blind trust in the stability of our mentally conditioned world must be shattered. Through violent natural events, the elemental intelligence will warn us that a world dimension, in fact the very one by which we orient ourselves, is being gradually dismantled. Life will certainly continue, but on another frequency. The elemental beings are using the increasing occurrence of natural catastrophes to sound the alarm and bring humanity to the point where, in good time, we consciously uncouple ourselves from the old world structure and follow the stream of change which guarantees the continuance of life on the earth's surface.

· · · · · · · · · · · · · · · ·

56. COMMENTARY: **The Earth Soul Awakens**

Since 1997, our daily reality has been occurring on two completely different planes which exist simultaneously. Without our noticing, every moment's reality since then has been woven together out of these two world dimensions. On the one hand, we live in an unstable and turbulent world, identified by the scars and trauma inflicted on it by millennia of human development and especially by the unusual aggressiveness of the past centuries. We are looking at a world dimension whose existence is seriously threatened by ecological damage and the emotional flood of human suffering.

On the other hand, a second, parallel reality is already pulsating in our bodies and environment. It is being established by the spiritual intervention of the Earth Soul and the concentrated efforts of the elemental beings, which are units of her consciousness. To be exact, the 'new' reality (the new space) is being created by transforming the old, exhausted power structures. Although still invisible, the new reality space can already be perceived by our feelings which are continually telling us: "All is for the best; look around you, see how life is beginning to shine."

Furthermore, I have observed that a special sort of elemental being has meantime appeared which has specifically developed itself to help with the earth

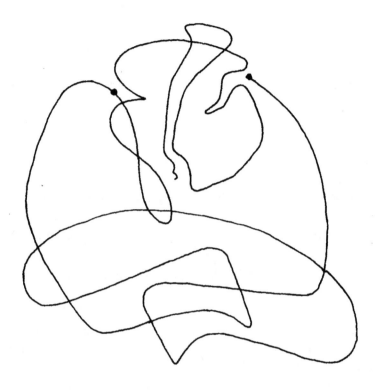

Julius, the old, wise being with whom
I conferred on the Island of Srakane.

change. We could call these beings 'midwives of the new world dimension'. They are distinct from the other elemental beings: first, they are not categorised in any of the four elements; second, they distinguish themselves by an extremely pure vibration that is best described by the colour white. I have already mentioned them as 'elementals of the fifth element.'

When, in July 1999, I encountered a great flock of these shining white elemental beings who were working on the construction of the new earth space, I asked them what their task was within the framework of Earth's consciousness. They set out to reply, gliding in and out amongst themselves and forming a broad circle around a bare piece of the surface. As I looked closer, I could glimpse the blurred contours of a sleeping giantess beneath the ground and recognise the Earth Soul. The giantess now began to move her arms and legs; then she raised her head until it penetrated the layer of earth covering her. I could perceive how slowly she opened her eyes. Obviously, she was seeing daylight again for the first time in a long, long while.

The accompanying message, put in human words, ran as follows: "The earth will awaken completely in her presence, and we are preparing ourselves to help her become completely herself" (cf. my book 'Touching the Breath of Gaia').

. . . .

57. COMMENTARY: **Environmental Spirits and Christ Consciousness**

The causes of this profound transformation of the Earth and her environmental spirits are hard to grasp. We may sense that the huge ecological problems now gathering like heavy clouds over the earth are its triggers. But what are the deeper causes?

I received an initial indication of the deeper connections on the 27th May, 2000, when I was in the midst of a forest in Saarland leading a group of geomantic researchers studying exercises for the perception of elemental beings. Completely unexpectedly, the giant figure of Pan appeared before me bearing all the characteristic features of the antique god of nature. But when he raised his arms, I could clearly see the stigmata, the wounds of Christ, on his hands and feet and in his side. Silver rays shot out of them to strike the corresponding places on my own body.

I was not now standing before a holographic fragment (fractal) of Pan that is incorporated within a specific landscape in the unity and wholeness of the natural world. I was standing before the integral Pan, the core figure, who holds all his parts bound in one unity and for this reason was honoured as the God of Nature by the Ancient Greeks.

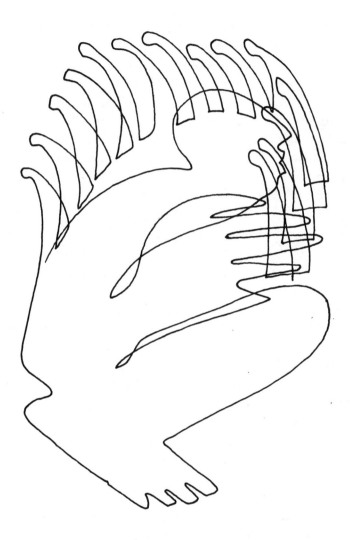

The elemental beings formed a circle
around the just-awakening Earth Soul.

Afterwards, I tried various ways to interpret this profoundly unsettling vision. Yet the message is really simple: The working of the Christ Consciousness in Earth's elemental world was brought to my conscious mind. A whole new dimension of earth change had opened up for me (cf. my book 'Daughter of Gaia').

In the Western World, the concept of Christ Consciousness is understood to point to a future aspect of God. Tibetan Buddhism recognises the future Buddha, called the Maitreya Buddha. But Christ's relationship with Pan and the world of nature is amazing. The incarnated Son of God is usually seen to be in an exclusive relationship with the human world. St. Francis of Assisi, much revered today, is the single Christian example having a relationship with nature. St. Francis also bore the stigmata of Christ and communicated with the moon, trees and birds.

Following in St. Francis' footsteps and with the help of a 'new' elemental being, I was able, in the year 2006, to make considerable progress. I discovered the elemental in Wasmuth Hausen in Bavaria on the reverse side of a stone highway cross that dated from the year 1704. As I was kneeling beside the crucifix, the elemental being's words rang suddenly in my consciousness: "Not human beings only, but also elemental beings participate in the experience of Christ's incarnation." In fact, they represent the consciousness of the bodily (i.e., earthly) material into which he incarnated. It is self-evident that it was informed of his cosmic presence.

It has been a lengthy process. It took a long time for the information to penetrate all the layers of earth consciousness and reach the earth's centre. At that moment the divine essence of the Earth Soul was touched and awakened, and this finally set in motion the complete transformation of her consciousness – and with it the consciousness of the elemental world.

. . . .

58. COMMENTARY: **Elemental Beings in Uproar**

It is hard even for elemental beings to grasp all that is happening today. This was made plain in quite a dramatic way when I went with a geomantic group in October 2006 to erect a lithopuncture stele by a stream in Odranci in eastern Slovenia. This was part of a lithopuncture project on both sides of the border between Hungary and Slovenia. It was financed by the European Union to encourage 'soft' forms of tourism in the Muranian region. In total, 17 stelae inlaid with chiselled cosmograms were erected.

The cosmogram for that point in Odranci was shaped by Katja Majer and denoted a focus point of the powers that are taking part in the construction of the

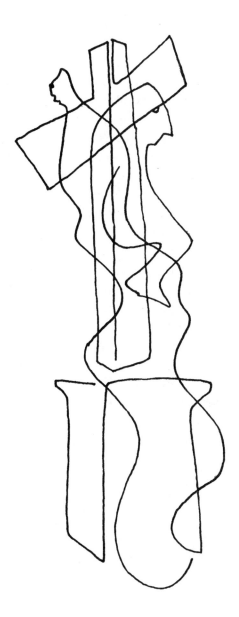

On the reverse side of the cross at Wasmuthhausen
bearing the figure of the dying Christ, there arose a 'new'
elemental being as the spirit of resurrection.

new, holy space. It signifies a new space/time structure which the Earth has for some time been trying to develop within the framework of her self-healing processes. Additionally, Odranci is a place that has a relationship with the Christ consciousness.

As we were erecting the stele, one of our participants, the sensitive Simona, felt increasingly sick. Weeping, she explained that the elemental beings of the stream beside which the stele would stand were in an uproar. They did not want to acknowledge the power that Katja had perceived there and to which the lithopuncture stone was dedicated. They would fiercely defend themselves against having to endure the placing of the stone in that location.

We immediately broke off our work in order to help the place's elemental beings join with the 'new' energies and qualities that are manifesting in consequence of the earth changes. Together we celebrated a ritual that my daughter Ajra and I had developed together a few years previous, specifically for such an occasion.

This is a recurring situation. One keeps coming across groups of elemental beings that are so deeply sunk in their own world that they have not noticed the extensive changes in Earth Consciousness around them. They remain stuck in their old consciousness condition without letting the new wind touch them. The healing ritual focuses on attunement to the new powers and qualities, while information on the cosmic moment, which pulsates in the heart of every human being, is transmitted to the elemental beings concerned. Because the eternal NOW vibrates at the core of our heart centre, the heart knows, at every given moment, what is the state of the cosmos, even if we are not consciously aware.

This is the form of the ritual: the participants stand in a circle and each one gives voice to the tone of their heart; from this arises a vibrational membrane through which the elemental beings can be led out of their separated time into the true present; the form of the ritual proceeds as we ask the beings to pass through the membrane.

After we had carried out this ritual, the stream's water beings had no problem accepting the stele upon which the cosmogram was carved. The stream is called the Črnec, 'Black Stream'.

· · · · · · · · · · · · · · ·

59. COMMENTARY: **Guardians of the New Space**

Those of us who are interested in the existence of elemental beings should not become confused by the new developments in Earth Consciousness. For this purpose I arranged a meeting with my elemental being teacher Julius in the summer of 2006. First, I tried to get a feeling from him, how he would classify the 'new'

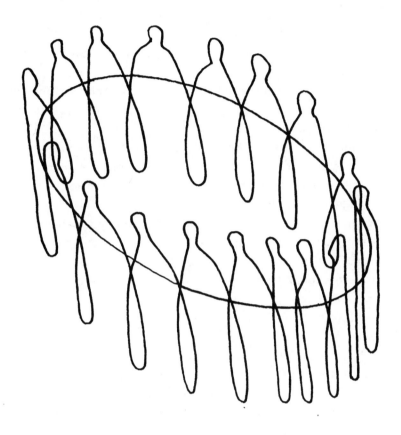

The group-membrane ritual to attune
with the elemental beings.

elemental beings. My consciousness interpreted his 'statements', assembled from various vibrations, as follows:

- We are dealing with beings of the Earth Consciousness that are not bound to processes that operate in the framework of one of the four elements or in the context of a specific place.
- These are beings that are specialised in the changing of the present space and time structures.
- They were formed by the Earth Soul to operate as media for communication between beings of different kinds, and also as mediators between humanity and the Earth Soul.
- They contribute to the construction of a holistically conceptualised earth space. They are able to 'glue together' different dimensions of being which are presently separated from one another while they create communication bridges between them.
- The beings of the fifth element are initiated in the secrets of human consciousness and the life of feelings. Therefore, they are able to approach human beings and support us in our personal change processes.
- They are in touch with information on Christ Consciousness and this is the source of their basic frequency of love and curiosity.

Further, I asked Julius to comment on the current processes of earth change. Here is my translation of his 'words':

"The Earth finds itself in the middle of the turbulence that is currently shaking our universe. The transformation processes of earth are developing parallel to the rhythm of this turbulence. In the universe, the situation is constantly altering and therefore you cannot expect any certain forecast. It is important to understand what the earth change is about. You should leave the responsibility for 'saving' the world to us, the experienced elemental beings. Believe in the resurrection of the new organism of earthly space and time, to help it manifest. Glide through the approaching epoch on the waves of change. The development of the universe is anything but linear!"

. . . .

60. COMMENTARY: **Experience on the Doga**

I discovered the Doga during a training seminar at Weissensee in Carinthia. The hill which bears this mysterious name is both a mountain of the heart and a mountain of change. A vital-energetic heart centre beats in the middle of the mountain. The shapes of Doga's slopes are incredibly animated, as if a constant process of change is happening in the belly of the hill.

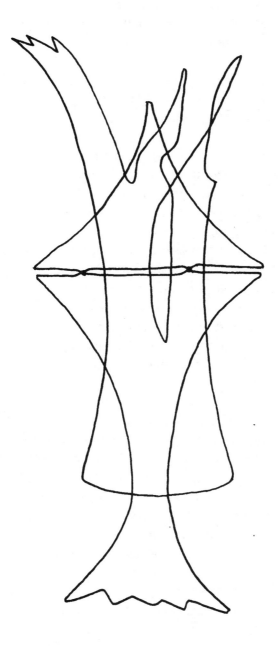

The spirit of an old oak tree with which I am
constantly conversing about the Earth Changes.

One gets the feeling that the Doga represents an age-old sacred place that has been reactivated for the purposes of the currently unfolding earth change. The dreamily beautiful landscape of the Weissensee is saturated with the quality of an island of light that radiates out from the Doga. This quality relates to the 'seeds of the new space' now just emerging. This means that in certain places the Earth Soul is already manifesting the quality of the future earth space as a model and a signpost, one might say, to guide us through the confusion of the epoch of change.

The slopes and plateau of the Doga have been cropped bald by cows. However, at the hill's western edge there is a flourishing hedge, thickly overgrown with trees. There I discovered a joyful group of beings of the ether element – the 'new' elemental spirits. To begin communicating with them, I proposed the following exercise to the training group:

- Imagine that there is a small white ball in the area between your hips.
- Tip your pelvis alternately forward and back so that the imaginary ball rolls to and fro on the rocking pelvic floor.
- Abruptly stop the rocking motion. In the same moment, imagine yourself opening the ball, as one might open a seed.
- With that, the corresponding perception channel opens of itself, and you glide unhesitatingly into the perceptual process.
- Repeat the exercise as needed, in succession.

For a long time I had been suffering from a persistent cough, so I took the opportunity to ask advice from the spirits of the Doga as 'masters of change'. The answer came to me immediately: "You have become too dense. The waves of change cannot run through you freely. Your body must be aired out."

At once I felt the cells of my body begin to pull apart from each other so that tiny free spaces, and bigger ones too, opened up between them. I repeated the exercise several times later when I was alone and my coughing stopped in a flash. (The exercise is recommended for all unusual bodily complaints).

To a greater or lesser extent, the epoch of great transformation is persistently laying claim to our bodies. A person may often think they are ill, but the problem is not illness but a reflection of our internal processes of change.

It is characteristic of the 'new' elemental beings that they love freedom and jest. When our communication had finished and we were raising our voices in harmony to signal the end of our visit and give thanks for the experience, I observed how, high above our group, the Doga's environmental spirits were practicing our pelvic rocking ritual amid loud roars of laughter.

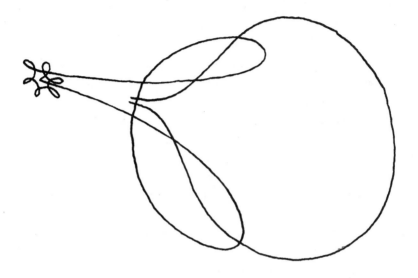

The light-island of the Weissensee constantly
balloons out from the heart of Doga Hill.

61. COMMENTARY: **Cosmic Elemental Beings**

The occasional emergence on the earth's surface of the so-called cosmic elemental beings also belongs to the phenomena of the present epoch of earth transformation. To avoid any possible confusion that may result from a meeting with the cosmic elemental beings, I will give a report on their existence.

The word 'cosmic' does not mean that those elemental beings have reached earth from out of the wide universe. Quite the opposite! The cosmic elemental beings are at home in the inner levels of the earth. We touched on earth's inner cosmos in the 42nd and 43rd commentaries in this present book. These elemental beings embody earth's memory and are the mediators of her experiences, which they have garnered over the millions of years of her interaction with the evolving beings and cultures that have settled on her surface. The memories are invaluable because, when confronted by a complex situation that calls for a decision, one can look back on them and find the reflection of similar connections and circumstances as those occurring in the present. The memory of previous decisions, reactions and solutions helps find the right path in a concrete situation.

The epoch of change in which earth and our civilisation now find themselves involves an unsafe transitional phase that requires the activation of all the spiritual-soul resources that Gaia has at her disposal, among them the recollections of similar epochs in the past which are stored in her memory. This is why the cosmic elemental beings from inward earth have begun to secure relationships with the life on the earth's surface. I have little doubt that the geomantic system of inter-dimensional portals mentioned in Commentary 29 has been awakened and activated by the guardians of the planetary memory – the cosmic elemental beings – to open ways to communicate with the earth's surface. Like the elemental beings of the fifth element, the cosmic elemental beings are free to choose which etheric form they use to emerge in human consciousness. They are sometimes sighted as highly technical UFOs and at others as humanoid beings but somewhat smaller in body and with exotic facial features. In my book 'Touching the Breath of Gaia', Chapter 45, I compared them to the extinct, so-called Neanderthal race.

They have one feature that is especially distinctive: through the energetic umbilical cord that links them to the collective memory of Earth, they dispose of a quite fantastic intelligence.

. . . .

62. COMMENTARY: **The Fairy Nature in Human Beings**

If one speaks about the present epoch of change, one thinks first of the alterations in the Nature Kingdom, about climate change and unusual global warming.

Cosmic elemental beings usually show
themselves in a form akin to humans.

Later, one may think about the changes in the human mind, in our consciousness. People are beginning to think holistically, becoming aware of the value of life and freeing themselves from materialist consciousness and the worn out thought-forms linked to it.

However, scant heed is given to the alterations on the emotional level of space. Yet this is precisely the sphere where the elemental beings are active. As has been mentioned many times, environmental spirits have no mental consciousness, but instead have an emotional one. They mediate between the etheric and material planes of space, but operate through the plane of feeling. The emotional plane is their home and their workplace.

The prime reason why the elemental world has been completely hidden from our modern human consciousness is that we have clung too tightly to our intellect and thereby totally suppressed its opposite pole, the emotional plane within us.

And now see the result – just as we are well on our way to becoming coldly calculating hominids guided only by reason, we stumble up against the lightning-woven, emotionally shattering world of the elemental beings. A rescuing hand is stretched out toward us! Let us not dismiss this fleeting turning point!

Our need is not primarily to recognise the parallel reality of environmental spirits and elemental beings, because for the most part these fulfil their tasks in the earth cosmos autonomously even if our civilisation misjudges them. Our need is much more to recognise our own fairy-like aspect. I have often emphasised that as incarnate beings we belong largely to the terrestrial world. In an odd and yet essential way we are also interwoven with Earth's emotional world.

Our fairy nature longs to be recognised and displayed. If we were to allow the fairy world's eternal sun within us to shine externally, the misery of our every-day world, oppressed with wars and sickness, would be instantly transformed into light. The magic wand which fairies use to do their work is not just an invented story. I am convinced that the fairy substance within us is ready to wield its magic wand. However, our consciousness must allow it and bid it welcome, or it will not prevail. We hold in our own hands the key to our fairy nature.

. . . .

63. EXERCISE: **Promote our Fairy Nature**

Our personal fairy nature lives its own life, disregarded by our waking conscious-ness but spun into our human emotional world. Must the two planes be forever separate? In no way! The time for change is now!

How can we integrate the light-filled, mythically vibrating world within us with our day-to-day experience? First of all, we must pay attention to the fairy-

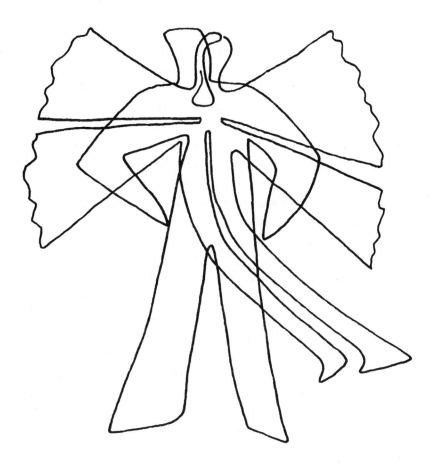

The fairy nature vibrates in humankind.

like quality within us. This quality is nothing very mysterious as our rational mind would like us to believe, but it does indeed go straight to our indisputable participation in the life of Nature and Earth, and thus to the presence of their elemental beings in us and around us. We are all dancing the same dance — although our logic would like to see it otherwise.

Secondly, we must practice maintaining, constantly and vigorously, the attention we pay to our fairy nature. For this purpose I am offering an exercise that aims to make playful contact with our inner child, be it boy or girl. However, the exercise will not work unless it is repeated several times a day — a few moments will suffice — over a lengthy period.

- Be aware that now, at this very moment, you are being accompanied by your inner boy or girl (decide for yourself which is more instructive, not which is simpler!). When you are walking, sense the inner child skipping at your side, when you are lying down, etc. — always in at least minimal contact with your body.

- Keep a watch out for the inner child who is accompanying you. It cannot move as quickly as a grown-up person. Even when you are in a hurry, help it come with you at its own pace. You may perhaps have to stride a trifle more slowly for a few moments. Take note: This is not so much about the imaginary child, but more about letting yourself fall into a totally different vibrational rhythm which your inner child can help you attain.

- For some specific moments allow the quality of the boy or girl accompanying you to rise spirally through your body and spread out through your aura. How does that feel to you? What does the environment around you look like at this moment? Try to keep constant in your life the sensitivity that unfolds in you at this moment.

For the exercise with the inner child.

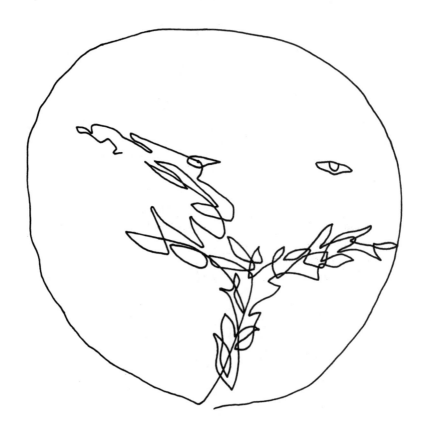

The elemental being of a plant.

About the Author

MARKO POGAČNIK was born in 1944 in Kranj, Slovenia, and graduated in 1967 as sculptor from the Academy of fine Arts in Ljubljana. He lives with his wife Marika in Šempas, Slovenia. They have three daughters and five grand children.

From 1965 until 1971, Marko worked as a member of an international art group called OHO in conceptual art and land art. Exhibitions include Information Show at the Museum of Modern Art in New York City (1970), Aktionsraum, Munich (1970), and Global Conceptualism Show 1950-80, Queens Museum of Art, New York (1999). Most of the collection of OHO works is housed by the Museum of Modern Art in Ljubljana.

In 1971, with his family and friends, Marko founded a rural artistic community and spiritual center called the "Šempas Family" in Šempas, Slovenia. The community lasted until 1979. Exhibitions by the Šempas Family include Trigon (1977) in Graz and the Venice Biennale of 1978. Since 1979 he has been engaged in geomantic and Earth healing work.

In the mid-1980s, Marko developed a method of Earth healing, "litho-puncture" (similar to acupuncture), using stone pillars positioned on acupuncture points of the landscape.

He is the author of numerous books, including *Touching the Breath of Gaia* (2007) and *Healing the Heart of the Earth* (1998). Visit his website at www. markopogacnik.com.

Bibliography

BLOOM, WILLIAM: *Devas, Fairies and Angels: A Modern Approach.*
Gothic Image, Glastonbury 1986

FINDHORN COMMUNITY, THE: *The Findhorn Garden Story: Inspired Color Photos Reveal the Magic.* Findhorn Press 2008

HODSON, GEOFFREY: *The Kingdom of the Gods.* Madras 1980

POGACNIK, MARKO: *Healing the Heart of the Earth.* Findhorn Press 1998

POGACNIK, MARKO: *Christ Power and the Earth Goddess: A Fifth Gospel.*
Findhorn Press 1999

POGACNIK, MARKO: *Earth Changes, Human Destiny: Coping and Attuning with the Help of the Revelation of St. John.* Findhorn Press 2000

POGACNIK, MARKO: *The Daughter of Gaia: Rebirth of the Divine Feminine.*
Findhorn Press 2001

POGACNIK, MARKO: *Turned Upside Down: A Work Book on Earth Changes and Personal Transformation.* Lindisfarne Books, USA 2004

POGACNIK, MARKO ET AL.: *How Wide the Heart: The Roots of Peace in Palestine and Israel.* Lindisfarne Books, USA 2007

POGACNIK, MARKO: *Touching the Breath of Gaia: 59 Foundation Stones for a Peaceful Civilization.* Findhorn Press 2007

POGACNIK, MARKO: *Sacred Geography: Geomancy: Co-Creating the Earth Cosmos.* Lindisfarne Books USA, 2008

STEINER, RUDOLF: *Nature Spirits: Selected Lectures.* Rudolf Steiner Press 1995

FINDHORN PRESS

Life Changing Books

For a complete catalogue,
please contact:

Findhorn Press Ltd
305a The Park, Findhorn
Forres IV36 3TE
Scotland, UK

Telephone
+44-(0)1309-690582
Fax
+44-(0)131-777-2711
eMail
info@findhornpress.com

or consult our catalogue online
(with secure order facility) on
www.findhornpress.com

For information on the Findhorn Foundation:
www.findhorn.org